The Abbey, ~~Beckenham~~ Ashurst Wood.

School Report of **M. A. B. Morpurgo**   age **9·5**

Easter Term, 19**53**

Form **III**   Average age **9·10**   No. of Boys **19**   Place

Subject	Remarks	Place
Scripture	Good and keen aB.	1
Latin	Rather disappointing, he can do some very good work when he makes up his mind but this is not very often. GtS.	9
Greek or German	He is progressing, but is very slow, and does not cover enough ground in the term. BCW.	
History	Fair. C—?	12
Geography	Good. C—?	3
Mathematics	Not a good Term. He could do much better. ECO.	5
French	His work is thoroughly unsatisfactory at present, he is both careless and inattentive. AdeC.	9
English Subjects	Rather disappointing. His work has been neither so neat nor so careful this term. With his intelligence he could do far better. It is possible that he wants more competition than can be supplied by his present Form + will do better in a different sphere. AJRG	7.

Head Master's Report

Rather inclined to think that his position at the top of the form was stale and unassailable – such an assumption has somewhat detracted from the value of his efforts.

       C.S.C.

Days Absent   **2**   Combined Order   = **6**

The Summer Term begins at 8.50 a.m. on **Wednesday April 29th/53**

Boarders must be in School by 6 p.m. on the day previous to this.

michael
morpurgo

MAGGIE FERGUSSON

michael morpurgo

War Child to *War Horse*

A biography by Maggie Fergusson
with stories by Michael Morpurgo

FOURTH ESTATE • *London*

First published in Great Britain in 2012 by
Fourth Estate
An imprint of HarperCollins*Publishers*
77–85 Fulham Palace Road,
London W6 8JB
www.4thestate.co.uk

Visit our authors' blog: www.fifthestate.co.uk

1

A catalogue record for this book is
available from the British Library

ISBN 978-0-00-738726-7

'A Fine Night, and All's Well' was first published in the *Radio Times* in 2010. 'Didn't
We Have a Lovely Time?' was first published in *Country Life* in 2010. 'A Bit of a
Daredevil' was first broadcast on Radio 4 in 2010. 'The Saga of Ragnar Erikson' was
first published on the Edinburgh International Book Festival website in 2010.
'A Proper Family' was first broadcast on Radio 4 in 2011.

Typeset in Minion by G&M Designs Limited,
Raunds, Northamptonshire
Printed and bound in Great Britain by
Clays Ltd, St Ives plc

For
Flora and Izzy

Contents

Preface   ix

1 Beneath the Hornbeam   1
    'Bubble, Bubble, Toil and Trouble'   33

2 Spotless Officer Number One   57
    'A Fine Night, and All's Well'   91

3 Situation Critical   99
    'Littleton 12–Wickhamstead 0'   135

4 A Winning Formula   149
    'Didn't We Have a Lovely Time?'   179

5 The Heat o' the Sun   187
    'A Bit of a Daredevil'   223

6 Better Answer – Might be Spielberg   233
    'The Saga of Ragnar Erikson'   269

7 Still Seeking   279
    'A Proper Family'   293

Bibliography   301
Acknowledgements   305

Preface

Buried in most of us is a desire to communicate with children on their own level. A child falls and scrapes his knee; we drop down to meet him eye to eye. This is the level on which Michael Morpurgo weaves his stories, sharing his thoughts with children in a way that they know is neither contrived nor condescending. Books such as *Kensuke's Kingdom*, *Private Peaceful*, *War Horse* and *Shadow* have become contemporary classics, establishing Michael as a kind of Pied Piper for a whole generation. His is a rare gift.

But Michael Morpurgo is very much more than a bestselling children's author. When his wife, Clare, was getting to know him nearly fifty years ago, she marvelled, in a letter, at his 'six selfs'. He is many people in one. He remains, in part, a boy of about ten, writing 'for the child inside myself that I still partly am'. He is a soldier, who won a scholarship to Sandhurst and might now be General Morpurgo had not providence and love combined gently to alter his course. He is a primary-school teacher, whose energy and charisma thrilled his pupils and maddened his colleagues in the staff-room. He is an entrepreneur, whose charity, Farms for City Children, has given more than 100,000 inner-city schoolchildren a taste of what it is like to live and work on a farm. He is a performer, who feels happiest on stage where he is able to forget himself as part of a cast. And he has, recently, become a crusader and statesman, using his fame as a soapbox from which to roar when he encounters injustice.

No wonder Michael's publishers have repeatedly urged him to write a memoir; but the one story he feels unable to tell is his own, though he is happy for it to be told. When he first proposed that I might write about his life, he was speaking on his mobile from Devon with such a big wind blowing in the background that it was hard to understand what he was saying. Once I had understood, I felt excited but uncertain. How clearly can one hope to see the shape of a life still being lived? And would it not be a mistake to write a book about Michael Morpurgo that had nothing to offer the children who love his work so much? So we struck a deal. I would write seven chapters about Michael's life; he would read them, reflect on the memories and feelings they stirred in him, and respond to each chapter with a story.

For the past two years, whenever Michael has been in London, I have bicycled from my home in Hammersmith to his riverside flat in Fulham and spent time there getting to know his 'six selfs' better. Looking out over the Thames, the tides rising and falling, seagulls crying, we have talked at length about his triumphs, about the struggles he has faced, and about the price he has paid for success. We have explored areas of his life that have remained obscure, perhaps, even to him. What has emerged is a story of light and shade: the light very bright, the shade uncomfortable and sometimes painful. Both light and shade are reflected not only in the chapters I have written, but in Michael's corresponding stories, some of which have required great courage in the making.

One day Michael Morpurgo must pass, in the words of the old saga-writers, 'out of the story'. Then the moment will come for somebody to lay another picture on top of this one, and to write a full biography. Here, meantime, is an attempt to catch an extraordinary man on the wing, while he is still in full flight.

MAGGIE FERGUSSON

michael morpurgo

1

Beneath the Hornbeam

In a corner of Michael Morpurgo's Devon garden, the ashes of three people share a final resting-place. The sitting room of his low, thatched cottage looks out on the spot where they lie. He passes it every morning on the way to the summer house where he writes. Above it, a hornbeam tree flourishes with such elegance and grace that you might imagine the ashes beneath must be mingled in invigorating harmony. But you'd be wrong. In life, these three people – Michael's mother, father and stepfather – caused one another untold pain, giving Michael an early education in what he describes as 'the frailty of happiness'. If you want to understand the thread of grief that runs through almost all his work, you should start here, beneath the hornbeam.

The first ashes to be scattered, on a cold, bright, blossomy day in the spring of 1993, were those of Michael's mother, Catherine, known from birth by her third name, Kippe (pronounced 'Kipper'). At her memorial service the congregation had sung the *Nunc Dimittis*,

Lord, now lettest thou thy servant depart in peace …

and they had sung it with full hearts, because for most of Kippe's life peace had been a stranger to her. She died an alcoholic, pitifully thin, stalked by depression, and convinced, Michael says, 'that she had failed in the eyes of God'.

How could her life have become so bitter? If Kippe had been a child in a story one might have said that, on her birth in the spring of 1918, the fairies had been generous at her cradle. The fourth of six children, she was beautiful – fair, with a tip-tilted nose and blue-green eyes – and her looks were coveted by her three sisters, who were plainer and more sturdily built. Her father called her his 'Little White Bird', echoing J. M. Barrie's fantasy of infant loveliness and innocence; and, complementing her face, she had a voice that would draw people to her for the rest of her life. Her younger and only surviving sibling, Jeanne, describes it as a 'brown velvet' voice, and in a recording made when Kippe was nearing old age it remains melodious, languid and gently seductive – the voice that lured Michael, unbookish boy though he was, into the wonders of words and stories.

Children outside the family were mesmerised by Kippe. Jeanne remembers, more than once, inviting friends home for tea, only to have them admit that what they really desired was to spend time near Kippe. They were fascinated not simply by her looks and voice but by her passionate nature. While other little girls played Mummies and Daddies, what Kippe wanted, from an early age, was to play 'Lovers' – and 'what Kippe wanted, Kippe got'.

Not that her parents went in for spoiling. Their rambling, Edwardian house, 'The Eyrie', near Radlett in Hertfordshire, had what seemed to Michael countless rooms, and was set in a large garden with a tennis lawn, an orchard and a dovecote. Yet money was always short. Kippe's mother, Tita, was a large, imposing woman who gave Michael his first inklings 'of what God might be like'. Before her marriage she had been a Shakespearean actress. She had a voice so deep and tremendous that she was on one occasion invited to read Grieg's *Bergliot* over a full orchestra conducted by Sir Henry Wood, and on another given the part of Abraham in a mystery play at the Albert Hall about the sacrifice of Isaac. Her mother, Marie Brema, had been a professional opera singer, the first from England to appear at Bayreuth. She created the role of the angel in the first performance of Elgar's *Dream of Gerontius*, and was once summoned to Buckingham Palace to sing for Queen Victoria. Both mother and daughter were close friends of Bernard Shaw, and when he came to write *You Never Can Tell* Tita was his model for the feisty and formidable Gloria ('a mettlesome dominative character,' in Shaw's own description, 'paralysed by the inexperience of her youth'). But neither Tita nor her mother had their heads turned by success. Both were fervent Christian Socialists and most of the money they made on stage was poured into Brema Looms, a workshop providing employment for crippled girls from London's East End.

In 1906 Tita, who in her late twenties had never so much as kissed a man, had met and fallen in love with a Belgian poet, scholar and nationalist, Emile Cammaerts. There were differences between them. Emile, who had spent much of his youth in an anarchist commune, spoke very little English, and was an atheist. Tita set about tackling both problems with a forcefulness that alarmed Shaw – 'For Heaven's sake,' he warned her, 'do learn to discriminate between yourself and the Almighty' – and she succeeded. A Brussels spinster was engaged to teach Emile English (they began their lessons by teasing out *Othello*, line by line) so that by the time he and Tita were married in 1908 his English was fluent. He had also converted to Christianity with a zeal that would never leave him. As there was little prospect of Tita's pursuing her stage career in Belgium, and as she felt she must look after her mother, they settled in London, before moving, as their family grew, to Radlett.

Tall, and with a fine, monumental head that would have sat happily amidst the emperors' busts that ring the Sheldonian Theatre in Oxford, Emile Cammaerts became revered in academic and literary circles both for his intellect and for his passionate devotion to Belgium. Invalided out of the First World War with a weak heart, he threw his energies instead into composing fiery, defiant, patriotic poems to encourage his compatriots. Lord Curzon translated his work; Elgar set his 'Carillon' ('Sing, Belgians, Sing') to music. He was Belgium's Rupert Brooke. When his fourth child's birth coincided with a significant Belgian victory over the Germans, he named her after the hamlet, De Kippe, where this had taken place.

Emile Cammaerts, 1943.

But while his Belgian patriotism remained central to him – he went on to become Professor of Belgian Studies at the University of London, and was appointed CBE for organising an exhibition of Flemish art at the Royal Academy in 1927 – Emile Cammaerts also, over time, assumed many of the trappings of the English establishment. He was a member of the Athenaeum, a regular writer of letters to *The Times*, a close friend of G. K. Chesterton and Walter de la Mare, and such a pillar of the Anglican Church that he considered, in his later years, taking Holy Orders. He was widely loved, and on his death in 1953 the Principal of Pusey House in Oxford described him as 'a man as near sanctity as I have ever met'.

To Michael, as a small boy, Emile Cammaerts seemed 'all that a grandfather should be'. He had a flowing beard, thick, tweed suits and heavy brown shoes. He emanated jollity. His theme tunes, in Michael's memories, are Mozart's horn concertos, to which he would bounce his grandchildren on his knee; and he had about him what his *Times* obituary would describe as an air of 'enchanted innocence'. Though he had made his career as an academic, his earliest published works had been plays for children, and he had written a study of nonsense verse. He would delight Michael with recitals of 'The Owl and the Pussy-cat', 'The Dong with a Luminous Nose', and, most memorably,

> There was an Old Man with a beard,
> Who said, 'It is just as I feared! –
> Two Owls and a Hen, four Larks and a Wren,
> Have all built their nests in my beard!'

Emile Cammaerts's reputation was considerably greater than his income, and with six children he and Tita were forced to run the household at the Eyrie along strict make-do-and-mend lines. Jeanne remembers Tita's darning broken bed springs with 15-amp fuse-wire; and avoiding, wherever possible, spending money on clothes, either for herself or for the children. There was principle at play here, as well as economy. Personal vanity was, in Tita's book, a vice second only to gossip. She had what Jeanne describes as 'an almost Islamic desire to hide her figure', and 'would happily have dressed herself in sacks'.

There was one area in which indulgence was encouraged. The early lives of both Emile and Tita had been bleak. Tita's father had separated from her mother soon after her birth, abandoning her to a lonely, rootless existence, trailing with her diva mother round the concert halls and opera houses of Europe. Wildly unfaithful, Emile's father had, similarly, left his mother, just before his birth, and had, finally, shot himself. Both Emile and Tita, as they grew up, had sought security and comfort in beauty – the beauty of the natural world, and the beauty of art.

At the Eyrie they set out to create a home in which their growing brood would be surrounded and sustained by music and painting and books. 'Every meal,' Jeanne laughs, 'was a seminar.' Even games of rummy and racing demon bristled with moral and intellectual competition. In the red-linoed first-floor nursery, parents and children gathered round a huge black table to read Shakespeare plays – Tita making a memorable Othello. On Sunday mornings, after church, they congregated by an oak chest filled with postcards of religious paintings by Giotto, Leonardo, Fra Angelico. Each in turn, the children were invited to pick out a postcard and to talk about what it told them of the life of Christ.

With such a rich diet of culture, there was little appetite for material comfort. Asked to choose between a new stair carpet and a gramophone recording of Schubert's trios, Jeanne and her siblings voted unanimously for Schubert.

Sitting in an armchair in an old people's home in Oxford, Jeanne, now in her late eighties, looks back with gratitude and love on the home that her parents created: 'They had no model to go on, but they were trying to make a perfect world for us.' And to some extent, for a while at least, they succeeded.

But, of the six children, the plain living and high thinking at the Eyrie suited Kippe least well. Her gifts were intuitive rather than intellectual, and at St Albans High School, though she shone on the lacrosse field, the teachers made it clear that she was a disappointment after her academic sisters. She was, perhaps, slightly dyslexic. During the family readings of Shakespeare she stumbled over her parts, and this was bitter to her because she had, in fact, a natural feeling for words and characters. The frustration and humiliation she suffered as a result led her to bully her younger, brighter sister, Jeanne.

Kippe went along with the family ethos of goodness and self-denial, but only intermittently. Sometimes she would tell her siblings that she had set her heart on becoming a nurse, and would post her pocket money penny by penny into the church poor-box. Jeanne remembers her reciting with feeling lines from W. H. Davies:

I hear leaves drinking rain;
   I hear rich leaves on top
Giving the poor beneath
   Drop after drop …

But increasingly Kippe recognised that what she really wanted was to act. She was so taken up with playing parts, in fact, that her sense of self was fragile.

Unlike her mother, moreover, Kippe minded about her appearance and her clothes. She had a natural taste for glamour and flamboyance, which was denied expression; and the passion that had made her such a thrilling playmate as a child proved, as she began to grow up, more dangerous and double-edged. At nineteen, she fell helplessly in love with a Cambridge friend of her elder brother, Francis. At about the same time she had a bad bout of flu. The two things together proved too much for her, and she suffered a breakdown. It was Jeanne who realised first that something was wrong, coming upon Kippe in their shared bedroom fingering a white-painted chair with the tips of her fingers and murmuring, 'It's so cold! The snow is deep.' For nearly three months, Tita and Emile took it in turns to keep a vigil by Kippe's bedside as she lay tossing and turning, sometimes calling out so loudly that she could be heard by neighbours beyond the Eyrie garden walls.

Looking back, and with the benefit of long hindsight, Jeanne wonders whether Kippe ever properly recovered; but she recovered sufficiently to leave home and return to the stage. After school she had won a place at RADA, and from there she went on to build a successful career in repertory. It was in the middle of a rehearsal in the Odeon Hall, Canterbury, in the autumn of 1938, that a man called Tony Bridge stepped on to the scene.

There was nothing remarkable-seeming about this new recruit to the company. A year older and slightly shorter than Kippe, he was not especially good-looking. Nor was he, in principle, 'available'. He too had trained at RADA, where he had met and fallen in love with a fellow student, Betty Mallett. Though not formally engaged, he and Betty were regarded, in his words, as a 'forever' couple. Yet within weeks of their meeting, Tony and Kippe – or Kate, as he called her, in affectionate reference to her *Shrew*-ish tendencies – were spending almost all their time together, heading off into the Kent countryside for long walks when they were not required on stage.

Kippe.

In Tony Bridge, Kippe had found a companion of real kindness, a man with what one of his friends later described as an extraordinary gift for 'ordinary human understanding'. The only child of lower-middle-class Londoners, he had a talent for amusing people, and for lightening and cheering any company in which he found himself. He made Kippe feel safe and happy. A friend, Mary Niven, remembers a joyful evening she spent with the two of them, during which they sang their way through *The Magic Flute*, Kippe as Papagena, Tony as Tamino: 'They triggered each other off. They were lost in delight.'

Not everyone shared their delight. Betty Mallett was, of course, devastated; and Tony's parents, Edith and Arthur Bridge, were disgusted on Betty's behalf. They did not warm to Kippe, whom they judged flighty and unreliable. Tony, meanwhile, was not all that Tita and Emile Cammaerts had hoped for Kippe. Quiet and unintellect-ual, he was, on his first visit to the Eyrie, thoroughly overwhelmed by the Cammaerts tribe; and they were underwhelmed by him. His kindness was mistaken for weakness. Kippe, her parents felt, needed somebody stronger.

Both families hoped that circumstances might drive the couple apart. Through the beautiful summer of 1939, their repertory company played to dwindling audiences until, on the outbreak of war, the Odeon Hall was closed. The following spring Tony Bridge was called up, and for the next eighteen months he was shunted from camp to camp around Britain, settling at last in the Scottish coastal town of Montrose. But separation only strengthened the desire for a more formal union, and on 26 June 1941, during a short army leave, Tony and Kippe were married at Christ Church, Radlett. They are captured in a photograph on the steps of the church, Kippe beaming and beautiful in a Pre-Raphaelite dress, Tony in his army battledress and heavy boots, the Cammaerts and Bridge parents flanking them, smiling as the occasion demanded.

Michael's parents' wedding, 26 June 1941. Left to right: Arthur and Edith Bridge, Jeanne and Francis Cammaerts, Tony and Kippe, Elizabeth, Tita and Emile Cammaerts.

The smiles are deceptive. On that early summer day, Emile and Tita Cammaerts, at least, were far from happy – and not simply because they had doubts about their future son-in-law. Less than three months earlier they had received the news that their younger son, Pieter, who had joined the RAF early in the war, had been killed, his body cut from the wreckage of a plane near the RAF base at St Eval in Cornwall. His funeral had been held at Christ Church. As his parents posed for Kippe's wedding photographs, the earth was still fresh on his grave.

Pieter Cammaerts was just twenty-one when he died, and his death cast a long shadow down the years. A difficult, unsettled child, he had followed Kippe to RADA and had proved himself an actor of real talent, leaving in the spring of 1938 with the Shakespeare

Schools Prize. At eighty-six, Jeanne still wipes tears from her eyes as she remembers his winning performance as Claudio in *Much Ado About Nothing*:

Ay, but to die, and go we know not where ...

A fable of heroism grew up around Pieter's last moments. The story that Kippe clung to – that she passed on to Michael, and that Michael has woven into stories of his own – was that the plane in which Pieter was flying as an observer had been damaged during an enemy attack, and the pilot wounded. Seizing the controls, Pieter had insisted that the rest of the crew parachute to safety leaving him to try to land alone. But a visit to the National Archives in Kew suggests that the truth is more prosaic. Sergeant Pieter Emile Gerald Cammaerts, serving with 101 Squadron, took off from RAF St Eval in a Blenheim bomber on the evening of 30 March 1941 on a mission to Brest – a mission that turned out to be fruitless ('Target area bombed but no results observed'). On return the plane overshot the end of the runway and crashed, killing Pieter and the pilot, and leaving the third member of the crew severely injured.

Pieter's siblings reacted in very different ways to his death. His elder brother, Francis, who had, at the outbreak of war, registered as a Conscientious Objector, was now moved to join the Special Operations Executive. He went on to become one of its bravest and most remarkable members, decorated with the DSO, Légion d'honneur and Croix de Guerre. But Kippe was too devastated to do anything but weep. 'She cast herself as Niobe,' says Jeanne. 'She was inconsolable.' For the rest of her life, if Pieter's name was mentioned, Kippe would walk out of the room; and on Remembrance Sunday every year she would take herself up to her bedroom and perform a private ritual, placing a poppy beside Pieter's photograph, and reciting Laurence Binyon's poem 'For the Fallen':

They shall grow not old, as we that are left grow old:
Age shall not weary them, nor the years condemn ...

With every autumn, the words seemed more poignant.

For Michael, growing up, Pieter was a constant presence. When he visited his grandparents at the Eyrie, he was 'the elephant in the room', never mentioned, deeply mourned. And wherever Kippe was, Pieter's handsome half-profile stared down from the photograph that she kept always on her dressing table. Michael so revered Pieter's self-sacrifice, and felt so desperately for his mother's sadness, that he would sometimes find himself weeping for the loss of the uncle he had never known. 'I think they had been really, really close, my mother and Pieter,' he says now. 'I think they had been *spiritually* close.'

Jeanne is impatient with this notion. She remembers Kippe and Pieter getting on particularly badly, and their shared love of acting being a source of friction rather than a bond. Kippe's grief, and her retrospective reverence for Pieter, she suggests, had their roots in a melodramatic need 'to be associated with somebody who had done something splendid in the war'.

There is another possibility. Kippe was stubborn. She had stood firm in the face of her parents' misgivings about her marriage to Tony Bridge. Yet their future together was fraught with uncertainty. Tony had no money and no home. Once the wedding was over, after a brief honeymoon in the Sussex countryside, he was to return to Scotland, and she to her childhood bedroom at the Eyrie. There was no knowing when the war would end, or when they would be able to live normally as a married couple. Kippe was still only twenty-three

Pieter Cammaerts.

and it would be surprising if, in the run-up to the wedding, she had not privately felt extremely anxious. Pieter's death may have given her just the excuse she needed, consciously or not, to vent her anxiety in grief – just as, in the years to come, it would provide an outlet for the sadness that gathered about her from other sources.

Eleven months after the wedding Kippe gave birth to a son and named him, after his uncle, Pieter. He was, from the start, the spitting image of his father – a father of whom he retains not a single childhood memory. Short leaves were few and brief and by the time Kippe realised that she was expecting a second baby, in the early spring of 1943, Tony Bridge was travelling east, via Basra, to the Iranian city of Abadan, where he had been posted with the Paiforce to guard the Anglo-Iranian Oil Company on the banks of the Shatt al-Arab waterway. It was here that he received a telegram from England announcing that a second son, Michael, had been born on 5 October. It was, he noted in his memoirs, 'joyous news'.

On the morning of Michael's birth *The Times* announced that Corsica had fallen to the French Resistance – the first department of France to be liberated. In the days that followed it became clear that the Allies had the Germans on the run. On 7 October the Red Army mounted a new thrust on enemy positions along the river Dnieper, breaking the Germans' 1,300-mile defence front; a week later Italy declared war on Germany. By the end of the month the Allies were bombing the Reich from Italian soil. In early December the British government announced that there would only be enough turkeys for one in ten families at Christmas, but any sense of joylessness was eased, on Boxing Day, by the news that the British navy had sunk the last of the great German battleships, the *Scharnhorst*, off the coast of Norway.

For Kippe, relief that the war might soon be over was mixed with apprehension. Since Tony had left for Abadan she had lived in a state of limbo, real life temporarily suspended. Now she was beset by anxieties. What would her husband do when he came home, and how would he provide for her and the boys? Where would they live? Would the Cammaerts family ever learn to respect him? And, more unsettling, did she respect him herself?

At the Eyrie, childhood rivalries and insecurities had continued to fester, and Tony Bridge had become a source of embarrassment to his young wife. His army career was unspectacular. Flat-footed and rather short-sighted, he had not been commissioned as an infantry officer, and had instead been enlisted into the Pioneer Corps – a blow to Kippe's pride. His letters home were few and dull, much taken up with complaints about the oppressive Persian heat and his troublesome eczema. Just before Pieter's death, Kippe's sister Elizabeth had married an officer serving on the North-West Frontier. Jeanne, meanwhile, was engaged to an officer in the 16th Durham Light Infantry. The letters Elizabeth and Jeanne received were frequent, vivid and entertaining, and they delighted in reading them aloud in the nursery at the Eyrie, reawakening in Kippe the feelings of inadequacy and failure that she had suffered as a child.

Yet all might have been well if, as planned, Tony Bridge had returned home in the summer of 1945. Instead, at short notice, his Iranian posting was prolonged, and just when – as Emile Cammaerts later put it – Kippe was 'keyed up' to welcome him back, and 'worn out by the preparations she had made to receive him and by a series of delays and disappointments', Jeanne's fiancé, Geoffrey Lindley, visited the Eyrie with an army friend, Jack Morpurgo.

The visit took place on 27 September 1945, and that morning Michael had spoken his first full sentence. Of Kippe's first impressions of Jack, there is no record; but nearly half a century on Jack's memories were vivid. 'The door opened,' he wrote, 'and a girl came in carrying a laden tea-tray. It was unmistakably an entrance; all conversation was silenced, Martha had upstaged a whole cast of Marys; but this Martha had all the advantages ... All my attention was centred on that tall slim figure, its every movement a delicious conspiracy between art and nature.' Here was a treasure, he reflected, 'who would outshine all else in my collection'.

He knew that she was married, but on the train back to St Pancras that evening Jack Morpurgo comforted himself that 'a girl as precious as Kippe had no need to waste her loveliness on the Pioneer Corps. "As a golden jewel in a pig's snout ..."' He was determined, from that first meeting, that he would have her.

Jack Morpurgo had all the qualities that Tony Bridge lacked. He was good-looking, witty, glamorous, faintly rakish. 'Confidence I never lacked,' he admits in his 1990 autobiography, *Master of None*, and self-assurance oozes from his description of himself at the time of his meeting with Kippe: 'a mature senior officer, his face hardened and blackened by years of sun and wind, his hair already touched with grey, the chest of his uniform-jacket blazoned with medal-ribbons, its epaulets sparkling with rank-badges'.

Born to working-class parents in the East End of London, thoroughly indulged by two adoring elder sisters and precociously clever, Jack had, at thirteen, won a scholarship to Christ's Hospital, a school founded by Edward VI for poor children. From that moment on, he was relentlessly determined to better himself. 'I wanted my parents to go,' he wrote, remembering their delivering him at Christ's Hospital for the first time. 'They did not belong in all this spaciousness. They could not match the blatant dignity that surrounded us, already even the elegance of my new uniform set me in another world.'

Jack's service with the Royal Artillery during the war, in India, the Middle East, Greece and Italy, had stiffened his ruthlessness. He had

Jack Morpurgo.

seen many men die. He had witnessed the defection of wives and girlfriends – including his own great love, Jane, from whose rejection he was still smarting when he met Kippe. He, and those serving with him, had learned that life could be short and uncertain and that they must take what it offered without hesitation or scruple. 'We were intensely loyal to those who served with us,' he wrote, 'but we would not have given a spent shell-case for convention or morality.' If winning Kippe meant destroying a marriage, breaking the heart of another man, and robbing two infant boys of their father, so be it.

In November 1945 Kippe caught the train up to London and she and Jack spent the evening alone together. By the end of the year they were engaged in what Jack later described as a game of 'Let's pretend' – 'but we were not children, we were in love'.

What happened over the next few weeks can be pieced together from a slim file of correspondence which remains, more than sixty years on, so distressing to Michael that he has never read it in full. Jack Morpurgo was cleverer than Kippe, and he knew it. His letters to her, typed on foolscap in faultless mandarin prose, are exercises in intellectual bullying. He bombards her with arguments until he has her boxed in on every side. Tony Bridge, he insists, is a mere 'basewallah' who has seen no real action. He is utterly undeserving of a wife like Kippe, whom Jack compares to Cleopatra. He flatters Kippe, quoting Keats to Fanny Burney, 'You have ravished me away by a Power I cannot resist …', but he also hints that youth is not on her side, and states baldly that he is 'not prepared to wait indefinitely'. When, briefly, Kippe summons up the strength to break off relations with him, he writes daily to his 'Lost Darling', protesting that she has condemned him to 'an eternity of bleakness' – yet slipping in a sly reference to Jean Lindsay, a pretty nurse with whom he spent time in Abyssinia, and who has been in touch and wants to see him.

Kippe's handwritten responses to Jack are, by contrast, short and simple, and filled with self-denigration and remorse. She begs his forgiveness for her 'failings' and her 'selfishness', for her inability to express herself – 'it's pretty poor to be able to say so little so stupidly' – and to see her way forward. She longs for guidance and comfort. Jack is sparing with his sympathy. 'You have this marvellous capacity for taking upon your own shoulders the burdens of all the world, and for blaming none but yourself for the mishaps that occur to others,' he concedes, but he warns that her misery and indecision will be causing damage to Pieter and Michael. And when Kippe admits that, in desperation, she has written a 'muddled letter' to Tony Bridge telling him what is afoot, Jack puts her swiftly into checkmate. He and Kippe cannot now stop seeing one another, he argues, because 'any break in our relations implies acceptance of some guilt, and will imply that to your husband'. Nor can Kippe any longer contemplate a future with Tony Bridge, who, knowing of her feelings for Jack, 'will pass his days with doubts'.

On receiving Kippe's 'muddled letter' Tony was granted compassionate leave. He made a painful progress back to England – Basra to Baghdad, Baghdad to Tel Aviv, Tel Aviv to Cairo, Cairo to Alexandria, across the Mediterranean to France, and, finally, by steamer into Newhaven. On Friday 1 February 1946 he and Kippe were reunited at the Rembrandt Hotel in Knightsbridge.

They travelled together to Suffolk, and for a week bicycled around Blythburgh, Walberswick, Southwold, Tony hoping that, surrounded by silence and sea breezes, by tall churches, fluent countryside and early spring light, they might somehow recover what they seemed to have lost. They returned to the Eyrie, and for most of that spring they remained together. But the atmosphere was fraught and Kippe was still in touch with Jack. On 4 April, having found Kippe in tears in Tony's arms, Emile Cammaerts sent Jack a letter, begging him courteously but firmly to leave his daughter alone. 'I don't know whether you realize what a terrible strain your present relationship with Catherine imposes upon Tony,' he wrote. 'I feel certain that he will not be able to stand it much longer. He is no longer the cheerful and easy-going man we used to know.' It was no good. Back in London Kippe and Jack went to see a divorce lawyer and, as Jack put it, 'prepared suitable evidence for inspection by a detective on an appointed day'.

It was to be, by today's standards, a brutally thorough separation. In the face of fierce opposition from his parents, who were about to lose their only grandchildren, Tony decided that it would be best for his sons if he removed himself completely from their lives. He was, after all, through no fault of his own, a complete stranger to them.

Both sons now speak of his decision with defensive pride: 'It was,' says Pieter, 'a very brave thing for him to do, to give us up. He thought, and I'm sure he was right, that it would be less confusing for us.' Michael compares Tony to Gabriel Oak – 'a man who didn't know the meaning of possessiveness or selfishness'. But Tony did not regard his actions as either brave or noble: 'It was,' he wrote towards the end of his life, 'just the way it had to be.' After bleak attempts to reignite his acting career in the West End, he emigrated to Canada, changed his name to Tony van Bridge, and eventually found work with Sir Tyrone Guthrie in Stratford, Ontario.

Despite all he had suffered, Tony remained, in a part of himself, devoted to his 'Kate'. In his 1995 memoir, *Also in the Cast*, the pages about her glow. 'I am glad that Kate and I married,' he insists; and the reader cannot help but feel that the urge to set down those words for posterity was his chief motive in writing the book.

*   *   *

In November 1945, the month that Kippe's affair with Jack Morpurgo began in earnest, the film *Brief Encounter* was released in British cinemas. We all know the story: a man and a woman, middle-class, in early middle age and married, meet by chance on a suburban railway station and fall in love. After much humiliation, guilt and anguish – played out against the strains of Rachmaninov's Piano Concerto No. 2 – they agree to part. So compelling were the performances by Trevor Howard and Celia Johnson that rumours flew about that they must genuinely be having an affair. But what impressed the *Times* critic was not so much the acting as the 'heroic integrity' at the centre of the film. In overriding their passions and returning to their dull but dependable spouses, the couple had, in the end, done 'the right thing'.

All over Britain the opposite was happening. Since the end of the First World War divorce rates had soared. By the middle of the Second World War they seemed to be out of control. In October 1943, the month that Kippe gave birth to Michael, the archbishops of Canterbury and York had spoken out jointly against 'moral laxity', urging Christians to remember that promiscuity and adultery were sins that degraded personality, destroyed homes, and visited 'years of terrible suffering' on innocent children. But the divorce rates rocketed again that year and the next. In 1945, 15,634 couples divorced; and by the time Kippe and Tony's decree nisi was granted the following year the number had nearly doubled to 29,829 – a misleadingly low figure, in fact, as by the middle of the year there were more than 50,000 service men and women waiting for divorces, and the Attorney-General had been forced to appoint thirty-five new legal teams to process their cases.

Behind these statistics lay innumerable tales of grief and heartache. Few divorces can have been less acrimonious than Kippe and Tony's. It was, as Tony later wrote, 'quiet and unsensational'. But it was, even so, 'full of suffering on both sides'; and it left Kippe with a burden of guilt that she would carry to the grave.

She had inflicted great pain not just on Tony, whose decency and acquiescence can only have made her feel worse, but also on her parents-in-law. By running off with Jack Morpurgo she had proved all their misgivings about her well-founded, as well as depriving them of access to their only grandchildren. For weeks Arthur and Edith Bridge fought their son's decision to give Kippe custody of the boys. She cannot have been unaware of their distress.

Then there were her own parents. Both Emile and Tita were children of broken marriages, and both, as a result, had an almost pathological horror of divorce. Ever since his father's suicide, Emile had been haunted by the notion that there was 'bad blood' in the Cammaerts family and that it might one day resurface. On hearing the news that Kippe was to marry Jack, Jeanne remembers, Tita clung to the arms of her chair until her knuckles turned white, while Emile muttered, 'I'll kill that boy.'

They pleaded with Kippe to reconsider, employing all the arguments that Emile would later publish in a treatise on marriage, *For Better, For Worse*: adultery was 'a sin'; second marriages were 'sham marriages'; it put a child's soul in danger to witness 'division in the very place where union should prevail'. But, as her mind was made up, the chief effect of their pleading was to make Jack Morpurgo determined that they would play very little part in his and Kippe's future. Though he generally disliked bad language, he referred to Tita simply as 'the bitch', and visited the Eyrie as seldom as possible. When he and Kippe finally married, in Kensington Register Office on 16 July 1947, not a single member of the Cammaerts family was present.

Kippe was forced to turn from her own family to the Morpurgos. Shortly after the marriage, she and Jack moved from his flat in

Clanricarde Gardens, Notting Hill Gate, to 84 Philbeach Gardens, near Earls Court. The tall, terraced house was somewhat beyond their means, so Jack's two spinster, schoolmistress sisters, Bess and Julie, moved in with them to help pay the bills and look after the boys. They were to remain a part of the household for the next quarter of a century, a Laurel and Hardy pair – Julie, who had been jilted when she was twenty-one, delicate and emotionally fragile; Bess big-hearted and controlling.

It was Bess who was deputed to take Pieter and Michael for a walk one afternoon, and to explain to them that Jack was now their father. A memory of their conversation remains with Michael, fragmentary but crystal-clear. 'We were on a railway bridge. I must have said something about my father, and Bess said, "Well, you've got a *new* father now, you know." And a train came by, and the steam came up in my face. And it just felt quite strange.'

Jack, in fact, never formally adopted Pieter and Michael; but he was determined to expunge the memory of Tony Bridge, and the boys implicitly understood that their real father must not be mentioned. From the summer of 1947 onwards, they took Jack's surname. 'No one ever said, "Jack is your *step*father,"' Michael remembers. 'And when my mother had two more children, Mark and Kay, no one talked about half-brothers and half-sisters. We were the Morpurgos: that's what they told the outside world. We children were part of that story; that sham.'

Pieter was just five at the time of the divorce, and had recently learned to write out his full name, PIETER BRIDGE. One of his earliest memories is of being told that he was a Bridge no longer, and of toiling over the new letters M-O-R-P-U-R-G-O. But visitors had only to look at Pieter to see that he was *not* a Morpurgo. He was

Michael and Pieter outside 84 Philbeach Gardens.

extraordinarily like his true father; a constant, vexing reminder to Jack of the man he had wronged. Like Farmer Tregerthen in Michael's story 'Gone to Sea', Jack was 'not a cruel man by nature, but he did not want to have to be reminded continually of his own inadequacy as a father and as a man'. From the start, he was unreasonably hard on Pieter, whom Jeanne describes as a 'sensitive, shivering child', and Michael was aware of being unfairly favoured.

Pieter and Michael, 1948.

Perhaps Kippe, too, was unsettled by Pieter's likeness to Tony; perhaps, because he was nervous and easily upset, he fuelled her guilt. Michael, by contrast, was a robust, sunny toddler, and with his mother, as with Jack, he had the closest bond. He remembers walking with her, hand-in-hand, through the smog that descended on London like a manifestation of post-war gloom. He remembers the thrill of being allowed to take charge of the ration book when they shopped together at the local International Stores, where he committed his first felony, slipping into his pocket a model Norman soldier with an orange tunic and an irresistible hinged helmet. He remembers stopping with her to talk to the weepy-eyed, skewbald milk-cart horse, Trumpeter, which used to stand shifting from foot to foot in Philbeach Gardens, munching from the sack of hay round his neck, giving off what seemed to Michael a fascinating odour of fur and sweat and dung.

But most vivid of all are his memories of bedtime, when Kippe would sit at the end of his bed and read to him. She read from *Aesop's Fables*, Masefield and de la Mare, from Belloc, Longfellow, Lear and Kipling. She had a way of making imaginary characters and places come alive, of conveying the music and joy and taste of language:

> Then Kolokolo Bird said, with a mournful cry, 'Go to the banks of the great grey-green, greasy Limpopo River, all set about with fever-trees …'

Michael rolled the words around on his tongue like sweets. When he was three, his mother found him rocking to and fro in his bed, chanting 'Zanzibar! Zanzibar! Marzipan! Zanzibar!'

Story-time over, Kippe would leave the door slightly ajar to let in a chink of light. The smell of her face-powder lingered in the room.

Sometimes there could be about Kippe an almost reckless *joie de vivre*. When one afternoon Pieter and Michael locked themselves into their fifth-floor bedroom while they were supposed to be resting, she shinned undaunted up a drainpipe, ignoring Jack's protests, and climbed in through their window to rescue them. When visitors came to the house she shone. 'As she opened the front door,' Michael remembers, 'it was as if she was walking on to a stage – beautifully dressed and made-up, charming, sparkling.'

But when the visitors left she tended to collapse, reaching for her cigarettes and smoking almost obsessively. And sometimes for days on end a sadness – what Pieter calls 'a wondering' – would settle upon her, and she became quiet and unreachable. Twice a year she would take Pieter and Michael on a bus to Twickenham to visit their paternal grandparents in their neat, modest, semi-detached house in Poulett Gardens. Michael remembers the uncomfortable formality of these visits – 'the scones, the clinking of spoons on teacups' – and the awkwardness as the conversation turned to Tony, his grandparents bringing out photographs and press clippings to show to the boys. On the way home, and for days afterwards, Kippe was silent. Michael knew that to ask questions would upset her further, so he too remained silent, aware simply that 'ours was a family which had at its heart a tension'.

In the wider world, too, he was becoming aware of complexity and shadows. The area around Philbeach Gardens had been heavily

Michael, 1948.

bombed in the Blitz, and the house next to number 84 completely destroyed. The cordoned-off bomb site was reachable via the cellar, and Michael particularly liked to play here alone. 'It was my Wendy house, I suppose. A rather tragic Wendy house.' Among the weeds and crumbling walls were remnants of life – bits of cutlery, a chair, an iron bedstead – evidence that in the very recent past 'there had been this terrible trauma' for the family that had lived there.

School, when it came, confirmed his sense that the world could be harsh. At three, Michael was taken to a playgroup in the hall of St Cuthbert's, Philbeach Gardens: a cosy, eccentric set-up, where the lady in charge kept order by issuing the children with linoleum 'islands' on which they would be asked to sit if they threatened to become unruly. At five, he moved on to the local state primary school, St Matthias, across Warwick Road. It seemed a cavernous, grim place to a small boy, with painted brick walls as in a prison or hospital, and windows so high that if a child tried to look out all he could see were small segments of sky. There was one magical element. Beneath the school lived a community of refugee Greek Orthodox monks: long, black-robed creatures who glided soundlessly in and out of a dark chapel full of glowing lanterns. But within the school itself the children were coaxed into learning through fear. Mistakes were met with a thwack of the teacher's ruler, either on the palm of the hand, or, more painfully, across the knuckles. Michael found himself frequently standing in the corner. Books and stories were suddenly filled with menace – 'words were to be spelt, forming sentences and clauses, with punctuation, in neat handwriting and without blotches'. He developed a stutter, his tongue and throat clamping with terror when he was asked to read or recite to the class; and he began to cheat, squinting across to copy from brainy, bespectacled Belinda, who shared his double desk, and with whom he was in love.

29

So it came as a relief when, just after his seventh birthday, plans were made for Michael to leave St Matthias and join Pieter at his prep school in Sussex. Kippe took him on a bus to Selfridges, and he remembers the delight of being measured up, of being the centre of attention, of watching his 'amazing' uniform (green, red and white cap; blazer 'like the coat of many colours'; rugby boots; shiny, black, lace-up shoes; socks; shorts; shirts and ties) piling up on the counter – 'all for me!' He had remained, despite everything, a happy child, 'very positive, full of laughs, a bit of a show-off', and the prospect of prep school was thrilling. 'I was really looking forward to it,' he says. 'I had no idea what was in store.'

It can be uncomfortable when family stories believed to be true are revealed as myth. When Maggie told me the truth about my uncle Pieter's death, it took a while to sink in. The story I'd believed for nearly seventy years had entered deeply into my imagination. So, in a different way, had the letters that Jack Morpurgo and my mother wrote each other when they fell in love – though I've not read them all. I wanted to work both Uncle Pieter and those letters into a story. As I turned it over in my mind it began to take the form of a letter itself – a confessional story/letter.

Bubble, Bubble, Toil and Trouble

To my mother, Kippe

Do you remember? You used to read to us every night, every night without fail. For both of us, Piet and me, this time just before bed was an oasis of warmth and intimacy. The taste of toothpaste still reminds me of those precious minutes alone with you, our bedtime treat. We'd climb into the same bed, browsing the book together before you came, longing to hear the sound of your footfall on the stairs. Sometimes I'd fall asleep before you came but would always wake for the story. You read to us only those stories and poems that you loved, often in a hushed voice as if you were confiding in us, telling us a secret you'd never told anyone else. We still love those stories and poems to this day, over sixty years later, but in my case with one exception.

Everything else you read us I simply adored. I never wanted your story-time to end. 'The Elephant's Child' from Kipling's *Just So Stories* was my favourite. Piet's was 'The Cat that Walked by Himself'. We both knew them off by heart. And then sometimes you'd read a poem by Masefield or de la Mare. It could be 'The Listeners' –

'Is there anybody there?' said the Traveller,
    Knocking on the moonlit door;
And his horse in the silence champed the grasses
    Of the forest's ferny floor …

Or maybe 'Cargoes', with all those wonderfully mysterious and musical names: 'Quinquireme of Nineveh from distant Ophir'. Or 'Sea-Fever':

I must go down to the seas again, to the lonely sea and
    the sky …

I may not always remember which poet wrote which poem, but I remember the poems, every line of them; and your voice reading them. And I mustn't forget Edward Lear's nonsense poems, those ludicrous limericks that made us all laugh so much.

There was an Old Man with a beard,
Who said, 'It is just as I feared! –
Two Owls and a Hen, four Larks and a Wren,
Have all built their nests in my beard!'

We all thought that the old man in question had to be your daddy, or Grad as we called him, who had a bushy white beard that smelt of pipe tobacco. I used to sit on his lap sometimes and explore the depths of his beard with my fingers, searching for any birds or birds' nests that might be there, but they never were. When I asked Grad once why there were no birds in his beard, he told me that they had been there, but they'd all grown up now and flown the nest 'like little birds do, like we all do in the end'.

*   *   *

It's not so surprising, when I come to think about it now, that you were such a compelling reader, such a magical storyteller. Until you married for the second time you had been an actress like your own mother, like your brother, like our first father too. It was in your blood to love words, to love stories (I think maybe it's in mine too – and Piet's, he's spent all his working life in theatre or television). You could make your voice sing and dance. You could be an elephant or a cat or even a crocodile – no trouble at all. You could do ghosts and pirates – Marley's ghost in *A Christmas Carol*, Captain Hook in *Peter Pan*. You simply became them. So Piet and I lived every story, believed every character. You brought them to life for us. Our imaginations soared on the wings of your words. And that was a fine and wonderful thing – mostly.

But the trouble was that with one poem in particular you were far too good, far too frightening. You scared me half to death every time you recited it. I don't think you realised it at first because I was adept at toughing it out. I'd feign terror, clap my hands dramatically over my ears while you were reading, make a whole big scene of being terrified, to cover up the fact that I was.

For obvious reasons you knew and loved Shakespeare. And, as I was later to discover, you were good at it on the stage too. You were Ophelia in *Hamlet*, Cordelia in *King Lear*, Rosalind in *As You Like It*: the reviews I read were all glowing. I found them after your death in among your papers in your desk, in an envelope marked 'good reviews, bad ones burnt'. Anyway, the trouble was that Piet loved one particular Shakespearean ditty of yours more than all the others, and at bedtime he'd ask for it over and over again. I dreaded it every time. I knew a terrifying transformation was about to occur. You'd simply become the three witches, sitting there around the fire over your steaming cauldron, chanting your hideous witchy spell. You thought, and Piet thought – or maybe he didn't, I'm still not sure – but certainly you thought that I was just messing about, playing at being scared as I put my hands over my ears and buried my head in the pillow. You would put on your tremulous witchy voice and that shrill cackle, and if I ever dared look up, I'd see your contorted witchy face, your fingers suddenly turned to claws, and I knew what was coming. Your screeching words would force themselves between my fingers into my ears and there was nothing I could do to keep them out. The moment I heard those first words of the witches' spell my soul was on fire with fear:

Bubble, bubble, toil and trouble,
Fire burn, and cauldron bubble …

I could tell that Piet was frightened too. He seemed to be enjoying his fear, revelling in it. But then he was brave. He'd even join in the chorus sometimes and I'd be screaming into my pillow by now to blot out the spell, over-acting like crazy, hamming it up, anything to disguise the real terror I was feeling.

Whenever you recited that horrible ditty I could never sleep afterwards, not for hours. The darkness around me was as dark as death, and full of watching witches, their eyes glaring at me, blood-red and menacing. I'd close my eyes to shut them out, but there was no shutting them out. Whether I was awake or asleep, they'd be there, haunting me, turning my dreams to nightmares. I'd wake up sweating, checking my nose had not been turned into a beak, feeling my hands and feet just in case they'd become webbed overnight.

* * *

I asked you about witches one day in the garden, do you remember? I was sitting on my bicycle and you were hanging out the washing on the line. I asked you whether they were really true. I tried to sound unconcerned, as nonchalant as I could. I tried to make out I was just inquisitive. I was longing, of course, for you to tell me the answer I wanted to hear, which was that all witches and their potions and spells were just in stories and poems and pictures, nothing but gobbledegook. But you didn't say that, did you? Instead you put on your witchy voice again and your witchy look and your witchy claws and chased me round the garden in and out of the sheets and pillowcases and pyjamas hanging from the line, and I cycled off screaming, and you practically split your sides you thought it was so funny.

But then I crashed my bicycle into the edge of the sandpit and was catapulted into the air. I had a soft enough landing in the sand, but I was shaken up, and now crying hysterically – the shock, I suppose – quite unable to pretend any longer. My heart was pounding with fear. You must have seen that the terror in my eyes was real, that I wasn't playing games any more. You caught me up then and hugged me to you, and that was the best thing you could have done. You hugged the fear out of me. We laughed and sobbed it away together.

You didn't do the 'Bubble, bubble' witchy ditty after that. But Piet did sometimes when he wanted to tease me. With him I knew it was always in fun, but it still frightened me even so. It gave me the shivers every time he did it, but the truth was that in time I found I was enjoying the shivers, just a little bit.

Although I wasn't ever comfortable with folk tales if there was a witch involved, with spells and curses and the like, I half-wanted to hear them, and later I read them myself. Maybe 'Hansel and Gretel' was the turning-point? Through that story I found out how to deal with witches. Just as Gretel had done, I'd creep up behind them and push them in the oven and that would be that. Once I thought I could handle a witch, I could really enjoy the tingle of terror in witchy stories. I became fascinated by them, and by spells and curses in general. Why else would I have done what I did in the bomb site in that spring of 1948 when you were away in America?

So now, all these decades later, it is my turn to tell you a witchy story. It's a story I should have told you, or rather confessed to you, a long time ago. But I could never bring myself to do it, until you were gone, until now.

Only three people in the world know this story, the three witches of Philbeach Gardens. I've never told anyone else because it's a story I've been ashamed of ever since it happened, some sixty-odd years ago. It still upsets me when I think of what I did, what we all did, and what happened afterwards. I still can't understand it or explain it. Maybe you can? I mean you've been alive and you've been dead, so you've been on both sides of the divide, haven't you? You'd know about these things. Anyway, here's our story, how it happened.

You remember when we all lived in London at number 84 Philbeach Gardens? And you remember the bomb site right next door to our house? I'd have been about six maybe, in my first year of proper school, at St Matthias on Warwick Road. It was an ordinary enough London County Council school, but strangely there was a chapel attached to it that we shared with Greek Orthodox priests who drifted around the place, black-bearded phantoms to us, so we kept well clear of them. Apples were the best thing about school. They were sent over from Canada for us because, just after the war, fruit was scarce. We were still on rations, weren't we?

Usually Piet would walk me to school, but if there was one of those pea-souper smogs, you'd take us and come and fetch us – for safety's sake, I suppose. I loved that, to see you waiting for us outside the school gates in the fog. But then, when we got home, you'd go and spoil it; you'd make us drink hot Bovril for tea to warm us up. You can't imagine how much I hated Bovril.

But Bovril aside, that was always the best time of the day, after school. What you won't remember, what you don't know, is what Piet and I and Belinda got up to down in the basement, when you weren't there. You remember Belinda from across the road? The three musketeers, you always called us. But we weren't the three musketeers at all, not for long anyway, not after what we found down in the basement that day.

You didn't like us to go down to the basement on our own because the wooden steps were too steep and they were rotten as well in places. That's why you kept the door locked. There was all sorts of stuff down there, anything you didn't want in the house or there wasn't room for. You kept suitcases there, among other things. We knew they were down there because we'd helped fetch them up with you before we went off on holiday to Bournemouth, the first holiday I ever went on, the first time I saw the sea.

We noticed then where you kept the key, up on the ledge above the door. I couldn't reach it, even standing on a chair, but Piet could. So that's how we got in there without you or anyone knowing. We just waited until the coast was clear, got the key, and down we went. The place was stuffed full of trunks and tea chests, iron bedsteads and mattresses, boxes of old clothes – wonderful for dressing up – and papers and broken picture frames. It was a real Aladdin's cave, full of treasures waiting to be discovered. But it was musty and dusty down there and full of cobwebs, and more than once when I came down the steps I saw rats scuttling away into dark corners. At least the light worked – only dimly. But it did mean that it wasn't as scary as it might otherwise have been.

There was a small fireplace in the basement: at one time someone had used it, because the whole place reeked of soot and smoke. There was a heap of ashes in the grate, and the feathery skeleton of a jackdaw or a crow lying on top, wings outstretched – it must have fallen down the chimney. There was a Belfast sink in the corner with a tap, always dripping away the seconds.

One trunk in particular fascinated us because it was covered in labels, and on every one of them a picture of a ship – one was called the *Mauretania*, another the *Queen Elizabeth*. Who knew what treasures it contained? But what excited us most about the trunk was that it was locked. We had to imagine what was in there, and our imaginings led us naturally to pirates – treasure chests and pirates go together, don't they. So that was partly, I suppose, why I came to think of that dark and dingy basement as a pirate's lair. The iron hooks hanging from the ceiling only served to confirm it. When we first saw the hooks, Piet and I knew at once that this place had to be Captain Hook's treasure cave. This was where Captain Hook from *Peter Pan* kept all his treasure and his spare hooks for his arm, in case he lost one in a fight, we thought.

Once we'd found that key, Piet and Belinda and I would be down in the basement whenever we could, mostly after school, mostly when you went away or whenever you were out and left us with Aunty B and Aunty J, our live-in babysitters. We got up to all sorts of tricks with them, which was wicked of us, I know that now. We only got away with it because they adored us. The best trick of all was to disappear down to the basement and then come up again after hiding away for a while to find them all of a fluster and running around the house like headless chickens looking for us. Poor Aunty B. Poor Aunty J. But I have to say it was fun, being so horrible.

In spite of the hours we spent down there, we didn't come across the witches' cauldron for some time. It was hardly surprising – there was just so much fascinating stuff to sift through and explore. The tea chests were stuffed with old photos and papers and newspaper cuttings, which Belinda would read out to us because she was the best reader. We found an entire treasure trove of family heirlooms, each one wrapped up in newspaper – pewter cups, china plates and ornaments, vases. But as soon as we found the witches' cauldron, nothing else mattered to us.

Piet discovered it under a pile of coal sacks in a dark, dank corner. It was heavy, black and pot-bellied, with handles, and stood on three clawed feet.

'Look,' Piet whispered – we always talked in whispers down in the basement. 'It's a witches' cauldron. *Bubble, bubble, toil and trouble.*'

'We could do spells and things,' Belinda said.

I was up those stairs like a bat out of hell. It was at least a week before they could persuade me to go down to that basement again, and then it was only because of Belinda, because I didn't want to look like a scaredy-cat in front of her.

You used to tease me about Belinda, Mum. Only gently, but it made me blush and get cross. You were right, though: I did love her. She used to sit next to me in class and she was very clever. She'd always be first with her hand up and would finish her letter-copying before anyone else. She often used to get ten out of ten for her spelling, and could read aloud almost as fluently as our teacher, Miss Cruickshank. What's more, Belinda could add up and take away in her head, without using her fingers. She was a genius. She could hopscotch better than anyone in the whole school, and stand on her head for over five minutes. Plus, she was pretty. She had red hair and her eyes were green as beech leaves in spring. She was also Piet's girlfriend, but we were young enough for none of that to matter.

I'd never have dared to do it if Belinda hadn't suggested it. We were on our way back from school one afternoon. She and Piet were walking ahead of me, whispering to one another. I caught up with them.

'What?' I said. 'What's going on?'

'You don't want to know,' Piet replied. 'It's about witches.'

'I'm not scared,' I told him.

So he went on, 'I was telling Belinda about the three witches and the "Bubble, bubble, toil and trouble" spell and she said why didn't we do it together, y'know, with the cauldron? We could make a fire, put in the frogs and newts and stuff, say the spell. We could be the three witches. I said you wouldn't want to do it.'

'I would,' I insisted.

'See?' Belinda said. 'I told you he'd do it, Piet. I'll make the hats. We've got to have witches' hats or the spell won't work.'

That was it. There was no way I could get out of it now.

It all happened while you were away. I think it was one of those times you went off to America with him, with our stepfather. I remember the postcards you sent us of the Empire State Building and one of the Statue of Liberty. I've still got them somewhere hidden away, in some trunk in our attic, I suppose. We didn't ever like you going off with him. But when you went away, there was always one major compensation. Aunty B and Aunty J would look after us, which meant of course that we could do pretty much as we liked.

Belinda set it all up, made the hats as she said she would, told us what to do and how to do it. She said it was the boys' job to make the fire, that girls didn't do that sort of thing. She sat on the locked trunk with the ship pictures all over it, kicking her heels, and watched as Piet and I did our best to get the fire to light. We got through half a box of pink-tipped Swan Vestas and still nothing would burn. Everything we tried was too damp – old newspapers, magazines, sacks, socks even. We tried blowing and fanning. Nothing worked. Belinda kept telling us we had to keep at it and it would light. 'Easy as pie,' she said. 'You've just got to blow harder.'

Then she patted the trunk. 'What's in this anyway?' she asked, her legs swinging, her heels drumming on the trunk.

'Dunno,' I said. 'It's locked.'

At that moment the lock flew open.

'It's not,' she said, and she got off the trunk and lifted the lid. We all peered in. There were letters and photos, hundreds of them. She picked one out.

'Who wrote this?'

It was your handwriting, Mum. And when Belinda started reading, it sounded just like your voice talking.

After just a few moments, Belinda stopped reading aloud and began reading the letter to herself.

'Golly gosh,' she whispered.

'What?' I asked. 'What does it say?'

'It's all about love,' she said. 'Listen.'

Darling J,
I love you, you know I do. But I just don't know if I can
go ahead with it. Don't think badly of me. I know I am
weak. I know I need your strength around me. I love you,
darling. Always.
Kate

She handed me the letter.

'That's our mum,' I told her. 'Sometimes she's Kate, sometimes
Kippe, sometimes Catherine. But that's how she writes, that's her
handwriting.'

'There's lots more like this,' Belinda said. Piet snatched the letter
out of my hand. 'You shouldn't be reading it,' he said, and there
were tears in his voice. 'It's private.'

That's when Piet spotted the photograph lying there in the
trunk in among the letters. He reached down and picked it up.

'It's their wedding,' he said. 'That's him, our real father, in the
uniform. And that's our mum.'

We stared at it in silence.

'She looks so beautiful,' Belinda whispered.

'That's private too,' Piet said, as he dropped the photograph and
the letter back into the trunk, and shut the lid.

I should never have said it, but I did. 'That letter, it looked dry, it
felt dry,' I said. 'If that one was dry, they'll all be dry.'

That's how we got the fire going, Mum, with your letters. So
that's my first confession. I'm not sure even now exactly what
made us do such a terrible thing. Make no mistake, we all knew it
was terrible, not just me. Piet didn't want to do it. I've got to tell
you that. But I talked him round. I persuaded him that burning
your letters wouldn't really matter because they couldn't be that
important. After all, why would they be left in a trunk in the

basement if they were? Eventually he gave way, but only reluctantly and because, like Belinda and me, he really wanted to get that fire lit and the cauldron bubbling.

We all wanted that, but if I'm honest I think there was another reason too. There were things in that letter, and probably in all the others, that I didn't want to hear about or even know about. I prefer to think of course that after failing so often to get a fire lit, we burned the letters in the trunk because they were our last hope. Anything that would burn was all right. But I know now that wouldn't be entirely true. What is true is that if we hadn't burned them, none of the rest of this would have happened.

Remember when we were a little older and you used to read us those C. S. Lewis books, the Narnia books? And how, although you loved them, I never really got on with them? Well, maybe what happened next was our Lion, Witch and Wardrobe moment. Only we didn't walk through the back of a bedroom cupboard into a never-never land and discover a rather goody-two-shoes lion walking about – I could never believe in that lion or the never-never land either. Our Narnia was real bricks and mortar, and we didn't get to it through a cupboard, but through a wall.

Piet was kneeling down, ready to light the letters we'd piled in the fireplace, and Belinda and I were scouting around for any bits of wood we could find – I broke up an empty tea chest, I remember. And there was our old playpen already in pieces, so we used that. The letters caught fire at once, and within moments there was smoke billowing out into the basement. Soon we were all coughing and choking, frantically trying to wave the smoke away. Piet saw it first because he was closer to the fireplace than we were.

'It's not going up the chimney at all,' he spluttered. I noticed then that he was leaning forward, hand over his mouth, peering into the chimney. 'It's going out the back. The smoke, it's going out through the bricks at the back of the fireplace. Look!'

Crouching down, through the clearing smoke, we could see that he was right. Piet had picked up the old chair leg he'd been using as a poker and began prodding at the bricks. 'They're loose,' he said. 'You can see them, they're moving – look!'

Now he was not just prodding, he was poking at them hard. That was when there was a sudden avalanche of bricks and the whole back wall behind the fireplace fell away. We were looking out through a huge hole into the bomb site beyond.

The bomb site next door had that high chain-link fence on the street side of it, remember? The sign read 'Keep Out'. You told us again and again never to climb the fence and go in there, that the walls were dangerous and could collapse at any moment, that there might even be unexploded bombs. More than once you told us about Malcolm, the teenage boy from down the street who used to go climbing the walls in there before the fence was put up, and how he'd fallen and broken his neck and how his legs didn't work any more – you pointed him out once in his wheelchair outside the corner shop. So Piet and I had never dared venture in there.

Belinda had though. She'd crawled in lots of times, she said, through a hole in the fence, and nothing had happened to her. And I'd stood there often enough, gazing into the bomb site from the street, fingers hooked into the fence, just longing to go in and explore. Now was our chance. More than a chance. That hole in the wall was an open invitation.

Once we'd scrambled through the hole and out into the bomb site we found we were not overlooked at all. We were well hidden from the road by the ruins and the thick undergrowth and trees, which seemed to be sprouting everywhere, even out of the walls themselves. The place was like a jungle and there was no one in it but us. Belinda discovered another fireplace, just like ours in the basement of the ruins of the house adjoining ours. We knew we couldn't light a fire for fear of discovery, but we had our cauldron and our hats and our 'Bubble, bubble' spell. We'd look for frogs and toads, find whatever we could and then imagine the rest, she said. We got lucky and found a frog and a few beetles and caterpillars. We managed to drag our cauldron through the hole, set it in the fireplace in the basement of the bombed-out house, and very soon we had collected enough hopping and wriggling and crawling things to make a proper witches' spell. But there was no water in the cauldron and no fire. We'd have to see if the spell would work without.

So there we sat, the three of us, in our witches' hats. We held hands around the cauldron, closed our eyes and chanted our 'Bubble, bubble' witches' ditty. Then, believing in these dark powers as hard as we could (the technique for me was much the same as praying, it had to be done with eyes squeezed shut), we put spells on all the people we hated. Belinda chose Miss Cruickshank because she was always picking on her in class for having inky fingers or a blunt pencil. She turned her into a frog – it would serve her right, she said, because she had poppy eyes. Piet chose Ma Higgins at the corner shop who we were sure cheated us whenever we went in to buy three pennyworth of lemon sherbets or humbugs or liquorice. She had a wart on her nose and he used his spell to make her grow at least twenty more. As for me, I chose Aunty B because she kept saying that Piet and I should be more grateful to our stepfather, that he was a much better father than our real dad because our real dad had gone off and left us. I knew that was a lie. So I decided to put my witch's spell on her. She had a big nose anyway. My spell would make her nose grow longer and longer, just like Pinocchio's when he told fibs. We sat there, eyes squeezed, for ages, until it came on to rain. Then we decided it was time to let the little creatures go and we went back through the hole into our basement, dragging the cauldron with us.

The days that followed were disappointing. Miss Cruickshank did not turn into a frog. Ma Higgins still only had one wart, and Aunty B's nose stayed just about the same. Our spells hadn't worked. We knew exactly why things hadn't gone as well as they should have done: we needed to light a real fire, to boil the water so that it bubbled and so that we could do the whole spell properly. Piet said that maybe it was also because we were being mean with our spells, that witches didn't have to do bad things, that maybe we could make good wishes come true using the same spells.

In any case, we knew we couldn't light a fire because we'd be seen. So for quite a while, even though we went on playing in the bomb site, we forgot about being witches and casting spells. Instead we played war games among the ruins – that was my idea. I liked war games and I liked hide-and-seek. So I decided one of us would be a German and go and hide while the other two counted to a hundred. Then the German would be hunted down and killed – shot or bayoneted. Bayoneted was best. I liked it when it was Piet's turn to be the German, and then Belinda and I could hunt him. But my turn always came round. Being the German could be a bit scary. One afternoon Belinda and Piet just left me hiding there in the bomb site and it got darker and darker and they never found me. I was there for hours. Afterwards they told me they'd given up because they couldn't find me, but I reckoned they were just having me on. I sulked for a long time after that. I was good at sulking, remember, Mum?

Then one day we woke up to the thickest, yellowest London smog we'd ever had, and we decided we'd chance it. Smoke and fog

– it would look the same. It even smelt the same. We'd light a fire in the bomb site and do the whole witches' spell as it should be done. We used the rest of your letters from the trunk and got a good fire going, filled the cauldron with water from the tap, and collected any little creatures we could find – worms mostly and snails (not the right creatures perhaps, but the best we could manage) and we boiled them, I'm ashamed to say. We sat there in our pointed hats, the smog and smoke swirling around us, waiting for the water to bubble. When it did, we joined hands and did our 'Bubble, bubble, toil and trouble' chant several times. Then we squeezed our eyes tight shut and each of us made a wish – a good wish, as Piet reminded us it had to be, not a wicked one, and we had to tell one another what our wish was.

'You go first then, Piet,' Belinda whispered after a while. Eyes closed, Piet chanted the 'Bubble, bubble' spell, and then began: 'I wish ... I wish that when I grow up I'll be a famous actor. I want to be like that one we saw in the film of *Henry V* – Laurence something. I'll wear armour like he did and a helmet, and charge into battle on my horse waving my sword, and I'll be shouting, "For Harry, England and St George!"' He opened his eyes and smiled at us. 'Be good, that,' he said. 'Your go, Michael.'

But I didn't want my go yet because I still hadn't made up my mind. The truth was that Piet's wish sounded so good that now I found myself wanting almost the same as he had wished for. But there was a difference. I didn't want only to be an *actor* playing Henry V, I wanted to be him, the real king, Henry V himself. I knew it would sound silly – I understood even then that it was an impossibility to make a wish like that come true, even if we got the witches' spell right this time. I'd have to think of another wish, one that had a chance of coming true. I needed time.

'No. You go next, Belinda,' I said.

Belinda rattled through the spell and then made her wish. 'I want to be like Florence Nightingale,' she said quietly. 'I want to nurse all the soldiers and sailors and pilots who were wounded in the war. I want to make them better again like she did.'

I could tell as she said it that Belinda meant every word. And that was what I had to do, I thought. I had to mean it. That way it might come true.

'All right,' I began, my eyes as tight shut as they would go, willing my wish to happen, 'I want to be like my uncle Pieter. I want to be a Spitfire pilot and shoot down German planes, and then the King would give me the Victoria Cross.'

I opened my eyes to find Piet frowning at me, angrily almost, and I knew it must have upset him somehow.

'You can't be him. He's dead,' he said. 'And I'm the one who's named after him, not you, so you've got to make another wish. It's all silly anyway. You can't be someone you're not. And besides, you didn't say the "Bubble, bubble" spell, so it won't work.'

I was about to argue with him when we heard the voice. It came from somewhere above us. We looked up. Through the smog we could see a young man sitting high up on a window ledge on the top of the ruins.

'Your brother's right, Michael,' he said. 'You can't be someone you're not, not your uncle Pieter, not Laurence Olivier either, not Florence Nightingale. I reckon you've got to be yourself.'

He climbed down and came over to us. He was wearing a light blue overcoat and a scarf. His face broke into a smile. 'I like the hats,' he said, crouching down beside us. 'And you make fine witches. You did all the "Bubble, bubble" baloney really well. Almost had me believing in it myself.'

Struck dumb, the three of us just sat there, simply gaping at him.

'All those spells,' the stranger went on, 'it's a load of twaddle, y'know. Nothing but hocus-pocus. And by the way, it's not "Bubble, bubble, toil and trouble", it's "Double, double toil and trouble". I was in the play once. I'm an actor; I know. I played Banquo, got myself murdered on a late-night walk. All this wishing you do – it's fine, and hoping is fine, too. And you're right, you can try, you must try to make your hopes and your wishes come true. But you have to be careful what you wish for. You have to think things through. They mustn't be just flights of fancy. Dangerous stuff, fancy. I've been watching you three for quite a while now, sitting and chanting your spells around your cauldron, playing your war games all around the bomb site. I know I shouldn't have been eavesdropping, but I haven't got much else to do these days. And when I heard you making your wishes just now, I thought I'd better speak up, tell you what I think, tell you what I know.'

We still couldn't say a word. He was holding out his hands over the fire to warm them.

'It really upsets me, y'know, to see you playing your war games,' he went on. 'And all of you just now, all of your wishes, one way or another, had something to do with war. And that worries me. I've been in a war. These ruins, that's what war does. That's bad enough, but it does more than that. Look around you.'

As he spoke, out of the smog the ruins seemed to grow and take shape and form roofs, chimneys, windows, doors. The houses rebuilt themselves before our eyes. We were still sitting over the cauldron, but now we were in the back garden of a house. There was blue sky above and butterflies chasing one another and sparrows bickering on the lawn. Nearby there were children playing in a sandpit, and a mother in a headscarf was calling out of the window for them to come in for tea. By the back door an old man, mouth wide open, lay fast asleep in a deckchair, his slippers on, an open book resting on his chest.

'And tell your grandad to come in too,' the mother was saying. 'And don't forget to wipe your feet and wash your hands.'

There was music playing on a gramophone from inside the house, and we could hear the rag-and-bone-man's horse clopping along the street: 'Any old iron? Any old iron?' came the cry.

As the sound of the horse's hooves died away the children went inside, one of them stopping to shake Grandpa awake. The old man stood up, looking directly at us, but not seeing us, and there was a terrible sadness in his eyes as he looked up into the sky. The fog came swirling down again around him, and around us. He disappeared into it and the houses were suddenly ruins again. When the fog cleared, moments later, the stranger was gone too, vanished. But we heard his voice again from high up on the wall above us – only his voice. He was nowhere to be seen.

'All of them are gone. Dead,' he said. 'One bombing raid, that's all it took. Mum, grandad, the children, the rag-and-bone-man and his horse too. All gone in one night. That's what war does. You remember that.' Those were the last words he spoke.

The three of us were still holding hands, and we soon discovered we'd all seen and heard the same thing. We had imagined nothing. We made a pact there and then that we would never tell another living soul. For weeks afterwards, Piet and I, when we were alone at home, couldn't talk about anything else. We were forever trying to puzzle it out. And at school, the three of us stuck together in the playground as if protecting our unspoken secret. When the usual war games started up around us, we never once joined in.

It was my idea to see if we could make it happen again, bring back the ghost of the stranger – because all of us agreed by now that that's what he must have been, a ghost. Piet and Belinda were more nervous than I was, but I persuaded them. We needed to find out who he was and why he'd come to see us.

We decided it would be sensible to wait for the next smog and light the fire under the cauldron just as we had before. But the smog never came, and in the end we lost patience. We would try bringing him back without the cauldron. After all he'd said it himself: the witches' spell was a lot of baloney.

Two or three times we sat there in the bomb site holding hands, the three of us willing him to come back, or at least to speak to us. Each time, nothing. We had no choice in the end but to risk it, to try the cauldron way again – it had worked before. And if we built the fire in the late evening, quite close to the hole in the wall, no one would see the flames from the street, nor the smoke in the gathering dark.

So one evening, that's exactly what we did. We used the last of the letters from the trunk, along with bits of twigs we'd found in the bomb site, and lit our fire under the cauldron. A few creepy-crawly creatures – spiders and beetles – had found their way into the cauldron on their own. Because they'd almost volunteered to be boiled, we didn't feel quite so bad about it. There we sat in the half-dark, holding hands, eyes closed and reciting 'Double, double toil and trouble', with the right words this time, and in unison, over and over again, wishing, hoping, willing the stranger to reappear.

But no voice spoke to us. No one came, nothing happened. We tried again and again. But it just didn't work.

'Maybe we imagined it all,' Belinda said. But she knew, we all knew that we hadn't. It must have been almost bedtime when we heard Aunty B and Aunty J calling for us up and down the street, and we had to give up. When we appeared, we made up a story about having been at choir practice in the church hall, which they seemed to believe (they always believed whatever we told them). Belinda went off home and that was that. Or so we thought.

That night Piet and I were shaken out of sleep by Aunty B and Aunty J. They were frantic, sobbing as they dragged us down the smoke-filled stairs and out into the cold night air. There we stood, shivering on the pavement. I was only half-awake and didn't understand what was going on until we heard the bells of the fire engine. Our house was on fire! We watched in fascination and horror as the hoses were wound out and the firemen went running into our house. They broke down the fence in the bomb site.

There were dozens of people in the street by now, all in dressing gowns. Belinda's mother, in her curlers, gave Aunty B and Aunty J tots of whisky to calm them down. As for Belinda and Piet and me, we stood together, watching the drama unfold, all of us knowing full well, of course, how the fire had started.

The fire officer was talking to Aunty B and Aunty J. 'It looks like some idiot, some old tramp maybe, has gone in that bomb site and started a fire to keep himself warm.' He shook his head. 'Though what an old witches' cauldron is doing down there, God only knows. We've managed to confine the fire to your basement, but it's totally burned out in there, gutted. There's only smoke damage in the house itself, though we've had to use a lot of water to get the fire under control, so it's a bit of a mess, I'm afraid. Still, we must be thankful for small mercies' – he ruffled my hair – 'these little mercies I'm talking about. You got them to safety and that's all that really matters, isn't it, when all's said and done?'

The three of us didn't dare look at one another, or at anyone else, in case the guilt showed in our eyes. We went to sleep in Belinda's house that night, and stayed there for a week or more while Aunty B and Aunty J got the house cleared up for your return. I remember them breaking the news of the fire to you on the doorstep and how you tried to comfort them as, tearfully, they relived every moment of it. You kept hugging them, telling them how wonderful they had been to save Pieter and me, and in the end that seemed to make them feel better.

But Piet and I didn't feel better. We haven't felt better about it all our lives, and to be honest, telling you about it now hasn't helped as much as I hoped it might. Hiding this terrible secret from you, for as long as we have, has been at least as bad as the guilt we felt on the night it happened. It seems confession is not enough.

The trouble is there's another secret we never told you. It's not as bad as the burning of your love-letters and your wedding photo, or setting fire to the house, but it was a secret we couldn't tell, because if we had told it, all the others would have come out too.

The Christmas after the fire Gran came to stay, if you remember. She gave you a present. You opened it and showed it to us, probably with tears in your eyes – you always had tears in your eyes when you spoke about him.

'Look, boys, what Gran has given us,' you said. 'It's a photo of your uncle Pieter in his RAF uniform. Doesn't he look fine?'

You passed it to Piet and me. It was the first time we'd ever seen a photo of him. Looking up at us, out of the silver frame, without any question, was the face of the stranger we had met in the bomb site that foggy day. We knew it at once.

That is the secret I feel saddest about now, because it might have been a great comfort to you if we'd had the courage to tell you.

Some time after you died, far from any of us, out in America, in Washington, I happened to find myself near St Eval in Cornwall at the RAF station where I'd been told Uncle Pieter's plane had crashed in 1941. I stood there on what was left of the runway and told him at last that I knew it had been him who came to see us in the bomb site all those years before. He didn't speak, I didn't see him – but he was there, I am sure of it. And you were there too, Mum, I'm sure of that as well. It was a spring day. The hawthorns were white in the hedges, the daffodils blowing in the wind, and the blackbirds calling to one another over the fields.

2

Spotless Officer Number One

Saturday 19 December 2009; the Dragon School, Oxford. The playing fields are white with frost, but the Lynam Hall is a hive of warmth and colour as parents and children cram in to hear Michael Morpurgo open the Dragon Christmas Sale. As he strides on to the stage, draped in a long, multicoloured, Dr Who scarf, he is running on empty. The last week alone has taken him to two bookshop signings in London, and stage productions of *The Best Christmas Present in the World* in Bristol and *On Angel Wings* in Winchester. Exhaustion shows when it comes to taking questions. 'By the way,' he tells a little girl in a lime-green top, after answering her question about where his stories come from, 'the colour of your shirt is *appalling*.' She blushes to the roots of her hair.

In talking to groups of children Michael adopts what the illustrator Emma Chichester Clark calls his 'angry headmaster mode', projecting a persona that is knockabout, bumptious and 'seemingly', he admits, 'rather over-confident'. But the man you discover when you spend time with Michael at his home in Devon is quite different: thoughtful, unsure of his gifts, frightened of the blank page, and prone to melancholy. This 'schizophrenia' (his word) bothers him. 'I'm comfortable in both parts,' he confesses, 'but I'm *un*comfortable with the fact that I seem to need two parts. And I am certainly uncomfortable with the effect that this has on the people I love.' He is referring to his wife and children, but they come later in the story, years after the seeds of his 'schizophrenia' were sown at The Abbey, near East Grinstead in Sussex.

In the second half of the last century, Sussex and Kent were honeycombed with prep schools. Middle-class boys were squirrelled away in them in such large numbers that, arriving at Victoria Station at the end of the holidays, they were obliged to join a scrum of children squeezing around a blackboard to get directions to the railway carriages specially reserved for the Abbey, Ashdown House, Brambletye, Fonthill Lodge, Hazelwood, Hillsbrow …

Many of these schools are still going strong, but the Abbey long since fell victim to financial mismanagement, closed its doors to pupils, and was sold to a property developer and converted into flats. Yet from the outside the house looks exactly the same today as the one to which Michael returns often in his dreams: an ugly, late-Victorian, mock-baronial pile; a jumble of turrets and mullioned windows and brick excrescences. A weather-vane pokes up, slightly cockeyed, amidst a coppice of top-heavy chimneys, and there is a bleak stone inscription – *PERSEVERANTIA* – above an ivy-clad front door. The buildings around the main house are now suburban dwellings, but their names hint at the past – one is called 'Gymnasium', another 'The Old Laundry' – and walking through the overgrown gardens that surround them is like stepping into the pages of Michael's books. There is the stream, swelled in Michael's imagination to a river, across which the 'toffs' and the 'oiks' fought their battles in *The War of Jenkins' Ear*; and the woods in which a blond boy called Christopher made a chapel with a log altar and a straw floor, and persuaded his contemporaries that he was Jesus come again. And at the bottom of the school park is the fence over which Michael – later Bertie in *The Butterfly Lion* – climbed, overcome with homesickness, in a bid to run away from school.

Visiting the Abbey on a drizzly afternoon in late winter, one feels that the dripping rhododendrons are haunted by the homesickness which Michael suffered from the moment he arrived. It was worst at night. There was something about the moment that Matron, strict but kind, called 'Lights Out!' that made him yearn for his mother. And though darkness was a relief, allowing the tears to roll down his cheeks unseen, sleep did not come easily. Beyond the dormitory window was a clock tower that chimed the quarters, 'slicing up the night'; and the night was dominated by anxiety about the following day.

In a tatty copy of the Abbey school magazine from 1957, after a 'hail and farewell' section in which the staff seem to have been drawn straight from a pack of Happy Families – goodbye Mr Kane, head of senior Classics; welcome Mr Bent, English master, and Miss Kitkat, junior matron – there is the précis of a speech given to the boys by a visiting headmaster at their summer prize-giving. Those who have won cups must win more next year, he insists. Those who have not must work harder. And those at the bottom of their classes should resolve to be 'at least halfway up' by the time he visits again.

Academic success mattered. Measured in 'pluses' and 'minuses', 'unders' and 'overs', the performance of every boy was calculated weekly and read out to the whole school on a Sunday evening. Those who did well became 'Centurions'. Those who did badly were punished. At worst, this meant a journey up the red-carpeted stairway, 'the Bloody Steps', to the study of fat-fingered Mr Crump, one of the triumvirate of headmasters, for a caning. Canings took place amidst a collection of African tribal artefacts and hunting trophies left by the Abbey's previous owner, gambler and mining millionaire Sir Abe Bailey: 'Swish. Then "Ow, sir!" You had to shake Crump's hand when it was finished.'

Michael had his fair share of punishment. Pigeonholed from the start as not especially bright – 'Very much below the standard of the form,' his Maths master noted at the end of his first term – he remained, throughout his time at the Abbey, somewhere around the middle to bottom of his year. He was not helped by his stutter, which grew steadily worse, tripping him up on his 'c's and 'f's and 'w's. If there was a poem to learn, or a string of history dates, he would lie in the early hours of the morning contriving ways of sliding over these troublesome consonants. This did not always work, and when it failed he was teased. Then he would blush, and then he would be teased again: 'You're going *red*, Mor*p*urgo ...' Anxiety brought on chronic eczema – cracking, weeping knee and arm joints, which Matron daubed with ointment at bedtime, before feeding Michael one tablespoonful of Radio Malt, to build him up.

He might have cut a pathetic figure had not the 'other' Michael Morpurgo, the waggish, confident doppelgänger who has accompanied him through life, come to his rescue. Perhaps it was his theatrical genes that enabled him to drop a visor of confidence over his vulnerability; or perhaps it was Jack Morpurgo. Jack's treatment of Pieter, who was even less academic than Michael, bordered on cruelty. Observing it, Michael had learned early that the only way to rub along with his stepfather was to devise ways to win praise, even if this involved deceit.

Edna Macleod, who, with her husband, Ian, spent so much time with Kippe and Jack that the joint families became known as the 'Macpurgos', remembers one Christmas morning on which Pieter got up early to make Edna and Ian breakfast in bed. Just as he was about to carry the tray into their room, Michael lifted it from his hands, walked through and presented it to Edna – 'getting all the kudos'. Michael was 'a monkey', Edna says, but also 'irresistible'.

At home, family and friends were enchanted by his 'intelligence and humour and charm'.

Very quickly, the same was true at school. Once it was clear that he was not going to shine academically, he found other areas in which he could come out on top. In the Abbey magazine the achievements of 'Morpurgo ii' are lauded on almost every page. He is Chapel Warden and Chief Chorister. He is the only boy wheeled out to play a violin solo, 'Highland Heather', in the Christmas carol concert. He is in the tennis team, and he is Captain of Cricket. He carries off the cups for Batting, Choir and Personal Merit. Above all, he is a hero on the rugby pitch. Reports of matches against neighbouring schools are peppered with descriptions of his triumphs: 'From a quick heel, Morpurgo scored a good try'; 'Morpurgo's covering and tackling were excellent'; 'Morpurgo found his swerve

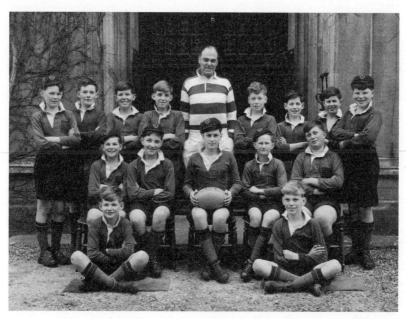

First XV at The Abbey, winter 1954. Mr Beagley stands centre back, Michael sits cross-legged, front left.

would not work on the slippery surface' but 'did some good defensive kicking' instead. Bookish he might not be, but the magazine editor is confident that 'a great Rugger future' lies before him.

His sporting triumphs brought multiple benefits. They had an anaesthetising effect on Jack, numbing him to Michael's mediocre academic reports: 'Far too inclined to flounder about in a sea of ink and inaccuracies' (Maths); 'His mapwork is untidy' (Geography); 'I do not understand him' (French); 'An exasperating boy' (English); 'Rather excitable and harum-scarum' (Headmaster). And they impressed the other boys, among whom Michael both relished and mistrusted his reputation as a 'clubbable and charismatic' hero. But, perhaps most importantly of all, they were rewarded with treats – rare, delicious opportunities to break the bounds of the Abbey and taste the wider world.

Like many of the other Abbey parents, Kippe and Jack barely ever came to visit the boys, so that even on 'Leave-out' Sundays the only hope of escape was to angle for an invitation from Humphrey and Peregrine Swann to join them, with their parents, for lunch at the Letherby and Christopher Hotel in East Grinstead. But success in sports, and in the choir, earned Michael visits to the cinema, and even, on one never-to-be-forgotten occasion, a trip to see *Così fan tutte* at Glyndebourne. Mr Gladstone, the most sympathetic of the three headmasters, drove the boys in his black Humber convertible, he and his wife, Kitty, in the front, Michael and two others in the back. They purred through the summer dusk, the Downs stretching before them like a Ravilious painting. The memory remains magical.

What did they wear for that outing? Such things mattered to Michael. His two most treasured possessions at the Abbey were the red ribbon he was awarded as Chief Chorister, and the green velvet cap that marked him out as Captain of Rugby. Like the children's television character Mr Benn, he felt most at home in a costume: 'I liked playing a part,' he says. 'It meant I could forget about myself.' And this was a relief, because he was unsure of his real identity. On the rugby pitch, while the other boys cheered his courage, he felt afraid and oddly detached. 'When I went in for a tackle, I did it closing my eyes because I was so scared,' he says. 'Part of me was there, in the scrum; but part of me was standing at the side of the pitch, watching.' This sense of involved detachment persists. As he talks at the Dragon School on that cold winter morning, his storyteller's costume – red trousers, black beret, stripy scarf – gives him the identity he needs to communicate with children, while at the same time enabling him to remain essentially hidden.

So how many people know Michael Morpurgo really well? 'Very few,' he believes. 'My brother, Pieter, and my half-brother, Mark, they know me.' But when I visit Mark, born to Kippe and Jack in 1948, at his home in the Scottish Highlands, he suggests otherwise. 'I wonder whether you will be able to get to the bottom of Michael,' he muses. 'I love him, but he's an enigma to me.' Peter Campbell, possibly Michael's closest school friend, agrees: 'You'll never really know Michael,' he says, 'and he'll never really know himself.'

Homesickness afflicted Michael throughout his years at the Abbey, and beyond. It began to take a hold about a fortnight before the end of the holidays, when his stepaunts, Bess and Julie, fetched their sewing baskets and got busy with nametapes. Soon afterwards the brown leather trunk was hauled out, packed, and delivered to the station to travel in advance – 'and you knew from that moment that you were on a wave that would carry you, like it or not, back to school'. Then came the last supper (always shepherd's pie), the last night at home, and the dreaded journey.

On Victoria Station, in those days, there was a small newsreel cinema, to which Kippe would take the boys for a final treat before surrendering them to the barrel-chested rugby master, Mr Beagley. This was a boon. The cinema's dark interior served as a kind of decompression chamber where, as Bugs Bunny or Mickey Mouse flickered on the screen, Michael could allow his 'home' self to slip away, and arm himself for school.

After that, it was best if Kippe left quickly. She was the focus for Michael's homesickness, but she was also an embarrassment to him. When they married, Kippe and Jack had decided that, as Pieter and Michael could not be expected to call Jack 'Daddy', they should cease to call Kippe 'Mummy'. They should address them both simply as 'Kippe' and 'Jack' – and any further children born to them should do the same. The boys at the Abbey, quick to spot chinks in one another's emotional armour, homed in on this oddity. 'Jack is not your *real* father,' they taunted, 'and Kippe is a *weird* name.' So it was a relief, really, when she turned to walk away, wrapped in her fragile sadness, smelling of face-powder. Michael could then settle into the corner of a railway carriage. To prevent himself from crying he concentrated on following raindrops down the thick windows with his finger, as the train wound out through south London, which was still pockmarked with bomb damage.

Yet, as the terms passed, Michael became aware that his homesickness was more habitual than real, and that there were things about school that he was growing not just to tolerate but to love.

The Abbey is set on high ground, and to the south its gardens tumble gently downwards, allowing wide views over Ashdown Forest. Between the formal garden and the forest were forty acres of school grounds, and on summer evenings the boys were left to 'play out' here, unsupervised, until the light failed. The memory of these evenings remains vivid and glorious – 'I was at that age when one is wide open to everything, antennae out.' These were hours of camps and camaraderie, of whittling arrows with sheath knives and exchanging secrets.

Winter evenings had a different charm. One of the headmasters, Mr Frith, regularly invited a group of boys to come to his study after supper and sit by the fire in their pyjamas. He served orange squash and Garibaldi biscuits, and read aloud from the novels of Dornford Yates: mild, sex-free thrillers, which had enjoyed a vogue between the wars, and in which the narrator-hero, Richard Chandos, drove about the Continent in a 'Rolls' tackling crime and hunting treasure. Michael loved these evenings – the warmth, the involvement in a story, the feeling of belonging. He slept well after them.

He was not, himself, a great reader – or at least not the kind that Jack Morpurgo would have wished him to be. The leather-bound copies of Dickens that Jack periodically put Michael's way were anathema to him, and to this day he has to overcome a psychological block before tackling large books, and cannot happily read for more than an hour at a stretch. But he was saved from Jack's contempt by a series called Great Illustrated Classics – easy-to-read, large-print abridgements which, borrowed from other boys and studied in secret, enabled him to pretend that he had read not only much of Dickens, but also of Homer, Dostoevsky and Sir Walter Scott. Privately, meantime, he was developing his own taste for really good yarns, in which pictures relieved his fear of text, so that the text could create pictures in his mind. He devoured the novels of G. A. Henty, of Kipling and, above all, of Robert Louis Stevenson: 'I *was* Jim Hawkins,' he says, remembering his first reading of *Treasure Island*. 'I was in that barrel of apples on the deck of the *Hispaniola*; I overheard the plots of mutiny.'

He was gripped, too, by the stories of real men. On the ground floor of the Abbey was a library, a dark, musty room, whose deep leather armchairs gave the atmosphere of a gentleman's club, and whose glass-fronted bookcases reached to the ceiling. The shelves were filled, for the most part, with books that had belonged to Sir Abe Bailey; and among these were bound copies of the *Illustrated London News*, stretching back to the mid-nineteenth century. Michael spent hours of his free time poring over black-and-white pencil sketches of soldiers fighting and dying in the Crimea and in the Balkan Wars.

History lessons fed his appetite for heroes. He remembers marvelling at the courage of Joan of Arc, steadfast at her stake as the flames began to lick around her; at the cunning of William the Conqueror, instructing his archers to fire into the air so that Harold's men would look up and get arrows in their eyes; at the valour of Simon de Montfort as he fell to his death at the Battle of Evesham. But one man preoccupied him more than any other, and that was Jesus.

The pupils at the Abbey filed into the school chapel every morning, and twice on a Sunday. But Michael, privately, went much more often. Apart from the 'bog', the chapel was the one place he could escape the other boys, and he liked being alone there with his thoughts, sitting before the altar where there was always a red lamp flickering. Though his faith was uncertain – 'I wanted to believe; I still do' – he felt drawn to the life of Jesus, told in stained glass. He longed to meet the man, yet at the same time felt sure that, were they to meet, Jesus would dislike him – 'because he was more perceptive than other people, and would see straight through me'. The mask he had developed to protect his more private, sensitive self from the sink-or-swim perils of prep school was already a source of confusion and guilt.

*　　*　　*

At home, Michael could allow his mask to slip, and his elation at the start of each school holidays was greater than any he has since experienced. Kippe and Jack had moved, in 1950, to a small village, Bradwell-juxta-Mare, on the Essex coast. With financial help from Bess and Julie they bought a large, haunted, sixteenth-century house, set in several acres of garden. In the post-war years, as domestic staff became for many a thing of the past, houses like New Hall had dropped in value. Buyers were struck less by the beauty of their architecture than by the number of windows that needed cleaning, floors sweeping, stairs running up and down. But Jack Morpurgo, socially ambitious and domestically impractical, had no such misgivings. What he saw in New Hall was a house that confirmed his transformation from East End working-class boy to English country squire.

Michael loved New Hall for other reasons. Its down-at-heel, rambling cosiness gave him a sense of belonging, and all the houses he has lived in since have been in some way attempts to recapture this. He and Pieter slept in adjoining attic bedrooms, with low sloping roofs, reached by a narrow staircase which the rest of the household rarely climbed. This was their private world, in which they made candles on a paraffin stove, read *Tintin* and *Asterix* and novels by Enid Blyton, all outlawed by Jack, and hoisted themselves out of the windows at night to sit in the leaded gully running between the roof and the house façade. The darkness was filled with the hooting of owls, the calls of wildfowl, and the mournful arhythmic clanging of boat riggings a couple of miles away, beyond the salt marshes, in the Blackwater Estuary.

The garden, too, was a boy's paradise, with a smooth front lawn for cricket and slip catching, and beamed stables with a sagging roof in which Pieter and Michael built a giant racetrack for their cars and played ping-pong on rainy days. To the back of the house the garden

Pieter, Mark and Michael outside New Hall.

had been allowed to run wild. Dog roses climbed over two old Nissen huts that had been used as a mess by RAF fighter squadrons flying out of Bradwell airfield during the war. There was an overgrown orchard with apple, pear, plum and damson trees, and a mulberry bush from which, in the summer holidays, Pieter and Michael harvested the purple, staining fruit in boiler suits.

Around the garden ran a high wall, up to which the sea would occasionally flood. The wall was a statement in mottled brick that New Hall was the big house; that its inhabitants lived somehow apart from the rest of the village. It taught Michael his first lessons about class division, because local boys liked to scale it, lean over the top, and jeer at the 'posh kids' on the other side.

When the Morpurgo brothers came out of the front gates these boys sometimes formed roadblocks, or kicked their bicycles, or threw stones. None of this deterred Pieter and Michael. If they loved the world within the garden wall, they loved what lay beyond it also. Bradwell-juxta-Mare was the sort of quintessentially English village that might have sprung from the pages of an Agatha Christie novel. Opposite New Hall was the home of retired Major Turpin; a little further along the road the three Miss Stubbings, spinster sisters, shared a cottage with wisteria around the door. And in the only other big house lived the Labour MP Tom Driberg. He struck Michael as 'fat and foul', though he knew nothing of Driberg's rampant homosexuality, which was still in those days a criminal offence.

Between the village and the sea lay a stretch of marshland that entered deeply into Michael's imagination – the marshland Paul Gallico captures in the opening pages of *The Snow Goose*: 'one of the last wild places of England, a low, far-reaching expanse of grass and reeds and half-submerged meadowlands ending in the great saltings and mud flats and tidal pools near the restless sea'.

It is a rich landscape for a storyteller, sunk so deep in time that distinctions between the ordinary and the fabulous begin to blur. Towards the end of the third century the Romans established a fort, Othona, on the coast by Bradwell. Four hundred years on, at the invitation of the Christian King Sigbert, a Lindisfarne monk, Cedd, arrived in a small boat. Using blocks of Kentish ragstone from Othona, he built a chapel in the sea wall. St Peter-on-the-Wall remains to this day, standing square against the huge Essex sky like a symbol of simplicity, perseverance and strength. Michael loved to sit alone by St Peter's, with the past for company. 'The Romans had been here, and the Saxons, and the Normans. And now me.'

There is an end-of-the-world feeling about Bradwell. Visiting from London, you follow the road east until it seems to go no further. On a summer's day, with the sun shining, the ditches frothing with cow parsley, the sea soughing across the marshes, it is easy to understand the melancholy magic the place held for Michael. But what must it have been like for Kippe, when Pieter and Michael went back to school in September, and the evenings began to draw in, and the days folded into one another with just the younger children and her sisters-in-law for company? In the village, she felt marked out as a woman with a past. The vicar, on discovering she was divorced, forbade her to take Holy Communion. So the square-towered church of St Thomas, which Kippe's upbringing and instincts might have moved her to seek out as a place of comfort and reassurance, became instead a source of anxiety and shame. Jack, meantime, was so often absent that he was not tuned into the nuances of village life. It was too far for him to commute from New Hall to London, so Kippe drove him to an early train on Monday mornings, and he spent the week in a pied-à-terre in London.

Perhaps to atone for the suffering she had inflicted on Tony Bridge, Kippe had resolved to be a faultless wife to Jack Morpurgo, never dissenting, never disloyal. She deferred to him in all things: the timing of meals, which gramophone records should be played, how her sons should be educated. Kippe had at first resisted the idea that the boys should be sent away to school, but Jack insisted, and she did not put up a fight. When the moment came to deliver Michael to the Abbey for the first time, she asked Edna Macleod to come with her for support. The journey was silent. 'When we arrived at the school,'

Edna recalls, 'Michael went into the loo, and didn't come out for a very long time. Kippe was chain-smoking. She turned to me with a desperate expression and said, "Oh God, Edna."'

Occasionally Kippe showed flashes of her old quicksilver spirit. At teatime on Christmas Day, for example, she would disappear up to her bedroom, put on a gymslip, arrange her hair in pigtails, and re-emerge to spend several hours in the persona of a naughty schoolgirl called Susie. She acted out her part with a mixture of flirtation and buffoonery which made Michael 'deeply embarrassed', but which Jack seemed to find 'funny, cute, rather sexy'. Then on 1 June 1953, flushed with patriotism, she draped herself in a Union Jack and climbed on to the roof of New Hall. The rain that was to drench the cheering Coronation crowds in London the following day was already falling steadily on Bradwell, and she stumbled and slipped as she picked her way across the wet slates. But she ignored Jack's begging her to come down, until she had her flag fixed and flying from a chimney stack.

Yet, like Bertie's mother in *The Butterfly Lion*, Kippe's 'good days' seemed outnumbered, to Michael, by days on which she was 'listless and sad'. More often than not she was physically exhausted. 'On minor, practical matters,' Jack had warned in a letter written during their courtship, 'I am dogmatic in my belief in the leadership of the male.' In practice this meant that, even when he was at home, it was Jack's prerogative to immure himself in his book-infested study, swathed in cigarette smoke, while Kippe managed the garden, the house, the shopping and cooking, and the four children. Having never involved himself in any of these tasks, Jack had no appreciation of the time and thought they demanded. Insofar as he noticed it at all, Kippe's exhaustion baffled and irritated him. Unable to share her difficulties, Kippe began, at Bradwell, to turn to drink for consolation.

In 1945 Jack had joined the editorial staff of Penguin Books, and had soon after been appointed chief history editor. But he was a man for whom ambition was doomed always to outstrip achievement, in every area of life. Even Kippe, so hard won, could not cure him of his roving eye, and rumours of his dalliances with other women rippled east from London.

Jack's restlessness and strivings were fuelled by insecurity. He longed to blot out not only his East End, working-class roots but also the deeper past of the Morpurgo family. Asked about his unusual surname, he would say that it was Italian. He rejected absolutely any suggestion that it was Jewish. In fact, as he must surely have known, his own parents had married in a synagogue. Originally from Marburg in Germany (Morpurgo is the Italianised 'Marburger'), the Morpurgo family had moved into Istria and Dalmatia in the nineteenth century and had become one of the most eminent Jewish dynasties in Trieste and Split. While Jack was busy establishing himself as an English squire, his Continental kinsmen were mourning the deaths of hundreds of Morpurgos in the Holocaust. On 30 September 1942 alone, three generations of one Morpurgo family – Aaron, Alida, Clara, Mordechai and Raphael – had been sent to their deaths in Auschwitz.

The Holocaust was avoided in conversation, both at home and at school. The boys were encouraged to dwell instead on the glory of the war and the courage of the British troops. They worked out the horror for themselves. Yet pupils at the Abbey were aware that the price of courage was often psychological damage and physical disfigurement. Down the road from the school, in the Queen Victoria Hospital in East Grinstead, the pioneering New Zealand plastic surgeon Sir Archibald McIndoe was devoting his life to rebuilding the minds and bodies of burned airmen. One of these, a Spitfire pilot named Eric Pearce, was a friend of Jack Morpurgo. His face, his hands and his ears had been so badly burned that, despite urgent warnings from Kippe ahead of his visits, Michael found it imposs- ible not to stare at him. 'He was a living monster. He had no eyebrows. All his skin was tightly drawn and white. And yet I was impressed by him as someone who had suffered, like Jesus.'

Another family friend had emerged from the war more profoundly, though less obviously, scarred. Edna Macleod's husband, Ian, known as 'Mac', was essentially a gentle, generous, humorous man – a welcome foil, when he visited Bradwell, to Jack's controlling egoism. But, as part of his service in the Royal Army Medical Corps, he had been one of the first to enter Bergen Belsen in the spring of 1945. For the rest of his life he suffered nightmares about the stench and sights and sounds that met the liberating forces: the cries, from those still able to cry, of *Nicht Krematorium! Nicht Krematorium!*; the tens of thousands of heaped corpses. 'He said they were moun- tains high, those poor, gassed Jews,' Edna remembers. 'Here and there a few were just breathing. He touched their lips with water.' When his memories overwhelmed him, Mac turned to drink; and, when he was drinking heavily, Edna visited Bradwell alone.

Eric Pearce and Ian Macleod were heroes; they had fought the good fight. Yet their reward was not glory, but brokenness. They presented Michael with a paradox that, even now, he struggles to comprehend. But the notion of glory remained seductive. In 1956 he was taken to the cinema to see *Reach for the Sky*, based on the true story of Douglas Bader who, despite having lost both his legs in a flying accident before the war, was called back into the RAF, fought in the Battle of Britain, and was imprisoned in Colditz, where his attempts to escape were so cunning and determined that his captors threatened to confiscate his prosthetic legs. It was a film calculated to fill small boys with dreams of heroism. Bader, as played by Kenneth More, is buoyant in the face of adversity, a man able to galvanise those around him without ever raising his voice or pulling rank; to infect others with resolution and hope in the midst of disaster. 'This is a story of courage,' the narrator intones as the credits roll. 'It has no end, because courage has no end.'

Michael Morpurgo shared some of Bader's qualities. At the end of his second term at the Abbey, when he was just eight, his headmaster's report noted that he was 'very much the leader of the younger generation of the school'. His contemporaries looked to him for guidance and found him 'charismatic'. In his final report, in the summer of 1957, Mr Gladstone wrote confidently that, 'although not a scholar', Michael possessed 'qualities that will ensure success'.

Pieter had by now moved on to Abbotsholme, a 'progressive' school in rural Derbyshire, where the headmaster, an old Christ's Hospital boy, had struck a deal with Jack over fees. For Michael, Jack set his sights higher. The reputation of The King's School, Canterbury, re-founded by Henry VIII in 1541, and with origins stretching back thirteen and a half centuries, had slumped somewhat between the two world wars. But, since the appointment of Canon 'Fred' Shirley as headmaster in 1935, pupil numbers had risen steadily as the school built up a reputation for academic, musical and sporting excellence. Shirley was a maverick and an enigma – to some a saint, to others a sadist. In a volume of recollections written after his death, one old boy offers what reads like a posthumous love-letter, while another paints a pen portrait of a monster and madman, who stood behind him brandishing an open penknife during rehearsals for a Shakespeare play, threatening to stab him if he did not speak clearly. Shirley's only daughter sums him up in a string of contradictory adjectives – 'devout, doubting, an ardent left-winger, a thorough snob, loving, self-centred, compassionate, hurtful'. But fans and detractors alike endorse Shirley's *Times* obituary, which described him as 'one of the most talked about headmasters in modern Britain', and 'one of the most successful'.

Shirley was a friend of Jack's, and, after conferring, the two men agreed that Michael should sit the scholarship examination. 'Everyone knew perfectly well that I was not scholarship material,' Michael remembers. 'I sat the first Greek exam in the lab at King's, and I knew I was doing really badly. As I was starting on the second, the headmaster's secretary, Miss Milward, called out my name. She marched me into her office and said that, because I'd only scored 2 per cent in the first exam, there was no point my sitting another Greek paper, and I was to do an intelligence test instead.' A few weeks later, on 17 June 1957, Shirley wrote to Michael: 'I have nominated you to [sic] a Lord Plender Scholarship – not at all on account of your marks in the exams! – but because I can give one of them for what is called "leadership quality" – so father gets the money value, and you can have your name up on the Abbey Honours Board; but it isn't a *King's* scholarship, so you won't be able to wear a gown!' The scholarship meant £100 off the fees – then £350 per annum – and was never officially entered into the school records.

Travellers to Canterbury today are greeted by a railway poster welcoming them to 'a city where the present keeps step with the past'. In fact, once you have moved through the wooden postern from the city into King's Mint Yard, it is easy to feel you have left the present behind, and have entered instead a world of cloisters, arches and twisting stone stairways. Lawns and passages have Arthurian names – the Green Court, the Dark Entry – and Tudor buildings jostle with medieval. Michael's house was Galpin's, Norman in origin. It was bordered on one side by the old pilgrims' lodgings and on the other by the thick, flint city walls round which a night-watchman walked in the dark. He came right past Michael's dormitory window, intoning 'Twelve o'clock, fine night and all's well' as the great cathedral bell chimed midnight.

Canterbury Cathedral, soaring into the sky in Romanesque magnificence, seems to keep the school tucked beneath its wing. The public generally enters it by the massive Christ Church Gate, but the pupils of King's slip in through a side door, which opens straight into what they call 'the martyrdom', where Thomas Becket was murdered in 1170. 'There is a cathedral in the school grounds,' a new boy once wrote home to his parents – King's pupils feel that Canterbury Cathedral is theirs. Standing in the nave on a Sunday morning, staring up into the fan vaulting, with the organ thundering and the voices of 650 boys singing 'All People that on Earth Do Dwell', remains for Michael 'one of the most extraordinary experiences on God's earth'. And even more moving were the early-morning Communion services held in the candle-lit dimity of the cathedral undercroft, in the Chapel of Our Lady, next to Thomas Becket's original tomb. The spiritual yearnings Michael had known at the Abbey intensified here, and it was a place in which he knew extremes of joy and desolation – 'because in that spiritual vein I could sometimes feel very unhappy, very isolated'.

His lonely, rather tortured piety is evident in a diary he kept during the spring and summer terms of 1960, when he was seventeen. Day by day, he noted his sporting achievements, adding occasional jaunty reflections on events in the wider world: Saturday 27 February, 'Princess Margaret is engaged to a photographer chap – Jones. 'Bout time too.' He rounded off almost every entry with an anxious, beseeching prayer, 'God, Please aid me to do my best this term, and to enjoy myself, if it be your will. Please.'

Academically, his performance remained mediocre. On arrival at King's he had been put in the B-stream, where he remained. Maths

Michael at King's School, Canterbury, 1959.

was particularly problematic. 'He is not quick to learn,' wrote the Maths master at the end of his first term, and his reports thereafter are beset with warnings that Michael might fail his O level – as indeed, on first go, he did. Even in English, and in creative writing, he showed little promise. In the composition section of the English Language O level, which he sat in the summer of 1959, he only just scraped through, with 56 per cent.

And yet, as his King's friend Peter Campbell remembers, 'he shone *personally*. He had an authority about him. He didn't need to be part of the group.' This is captured, for Campbell, in a photograph of the Rugby XV taken in his and Michael's last year at the school. Fourteen of the fifteen – Campbell among them – are clearly part of a team; but Michael stands on the edge, chin defiantly in the air, staring outwards. This independence made him likeable and impressive both to his peers and to the staff. 'He never makes a fuss, and so far as I know he never causes a harsh word or gets one,' his housemaster, Richard Roberts, wrote at the end of his first term. 'He has done well to qualify for promotion in the Corps so young.'

The Cadet Corps had quickly become central to Michael. One afternoon a week, it involved his dressing up in khaki tunic, blue beret, brass badge, puttees and boots, and reporting for duty to Colonel Kem Gross, whose job it was to initiate the pupils of King's

First XV, King's School, Canterbury, spring 1962. Michael stands on the far right, next to Peter Campbell. Sebastian Barker is fifth from the left.

in the arts of rifle-loading, marching, map-reading, fieldcraft and command. These were skills well suited to a boy like Michael, with natural authority and an ability to get others to do his bidding without raising his voice or becoming unpleasant. Yet what appealed to Michael most was not so much being in charge of other boys as feeling at one with them, in an organisation that 'gave a frame to human activity'. And of course the uniform helped. Several of his diary entries refer to the efforts he put into working up a really good shine on his belt and boots and badge, and the results impressed his contemporaries. 'I saw him as Spotless Officer Number One,' says the poet Sebastian Barker, who was a year below Michael at King's. 'I still remember those pink cheeks of his beaming from his army uniform with white-washed canvas sparkling round his ankles, and him with a straight back like a rifle standing to attention.' Mark Morpurgo, who arrived at King's in 1962, remembers Michael marching at the head of the Cadet Corps, so impeccably dressed that 'he looked like an officer in the SS'.

This was not a game to Michael. As he marched in formation across the Green Court, he thought about the courage and sacrifice of Eric Pearce and Ian Macleod, and of those he would never meet – his uncle Pieter, and the 258 King's Canterbury old boys who had given their lives in the two world wars. These were the men he wanted to model his life on, and becoming a soldier seemed the best way to do it. Shortly after his sixteenth birthday, he applied for an army scholarship, which would pay his last two years' school fees on the understanding that he would move straight from King's to Sandhurst to train as a Gunner in the Royal Artillery. As the exam approached, the pious pleadings at the end of his diary entries reached fever pitch. Even reading them now, half a century on, one breathes a sigh of relief on reaching the entry for 18 May 1960, when success was confirmed in a telegram from Sandhurst.

'Spotless Officer Number One', January 1961.

'Praise be God,' writes Michael. 'Dear Lord I shall try sincerely to show my infinite thanks by being a better Christian.'

Sandhurst had not only given him a scholarship, but the top scholarship of the year. Within weeks this resulted in an invitation that a teenage boy could scarcely have dreamed of – to accompany the Queen and the Duke of Edinburgh on a three-week tour of India, as guests of the Indian government, marking the thirteenth Republic Day celebrations. While his contemporaries returned to King's for the start of the Easter term in January 1961, Michael found himself instead boarding a plane at RAF Lyneham, and flying, via the Libyan desert, to Bombay.

What knowledge he had of the sub-continent came from Kipling and *Tintin*, and he was overwhelmed, at first, by the dirt and squalor, the seething crowds, the smell and the ceaseless movement. 'The work never stops, the noise never ceases,' he wrote in his diary. But he warmed immediately to the Indian Army officers deputed to take care of him – 'kind, hard-working, hospitable, grateful and proud' – and he was moved by the spirit of the Indian people: 'They are a people living with a hope,' he wrote. 'A hope of making India a great, happy and prosperous nation.' As he was driven through the shanty towns on the outskirts of Bombay, an Indian Army major assured him that 'soon there would be no more poverty of this sort'.

His unease at the poverty did not detract from his delight at the pampering and exoticism lavished upon him by his hosts: the white-turbaned servants who stood, silent and ramrod straight, behind his chair at dinner; the Camel Corps, followed by painted elephants, who paraded through the streets of Delhi on Republic Day; the introductions to men and women familiar to him from newspapers and postage stamps. At breakfast in the Prime Minister's palace – an occasion made extra thrilling by the presence of a baby tiger, which wandered among the guests on a lead – Michael chatted not only to

Michael meets Pandit Nehru, 28 January 1961.

Pandit Nehru ('one of the most outstanding personalities I have ever come across', he noted in his diary, 'very affectionate and always interested') but also to his daughter Indira Gandhi ('I'd seen her before on television, and there she was, shaking my hand, no taller than I was').

In the midst of all this, his thoughts strayed occasionally to King's Canterbury, and the chilblains and burst pipes that always accompanied the beginning of the Easter term. 'Aren't you supposed to be back at school?' the Duke of Edinburgh demanded when they were first introduced. 'Yes, sir,' Michael replied. 'That's one of the best things about it all!'

India reinforced Michael's conviction that he was on the right path, that the army was the place for him. Only one person struck a note of caution. On arrival at King's, each boy was appointed a tutor whose job it was to keep an eye on his development, not only academic and sporting but also spiritual and psychological. Michael's tutor, Sydney Sopwith, was generally acknowledged to be one of the kindest and most remarkable on the staff. Born at the height of Queen Victoria's reign, he was a Mr Chips figure, a widower who had devoted his life to passing on to generations of boys his love of English literature. He was in his seventies by the time Michael arrived at King's, small and balding, and brimming with the accumulated wisdom of nearly sixty years' teaching. Over tots of sherry in his tiny flat in Lardergate, Sopwith tried gently to suggest to Michael that there was a life full of promise and richness beyond the rugby field and the Corps, and that literature had more to offer him than he might dare believe. He lent him books to read, and introduced him to the poetry of Wilfred Owen and Siegfried Sassoon; and Michael responded. His love of words was dormant, not dead. Yet, outwith Sopwith's sitting room, this delight and excitement were difficult to sustain. In English lessons, set texts remained a chore; and at home, in the holidays, expressing a feeling for poetry or words made him vulnerable to ridicule. Jack Morpurgo allowed himself, occasionally, to be sentimental; but he despised sentimentality in others. He was the literary authority in the household. He did not brook competition.

So as the summer term of 1961 drew to a close, with A level exams in English and French successfully completed, Michael turned his back on his studies without regret. But the end of academia did not mean the end of school. One strand of Fred Shirley's strategy in effecting the metamorphosis of King's from minor to front-rank public school was to invite boys to return to Canterbury for what would now be considered their 'gap' years. It was good for them, he argued, to spend a few months divesting themselves of what he called the 'exam-grab mentality', and developing more fully as human beings.

This system had obvious advantages for Shirley. It meant that there was always a group of older boys able to devote themselves exclusively to music, drama and sport, bringing glory to King's in all these fields. But there were other, more subtle, benefits. Shirley was a control freak. It suited him to surround himself with a close inner circle of favoured senior boys in whom he could invest temporary power, thus keeping some of his masters relatively weak. The King's monitors, who strode about the school like a bench of bishops, purple gowns flying from their shoulders, were often made to feel more powerful, more in the know, than heads of department, or even housemasters.

For Michael, Shirley had even higher things in mind. Their first meeting, just after Michael arrived at the school, had not been auspicious. Shirley had spotted him across the Green Court, pointed at him, and called him over. 'Mmm,' he said. 'Morpurgo. Know your father.' Then he poked him in the stomach: 'White belly. Do your jacket up. White belly! Do it up!' But from then on, he kept an eye on him. Michael's lack of academic prowess made him, if anything, more interesting to Shirley, who, as his *Times* obituary reported, liked nothing better than '"getting hold" of a boy with moderate natural gifts, and pouring into him his own liveliness and single-mindedness'. During the summer holidays following A levels, he telephoned Michael at home and asked whether he might return to King's in the autumn as Captain of School.

It is hard to exaggerate the authority that this position conferred on a not-quite-eighteen-year-old boy – an authority epitomised in Michael's being presented with a private key to the cathedral ('Shirley's Temple' to the boys), so that he could wander there alone after the public had left in the evening. If Shirley was absent it was the Captain's job, effectively, to run the school; and Shirley was absent often. Every Thursday he took a day's holiday and set off, sprucely dressed and wearing a rather rakish wide-brimmed hat, on a marathon hike across the Kent countryside. He had regular govern-ors' meetings in London, and meetings in Oxford and Cambridge; and not infrequently he lapsed into a mysterious malady and refused to leave his bed. Even when he was at home, and fit, he often preferred the Captain of School to address the boys on his behalf when they assembled in the monstrous Shirley Hall after breakfast. On these occasions he would leave in the Captain's pigeonhole small, square cards with hastily penned instructions. Sometimes, these were reasonably clear:

1. Hats.
2. Orchestra.
3. No contemptuous reports on the cricketing abilities of other schools – however tempting.
4. Why do the monitors still read so badly?

Sometimes, they simply offered a biblical reference: 'S. Matthew 5 v. 5'. Then it was up to the Captain to puzzle out the point that Shirley wished him to make.

Michael, as Captain of School, was to take on responsibilities greater than any who had gone before him, because his last year at King's was Fred Shirley's also. At seventy-two, after twenty-seven years as headmaster, Shirley was determined to go out in a blaze of glory. Tributes were paid to him in words, in paint and in bronze, and, as proof that King's had 'arrived', he busied himself welcoming important guests. Dame Peggy Ashcroft visited, and Joyce Grenfell. Somerset Maugham, an old boy, came to open the Maugham Library (he had paid for its construction, and it would later house the collec-tion of books he gave to the school). It was Michael's job, on these occasions, to don Court Dress (gown, breeches, black tights,

*Michael escorts the Queen Mother during her visit to King's
School, Canterbury, 12 July 1962.*

ribboned pumps), to make conversation with the grandees as he guided them round, and to lead the school in giving them a rousing 'three cheers' as they departed.

Shirley's crowning moment came on 12 July 1962 when, descending through heavy clouds in a red helicopter, the Queen Mother arrived at King's to attend a thanksgiving service conducted by the Archbishop of Canterbury. After lunch at the headmaster's house ('roses, Liebfraumilch, cold chicken', notes the school magazine), she was accompanied by Michael first to unveil a plaque to Shirley in the Shirley Hall, then to the cathedral. As he escorted her up the nave to a fanfare of trumpets, the wife of a school governor leaned towards him and whispered in his ear, 'You'll never be so important again.'

Two weeks later Michael packed his school trunk for the last time. Bidding him farewell, Fred Shirley held him in a long, silent handshake, 'as close to a hug as could be allowed'. 'I think on sober reflection,' Shirley wrote, penning Michael's leaving note, 'he has proved the best, most competent, and to the boys most acceptable Head of School in my time.'

Shirley's adulation might have been off-putting to both boys and staff; but half a century on those who remember Michael at King's speak warmly of him. 'He was much liked and even loved in his fantastically authoritarian appearance and school role,' says Sebastian Barker. 'There was something cuddly about him even then.' Richard Roberts apologises that he can recollect nothing even faintly critical – 'I'm so sorry. I've tried desperately hard …'

The head of the Cadet Corps, Kem Gross, could hardly contain his pride that it was in the army that this golden boy was now to make his mark on the world. He had appointed Michael his Company Sergeant-Major, and he was confident that he would go on to take the Sword of Honour at Sandhurst, and either die a glorious death in some corner of a foreign field or rise swiftly through the ranks to Field Marshal. It was a shock, not just for Gross but for the entire school, when in the summer of 1963 news reached King's that Michael Morpurgo had abandoned Sandhurst, had married, and was shortly to become a father.

I wonder whether the Captain of School at King's still has a key to the cathedral. It seems extraordinary to me now. Peter Campbell and I used to explore there together in the evening after choir practice. Once we climbed a mysterious winding staircase and came out above the ceiling of the nave. 'It was like a landscape of sand dunes up there,' Peter says. But my clearest memory of being in the cathedral after dark is of the night I got locked in, again after choir practice in the undercroft. It was terrifying, a ghost lurking in every transept, in every choir-stall.

A Fine Night, and All's Well

I was new, a new boy, a young boy, in an old school – the oldest
school in the country, they told me. Outside our dormitory
window there was a Norman staircase and the medieval monastic
buildings of the Green Court; and beyond that, there was the great
cathedral itself, and Bell Harry ringing out the hours, day and
night.

We were expected to know the history of the school and the
names of every building: house monitors could stop and test us
any time. One of them – we already called him 'Flashman' – would
go on questioning us until we got something wrong. Then he
would give us ten minutes to change into our PE kits, to run
around the Mint Yard a dozen times and afterwards report to him
in his study, fully dressed again. The last task alone was almost
impossible for us new boys as we were still all fingers and thumbs
with our uniforms, trying to get to grips with wing collars and
collar studs that seemed to have minds of their own.

The uniform was just part of the ritual of the place: boater,
pinstriped trousers, wing collar, black jacket and waistcoat – with
the middle button always done up if you were a new boy. As new
boys, we had to navigate our way through a sea of hazards. We
learned quickly enough that the only way to keep out of trouble
was to know our place, be on time and have that middle button
done up. I longed simply to get through each day, to be in my bed

and alone in the darkness. Only then could I put Flashman out of my mind and begin to dream that I was back home again.

But Bell Harry would remind me every hour, on the hour, that I was not. Lying awake, I'd listen for the night-watchman to come on his rounds, pacing the precincts and the city wall. Sometimes his footsteps stopped right outside our dormitory window and I'd hear him calling out: 'Twelve o'clock. Fine night and all's well.'

I took some comfort from that. Hoping it would be true for me the next day and praying that I would manage somehow to avoid Flashman and get through unnoticed and unpunished, I would fall asleep at last.

But my prayers weren't working. As the weeks passed it became obvious that Flashman had it in for me in particular. He used the strangeness of my name as his main weapon, teasing me about it every night. Then one night it got nasty. We were reading in the dormitory before lights out when I looked up and saw him there with his usual three cronies, standing at the end of my bed. I steeled myself.

'D'you know what someone told me, *Morpurgo*?' he began. 'Someone told me your name's Jewish. You're a Jew boy, aren't you?'

There was real menace in his eyes, naked dislike. I didn't argue, I didn't say anything.

'We don't like Jew boys, do we?' he went on. 'Gone all dumb, have we? Scared out of our little Jewish wits, are we?'

I am sure that worse would have happened had Mr Robbins, the housemaster, not come in at that moment to turn the lights out.

After that, fear of Flashman taught me wherever possible to go round in a protective band of others, a cocoon of friends. Perhaps we were all doing the same, finding strength and comfort in numbers. I wasn't the only one finding it difficult to settle into this strange place.

I made these friends mostly on the rugby field or in the choir, singing Thomas Tallis or Orlando Gibbons in the cathedral or crashing through a tackle to score – life was getting better. I didn't excel at either singing or rugby, but did both just about well enough to be up there with those that did.

Schoolwork though was a real problem. I couldn't seem to make any headway and all too often I found myself in detention or playing catch-up, forever trying to explain why I had not yet done the work I should have done. For some reason, History seemed particularly difficult. It was towards the end of term that Mr Kennedy set us an essay on the murder of Thomas à Becket. I was struggling. We all knew the story, sort of: how the archbishop had been struck down in the cathedral in 1170 by four dastardly knights sent there by his erstwhile best friend, King Henry II. The trouble was that the essay had to be at least two sides long and however large I wrote I hadn't been able to manage more than half a side. I did what I often did when confronted with a task I found too challenging: I procrastinated and worried about it. My tutor, Mr Skipness, tried to help me. He suggested that for inspiration I should go and stand on the stone in the cathedral that marked the very spot where Becket had been murdered. He told me exactly where it was and how to get there. I couldn't help thinking at the time that it was a pretty silly idea; but I didn't say so of course, I just didn't do it.

It was nearly the end of term and the choir was practising hard for the carol service. Mr Hedred, our hyperactive genius of a choirmaster, gathered us for one last rehearsal in the undercroft of the cathedral, the crypt, our usual place for choir practice. It was a warm, dimly lit place of arches and flickering shadows – everywhere the scent of candles and ancient stone. I was sitting as always next to Peter, my best friend – fly half, and a brilliant one, in our rugby team – among the trebles. Peter had perfect pitch and a more musical voice than mine, which was fine for me because it meant that I could follow him. We sang so well that evening that Mr Hedred ended choir practice early. He told us that we were the best choir he'd ever had, so we were all glowing as we stood up to go. That was when Peter told me that he had finished his Becket essay.

'Done yours?' he asked.

'Course,' I said.

None of the rest of this would have happened if I hadn't told that little lie.

That was when I panicked. In desperation I decided I had no choice but to do just what Mr Skipness had suggested. As Peter and the others drifted away through the undercroft towards the door to the cloisters, I wandered off into the shadows and made my way up the steps and into the nave.

There was an echoing emptiness as I stood there, alone at the heart of the cathedral. I tried as hard as I could to calm my fears, thinking that if I turned back now, it wouldn't be too late to catch up with the others – I could still hear the murmur of their voices. But then ahead of me, somewhere between the nave and the choir, I saw a flickering light that seemed to beckon me on. Without thinking I walked towards it, down some steps and into a kind of side chapel.

Looking around, I could hardly believe it. It was almost exactly as Mr Skipness had described. There was the small square tile on the floor that he had told me about. This must have been it, the very place where Thomas à Becket had been murdered.

I stood there and closed my eyes. In my mind I pictured the knights bursting into the cathedral, swords drawn, and the archbishop telling them that this was a holy place and to put up their weapons. In horror, I watched as they hacked down one of his servants and then came on towards him. I saw him kneeling down, crossing himself and praying out loud as the first sword struck. The whole horrible deed was played out like a film in my head. I opened my eyes. I couldn't bear to watch any longer.

The man who stood before me was dressed like a bishop, in a white cloak, his face shaded under a hood. He held a crozier in his hand.

'You don't want to think about it,' he said. 'And neither do I. It was a painful business, but over soon enough.'

The voice was far and yet near at the same time, the voice of a ghost. I ran. The only way out I could see was a small wooden door which I hoped might take me back to the cloisters. I lifted the latch. It wouldn't open. I hammered on the door.

'It's locked,' the voice said. 'Don't worry. I shan't harm you. Thomas Becket never harmed anyone in his life. Why should he start now?'

As I turned to face the ghost, he seemed to be floating over the floor towards me, caught up in his own source of light. He lifted his hood so that for the first time I could see his face. He was younger than I thought Thomas à Becket should be, with bright, smiling eyes. He held out his hand.

'They've all gone,' he said. 'Everything's locked up.' He took me gently by the elbow. 'But I have my own way out. Don't worry. Come along.'

As he led me through the vastness of the empty cathedral, he talked, answering all the questions I wanted to ask but didn't dare.

When we reached the choir he stopped and looked up at the high altar. He sighed.

'Henry was not a lucky name for me, not one I have any cause to be fond of. Michael, on the other hand, is a fine name.'

'You know my name?' I breathed.

'I know everything about you, about everyone in this place. I've lived here, in one form or another, for nearly a thousand years. I've always made it my business to keep an eye on the place, to know who's who and what's what. I am able to go seen or unseen, as I wish, to look deep into hearts and minds – we can, you know. There's a lot I like about being a ghost. I'd rather be alive, of course I would; I died too young. But it doesn't matter now. What's a few years here or there? We're all of us a long time dead.

'Up there just above the altar, that's where King Henry had me buried. You should have seen the tomb. Never saw so much gold in all my life – all to appease his conscience. He lay right there, flat on his face, and sobbed like a baby asking for forgiveness – as if anyone was fooled by his crocodile tears. And then another Henry, the eighth Henry came along, dug up my bones and took away the gold. He was fond of gold that one, gold and wives. So you can see I have good cause not to like the name Henry very much.'

I was following him up the steep winding stairway and finding it difficult to keep up. I thought that the steps would go on for ever, that he was taking me all the way to heaven. Then I felt the cold night air on my cheeks, and saw the stars and the moon above me.

'The top of Bell Harry,' he said. 'Look!'

Spread out beneath were the evening lights of the city and, right below us, the school: the Green Court, the Mint Yard and Galpin's, my own house. I could see there was a light on in my dormitory, where Flashman, I was sure, would be waiting for me. Suddenly I didn't want to go back.

The ghost seemed to anticipate my every thought.

'You mustn't worry about Flashman,' he said. 'One way or another you'll find your own way to deal with him. And you'll finish that essay too. Which reminds me. Whatever you have heard, when those knights came for me – and you're right, they were dastardly – I didn't just kneel down meekly and let them get on with it. I fought like a tiger, wielding my crozier like a broad sword. I fought them to the end. The only way to live and the only way to die.'

As he spoke I felt his arm around my waist.

'You'll be fine, Michael,' he said. 'I've got you.'

And with that we lifted gently off Bell Harry tower and floated down over the school, past the Norman staircase, to land right in the Mint Yard, just outside my house. I was so amazed and disorientated that I stumbled when I touched the ground. It took me a while to catch my breath.

'You all right?'

I turned. It was the night-watchman, standing there in the light of his lamp, smiling at me. But he was Thomas à Becket too. He had the face of the archbishop, the face of a saint.

'I'd best be off,' he said. 'Got my rounds to do. I like to keep an eye out.'

'What's it like being a saint?' I asked. It just slipped out.

'It doesn't cut any mustard, not where I come from. It's what you do you'll be remembered for, not the honours or the titles or the money. Just do the best you can. That's what I did. And that's all that I can tell you on the subject.'

He turned as if to go, but then something else occurred to him: 'Except to say that you boys, you sang like angels tonight, like angels,' he said.

And with a wave of his hand he walked away.

A window opened. 'Hey, Jew boy!' It was Flashman. 'What the devil do you think you're doing out there at this time of night? Get upstairs to your dormitory. Now!'

I got up early in the morning to write my essay on Becket and handed it in on time. When Mr Kennedy gave it back to me a couple of days later, he said, 'Entertaining, Morpurgo. But stick to the facts. Becket did not fight back. He submitted courageously to his fate. It is well known, well documented. You can't improve on truth, Morpurgo. Fiction is for fantasists.'

As for Flashman, my moment to settle the score came a week or so later. We were out on the rugby pitch when I saw him come charging out of the scrum, ball in hand. I raced after him, chasing him across the pitch, and launched myself headlong at him. The impact knocked the air out of both of us. I was up first and glaring down at him as he lay at my feet. I didn't have to say a word; I knew from that moment on that neither Flashman nor his cronies would ever bother me again.

On the last night of term, after the carol service, I lay awake in my bed, listening out for the night-watchman. As Bell Harry tolled the final stroke of midnight I heard his familiar footsteps on the walk outside our window.

'Twelve o'clock. Fine night and all's well,' he called out.

And all *was* well too.

3

Situation Critical

One evening during the Easter holidays of 1962, the Morpurgo family – Kippe and Jack, Pieter, Michael, Mark and Kay, and the aunts, Bess and Julie – drew the curtains in the sitting room and gathered in front of the television to watch *Great Expectations*. This was not the famous David Lean version, but a new adaptation by the Canadian Broadcasting Company, and it was a rare treat. The television, first rented for the wedding of Princess Margaret in 1960, was controlled by Jack and switched on only occasionally. So there was an atmosphere of cosy excitement as the machine warmed up, and the orphan Pip appeared on the screen, running from the marshes into the graveyard, darkness falling and trees swaying and whipping about him. Then up from behind a gravestone reared Magwitch, his hair cropped and filthy, his face full of rage and terror and hurt. 'My God,' breathed Kippe, gripping Michael's arm. 'It's Tony. It's your father!' Jack rose from his armchair and left the room.

Since Michael was a small boy Tony Bridge had hovered on the periphery of his consciousness. The teatime visits to Poulett Gardens ceased after the move to Bradwell, but the Bridge grandparents continued to send Pieter and Michael cards for Christmas, Easter and birthdays, and often, enclosed in these, were newspaper clippings about Tony's theatrical successes in Canada – silent reminders to their grandsons that Jack Morpurgo was not their father, that their real father was alive and well and not to be forgotten. In one of

Tony Bridge as Magwitch in Great Expectations, *1962.*

these clippings, Michael found a reference to the fact that Tony had acted in Canterbury before the war. He knew, while he was a school-boy at King's, that he was living in the city where his parents had met and fallen in love, and the knowledge pleased him.

Now, having seen him almost in the flesh, Michael began to think more about his father. He questioned Kippe, hard but fruitlessly; and he continued the questioning with Pieter, and in his own head. What was this man like? Why had he been airbrushed from their lives? And how had his absence affected the way Pieter and he had developed? Would he, for example, have felt drawn to the army if he had been brought up by Tony Bridge rather than Jack Morpurgo?

Looking back now on his decision to go to Sandhurst, Michael finds it hard to judge how far his own ambitions had been shaped by Jack's. Jack had had a 'good' war, and was proud of it. In a telling fragment of memoir, written in old age, he describes his delight when, walking through Whitehall with Kippe one morning in 1946, he was recognised as a field officer by the Horse Guards, who 'sat to attention on their horses and saluted me with their sabres'. These things mattered to him, just as it mattered that, when Michael won his army scholarship in 1960, it was announced in *The Times*. Pieter, having left school at fifteen, had taken employment as an assistant stage manager with a travelling theatre company, and Jack had written off his future. But Michael, in going to Sandhurst, knew that he was doing 'something that could make Jack really proud'. The prospect pleased him.

This was not purely selfish. When Jack was happy, life became easier for everybody, particularly Kippe. During his years at King's, Michael had watched his mother become steadily sadder and more withdrawn, bowed by Jack's bullying when he was at home, and by rumours of his philandering when he was away. In an attempt to shore up their marriage they had moved, while Michael was at King's, from New Hall to Oxhey Hall, an old Tudor hunting-lodge near Watford, handy for the Metropolitan line on which Jack commuted into London. It was here that Michael first became aware that Kippe was drinking too much. He watched her one evening flop drunkenly from her bedroom window and vomit into the flowerbed below. If, by being a successful soldier, he could make Jack proud, he might pour balm on a situation that was growing progressively more distressing.

*   *   *

The Sandhurst term was due to begin on 3 September, and before that Michael was to join Kippe and Jack, Mark and Kay for a final family holiday. Jack had been commissioned by Eyre & Spottiswoode, 'in association with the BP Touring Service', to write *The Road to Athens*, a guidebook for holidaymakers planning motor tours of Greece, and in early August the family set off in his maroon Daimler – one of the perks of his new position as Director-General of the National Book League.

Jack had, officially, left Penguin in 1955, but he remained thick with the company's mercurial founder, Sir Allen Lane, and nursed hopes that he might one day be appointed his successor. So when Lane mentioned that his twenty-year-old daughter, Clare, was planning to spend the summer hitchhiking round Greece with her sister Christine, Jack invited her to come and see him in his offices in Albemarle Street. 'He was flirtatious and charming,' Clare remembers, 'and I liked him very much.' He took her on to dinner with Kippe, and they arranged that Clare and Christine should meet up with the Morpurgos in Corfu at the end of the holidays.

What Kippe and Jack told Michael about Clare he cannot now remember; but the first thing he did, on arriving in Corfu, was to make a bee-line for her hotel. It was late evening, and dark. Clare was getting ready for bed when the proprietor knocked on her door to say she had a visitor. Rather than come downstairs, she stepped in her long white nightdress on to the balcony of her first-floor room, and saw Michael standing below in the half-light, on a rubbish heap. First impressions, on both sides, were good. Michael was bowled over by Clare's beauty. With her long, black hair, green eyes, high cheek-bones and open smile, she must have looked, on that first encounter, not unlike Olivia Hussey in Zeffirelli's *Romeo and Juliet*, and she was warm and easy to talk to. Clare, who was already juggling more than one boyfriend, felt Michael might be a perfect

Clare, 1962.

match for sixteen-year-old Christine. They arranged to meet on the beach in the morning.

The following day was spent talking, walking, swimming. Michael remembers Clare's 'amazing green bathing costume with a very low back'. Clare was struck by how good Michael was at listening, 'not at all flirtatious, but interested and interesting'. Christine remembers that they talked only to each other, leaving her to make conversation with fourteen-year-old Mark. Michael and Clare arranged to meet the following day, and the one after that, and then made plans to see each other in London. On 3 September, when Kippe drove Michael to Sandhurst, Clare came too. She sensed that Michael was anxious and unhappy; and she was right. For as long as he could remember, he had set his sights on soldiering. Now, alongside the habitual twinges of start-of-term homesickness, he felt a bat's squeak of doubt about the future.

To begin with, Michael was too fully occupied, and too exhausted, for his doubts to develop. He had been placed in Victory College, in Alamein Company, and from 6 a.m., when he and his fellow cadets presented themselves for drill on the parade ground, his days were filled with exercises, inspections, kit polishing and running with weights up and down Sandhurst's notorious 'Heartbreak Hill'. All this took place to the accompaniment of volleys of abuse from Sergeant-Major Bostock, later the model for Sergeant Hanley in *Private Peaceful*: 'What are you, sir? I'll tell you what you are! You are an *effing* waste of space, sir! Get running, sir, or I'll castrate you with the rough end of a ragman's trumpet, sir!' The aim was to test the cadets' physical and mental endurance, and to knock out of them any vestige of public-school arrogance. 'They beat you down to nothing,' says Peter Campbell, who had also gone on from King's to Sandhurst, 'before building you up again.' He doubted, from the start, whether Michael would stay the course. 'Just a few months ago, he'd been the highest of the high. Now he was the lowest of the low, no longer giving orders, but taking them. Mike has never liked being told what to do.'

For several weeks Michael could only speak to Clare in snatched, reverse-charge calls from the telephone box below Victory College; but they wrote to each other almost daily. 'For the first time since I left school,' Clare confesses, 'I'm longing for the days to go by quickly. If your letters to me come even in the second post, I go quite mad.' Then, in late October, Alamein Company 'Passed off the Square', and the occasional evening out became possible. Michael's fellow cadet Eddie Tait also had a girlfriend in London, and he had a car – a 'Frogeye' Sprite. He would drop Michael in Holland Park, where Clare was living with her mother, studying for A levels in English, French and Biology.

Clare had turned down three proposals in the months running up to her meeting with Michael. The relationship between her parents, Allen and Lettice Lane, had been so fraught and unhappy that she had decided that marriage was not something she would ever want for herself. So it surprised her, that autumn, to feel an increasingly clear sense of commitment to Michael. She had never encountered a character so multifaceted. One moment he was larking about, the next following Canon Shirley's example and leaving her references to Bible passages to ponder in his absence. 'Darling, darling, I love you more and more each time you show me one of your six selfs [*sic*],' Clare writes in one letter; and in another, 'I love you, I LOVE YOU, you smooth, rugger-playing, choir-boy humanitarian.' She was overwhelmed by Michael's warmth and 'superhuman generosity'. He was being paid a meagre 12*s*. 6*d*. a day, but, as that first term came to an end, he presented Clare with a pink tourmaline necklace, which Kippe had helped him choose and on which he had blown all his savings. 'No one,' she says, 'had ever been so kind to me.'

Not everybody was pleased with these developments. Clare's parents spent their weeks separately but met up for weekends at Priory Farm near Reading, and on Sundays, after church, Clare often collected Michael from Sandhurst and drove him there for lunch. These were uncomfortable occasions. Whereas in some businessmen success breeds an avuncular generosity towards the younger generation, in Allen Lane it seems to have had almost the opposite effect. 'He just did not like young men,' says Clare, while Christine's husband, David Teale, recalls Lane's uncanny ability to sense the chinks in people's psychological armour, 'and then blow them to smithereens'.

Penguin Books had made Lane a millionaire several times over. He was suspicious that Michael was after Clare's money, and he remained suspicious even after commissioning a secret report from his handwriting expert, Mrs Jacoby, who assured him that Michael's was not the hand of a gold-digger, but of a 'very intelligent, kind and sympathetic man of high moral principles'. Lane also found him dull – 'Michael Morpurgo's never going to set the Thames on fire,' Christine remembers her father saying, again and again – and the prospect of Michael's becoming an army officer seemed to him contemptible. Jack Morpurgo, in his biography *Allen Lane: King Penguin*, attributes Lane's dislike of soldiers to his guilt at not having fought in the war; but Christine thinks this nonsense. She believes her father's hatred of the armed forces had its roots in the death of his beloved brother, John, serving in the navy in 1942 – a bereavement that left him inconsolable, unable to eat or sleep.

Lane never found it easy to form close relationships. 'I have,' he once confessed, 'a little barrier around myself that I find it very difficult to let anybody inside' – and from John's death onwards that barrier was reinforced. The only people for whom he might occasionally let it down were his blood relations, and particularly his daughters, Clare, Christine and Anna. He was a marvellous father, arranging bicycling holidays with the girls in Normandy, or allowing them to accompany him on business trips around the world. As soon as Clare was old enough, he began to take her out in the evening, to restaurants and the theatre. She was his constant companion. He was not going to lose her to another man without a fight.

So, when Michael began to turn up at Priory Farm, Lane either ignored or humiliated him, and he encouraged other weekend visitors to join in the sport. The army was a particularly rich source of ridicule. How did Michael envisage Clare's future, Lane would ask – as an officer's wife in Poona? His guests, often toadying for positions at Penguin, fell about with laughter.

But Clare stood her ground. She was, in fact, very willing to become an officer's wife, if that was what Michael really wanted. What worried her was not her father's disapproval, but the unease

Clare and Allen Lane, 1955.

she sensed in Michael himself about the path he had chosen. 'I kept asking him, "Why? Why are you doing this?"' Michael's response was increasingly uncertain.

In mid-December 1962 the officer cadets of Alamein Company were instructed to prepare for a final exercise, 'Exercise Climax', before the Christmas break. As they drove out through the gates of Sandhurst in whining three-ton lorries, snowflakes began to drift from a leaden sky. It was the beginning of the coldest winter Britain had known for 200 years.

On freezing Berkshire heathland, in the last of the afternoon light, Michael and his Nigerian companion, Sam, dug themselves into a frosty trench. The snow was now falling in flakes so huge that if they looked up from their digging they were blinded; but while the light lasted their spirits were high.

Out somewhere beyond the trench was an 'enemy' of Argyll and Sutherland Highlanders, who might attack at any moment. Michael and Sam, and the rest of Alamein Company, had been instructed to remain on 'stand to' all night, watching, eyes peeled, for shadows drifting through the darkness towards them. They had been ordered not to talk, just to watch.

As dusk fell, what had initially seemed like a game became fraught, for Michael, with irrational fear. He could hear the voice of the enemy somewhere out in No Man's Land, laughing, taunting; but, blinded by the snow, he could see nothing. The frost began to gnaw at his bones. He could no longer feel his fingers; his kidneys ached. Beside him, curled up in the trench, Sam began to sob with cold.

Michael longed, but did not dare, to sleep. Instead, he began to think about other soldiers, and other freezing nights. In Greece, over the summer, he had read *War and Peace*, and he thought now about the troops around Napoleon retreating through the snow and ice from Moscow. Then he thought of the Italians, high in the bitter cold of the Alps, fighting the Austrians in the First World War, and then of the soldiers in the Serbo-Croat wars he had read about as a schoolboy, poring over the *Illustrated London News* in the library at the Abbey.

At some point towards dawn, these thoughts became almost hallucinatory. Crouched in his trench, looking out over No Man's Land, he began to imagine that he was a young soldier in the First World War. A figure in grey moved towards him in the snow, waving a white flag. No one fired a shot; the longer no one fired, the more certain he became that he should climb out of his trench to meet his enemy.

The Christmas truce of 1914, which Michael had first learned about reading *Eagle* at prep school, became, that night, absolutely real for him. Entering into it imaginatively, he found himself, though physically frozen, 'warm to my very soul', and he questioned more urgently than ever the course his life had taken. If peace was what he really cared about, why was he training for war? 'I had always wanted

Clare and Michael at the Beagle Ball, Sandhurst,
20 December 1962.

to fight the good fight,' he reflects, looking back. 'That night, I began to wonder whether there was another way to fight it.'

From then on, things moved swiftly. On the evening of 20 December, at the Beagle Ball, the Sandhurst cadets celebrated the completion of their first term. Photographs show Clare on Michael's knee at the end of the evening, staring into the distance in a daze of happiness, while he looks at her, besotted. Two evenings later they met for dinner at the Maison Basque in Albemarle Street and, without much planning on either side, got engaged.

'Nowadays, I can't buy a dress without taking it back to the shop,' Clare says. 'So it amazes me how easily it all happened. Michael was saying he'd be another two years in the army, and I said, "Don't worry, I'll wait. I'll marry you, if you like." He said, "Would you?" And that was it. It was unsoppy, unheavy stuff, and we didn't doubt what we'd done at all.'

The following day they went their separate ways for Christmas, Clare to her father's house in Spain, Michael to Oxhey Hall. 'We woke this morning to hear Michael coming down the drive whistling the Scipio march,' Kippe wrote to Clare on 23 December, 'a very tired but very happy soldier. He told us your news with our early morning tea … I could not be more delighted, we already feel you are part of the family. It's almost too good to be true.'

They planned to marry in the summer of 1964, after Michael had completed his army training. Back at Sandhurst, at the beginning of a snowy spring term, he wrote out a list of things Clare might reflect on to buoy her up through the long wait. One was 'the knowledge that nothing really matters – that no two people could possibly love as we do, that Clare and Mike will never, never be separated by anything or anyone'. Another was 'the nasty thought of little Michaels, or even worse, little Clares!' These were to appear much sooner than either of them had planned. In late May Michael took a call from Clare in the telephone box below Victory College. She was pregnant. 'I remember going warm all over,' Michael says. 'I knew something huge had happened. But I also knew that I wanted to be with Clare for the rest of my life, and that I wanted to have this baby.'

His clarity and conviction were put to the test when, on 12 June, he and Clare met Kippe and Jack to break the news. Clare had already spoken to Allen and Lettice Lane. Despite their misgivings about Michael, they had put a good face on the engagement, and they were now happy at the prospect of becoming grandparents. Jack, too, had expressed cautious approval of the engagement. 'Piety and pomposity become me ill,' he had written to Clare, 'but I would be failing in paternal duty did I not show awareness of the problems you have before you: so long to wait, professions to win and once won to hold in not entirely easy circumstances. However the stable counts and yours (at least) is accustomed to breeding winners.' But a baby, at this stage, was another matter altogether. It would ruin Michael's future in the army, and might even involve Jack's having to pay back the Sandhurst scholarship money that had seen him through his last two years at King's. Clare, Jack insisted, must have an abortion. Kippe, who had at first been thrilled by the news of the pregnancy, toed his line.

The following morning, back at Sandhurst, Michael poured out his disgust in a letter to Clare. It had been a 'beastly, nasty, heart-breaking evening', and he was ashamed of his parents' 'mule-headed stupidity'. 'This is our child, darling, yours first and then mine,' he wrote. 'The thought of an abortion made me physically sick – I've thought about that and my parents' complete selfishness all day.' News of the meeting filtered back to Allen Lane, who was incensed that Jack Morpurgo should tell his daughter what to do.

Michael and Clare's engagement was announced in *The Times* on 18 June, but news of the pregnancy was kept from their wider families and friends. At Clare's twenty-first birthday party in the barn at Priory Farm on 6 July, she danced all night, deaf to her mother's warnings about the effects her energetic rock 'n' roll might have on her baby. And she wore a plaster round her finger so that no one would know that she and Michael were, in fact, already married.

In order to extract Michael from Sandhurst for a secret wedding, Kippe had, on 25 June, sent him a telegram: 'URGENT YOU GET HOME SITUATION CRITICAL MOTHER'. Three days later, on 28 June, Michael and Clare, Allen and Lettice Lane, Kippe and Jack, foregathered at Kensington Register Office, and then drove through the rain, in near silence, to Lettice's flat at 23 Holland Park. It was, Michael remembers, 'an absolutely horrible day'. Clare's parents were barely speaking to his, and he himself was overcome with shame at having deceived his senior officers. After wedding cake and one bottle of champagne, he and Clare set off for Caversham, where Michael took and failed his driving test. They moved on to The Compleat Angler in Marlow. 'And then,' says Michael, 'it became funny. We sat in our attic bedroom, and we didn't know what to do with ourselves. So we went out to a movie, *Barabbas*, and then came back to the hotel and ate steak Diane.' The other diners could not disguise their fascination with this mysterious couple. It seemed likely they were on their honeymoon – Clare's pregnancy was beginning to show – yet neither looked more than about fifteen years old.

Early next morning Clare drove Michael back to Sandhurst. He had known for six months now that he must leave the place, but making the final break had defeated him. He had no idea what he was going to do with himself when he left, and the prospect of abandoning his fellow cadets in Victory College filled him with gloom. During the rigours of the Sandhurst training they had supported one another through thick and thin: 'We were cemented together.' To say goodbye to them now felt like betrayal.

In the end, however, there were no goodbyes. That summer, Alamein Company was sent on an exercise to Schleiden in Germany, and from here Michael wrote to inform his Commanding Officer of his decision. The moment he returned to Sandhurst he was summoned before a board of high-ranking officers, 'civil but cold', and urged to change his mind. When it became clear that he would not, he was ordered to leave immediately, without speaking to anyone.

In *The Nun's Story*, when Audrey Hepburn has finally persuaded her abbess that she has lost faith in her vocation to religious life, there is a chilling, silent, final scene in which she takes off her habit, resumes her civilian clothes, and walks out alone into the street. This scene spooled through Michael's mind as he laid aside his army uniform, and walked out through the Sandhurst gates. He felt no excitement, only guilt – 'and when, occasionally, I have passed that place since, I have felt a shudder of shame'.

Michael's future was now unclear. The Damascene moment on the frozen heathland when he had become suddenly certain that he must leave the army had been accompanied by no corresponding inspiration about what he should do instead. A family friend offered to help him into a job with Imperial Life, but the thought of any kind of professional or business career appalled him. In order to play for time, and to gain some sort of qualification, he decided he must apply for university. Canon Shirley was mobilised, and imme-diately set about bringing 'personal pressure to bear' on J.N.D. Kelly, principal of his old Oxford college, St Edmund Hall. Shirley suggested that Jack Morpurgo and Allen Lane might also get involved in some string-pulling with A.L.P. Norrington, Vice-Chancellor of the university: 'They should both take him out to lunch. He knows all about nepotism and undue influence – got his own boy into a good job in London at the Oxford Press. Scripture teaches the use of *importunity*!' Whether anyone spoke to Norrington is not clear, but when Michael travelled to Oxford it was for an interview not at St Edmund Hall but at Christ Church, where Jack Morpurgo had had a word with his old friend J. H. Plumb, hero of Bletchley Park and a formidable scholar, later knighted for his services to eighteenth-century British history. In a short but excruciating interview Michael was questioned by an English don about aspects of *King Lear*. 'I floundered horribly,' he remembers. 'We both knew it was hopeless.' A letter of polite rejection followed.

In the end, it was Kippe's sister Elizabeth who came to the rescue. Her sister-in-law Muriel Hudson was tutor to women students at King's College London, and, having met and talked to Michael, Dr Hudson arranged that he should come to King's to study French, English and Philosophy – not for a full-blown Honours degree, but for what was known as a general degree.

Michael was due to start at King's in the autumn of 1964, and to fill the intervening months he answered an advertisement from Gabbitas-Thring for a post as junior master at a prep school, Great Ballard, near Chichester. He was to teach everything from Maths to rugby. Clare was to help a bit with art. It would be pleasing, with hindsight, to claim that both felt drawn to work with children – and in Clare's case it would not be entirely wrong. In a number of her letters to Michael at Sandhurst she considers teaching, and she would later go on to get both a Montessori qualification and a BA in Education. But Michael, at this time, had no particular interest in children. He had never especially enjoyed the company of his half-siblings, Mark and Kay – when they were small, he had found them whiny and irritating – and he didn't expect to like the pupils at Great Ballard any better. 'It was just a wage,' he admits. 'I fell into it.'

So it was a surprise to find that teaching came naturally to him: 'After a few minutes in the classroom, I knew this was something I could do.' For the children, the energy and enthusiasm of a master young enough to be their brother were thrilling. And, because they liked him, Michael found himself warming to them in return.

What he never warmed to was the staff-room. 'It had a nasty atmosphere, full of fear,' he says. He felt he neither belonged nor wanted to belong there: 'I didn't want to fit in with the dowdy old staff.' The joint headmasters, Peter and Michael Sugden, had appointed him to teach for an academic year, but during the Easter holidays he decided he could not face another term, and handed in his notice.

Despite mixed memories of Great Ballard, both Michael and Clare look back on this time as a sort of idyll. They had rented a tiny, thatched house, Wyndham Cottage, on the edge of a village called Rogate, and the long drive across the South Downs to school every morning was glorious. Sometimes, Clare drove Michael in her dressing gown; sometimes, ignoring the fact that he still had not passed his test, he drove himself. He felt proud to be in regular, salaried employment; proud that, in the teeth of opposition and discouragement, he and Clare had won through.

Jeannie Hyde Parker, whose parents owned Wyndham Cottage, was twelve when Michael and Clare arrived, and used often to bicycle over to visit them. They seemed to her like a couple from a fairy tale – Michael 'drop-dead gorgeous', Clare 'the most beautiful woman I had ever met'. Overcome with envy of Clare's looks, she slipped her mother's hand while shopping in Liphook one Saturday morning, ran to the chemist, and spent her pocket money on a bottle of black hair dye. But what struck Jeannie's mother, Lady Leslie, even more than the youth and beauty of her new tenants was the sense of mystery that surrounded them. They were like the babes in the wood. 'Nobody ever came to visit them. We guessed perhaps they had eloped, or had been cut off by their families.'

This was not far from the truth. Blissfully happy though they were together, Michael and Clare were aware of living under a cloud of disappointment and disapproval from both sets of parents. Allen Lane, for one, was not expecting the marriage to last. He had told Clare outright that once her baby was born she might consider divorce. Jack, meanwhile, was reeling from a double blow. Not only had he lost control of Michael, on whom he had pinned such high hopes, but his friendship with Allen Lane had been irreparably damaged. Shortly after the wedding Lane had sent an emissary, Harry Paroissien, to take Jack out to lunch, and to suggest that, if he would help support Michael and Clare to the tune of £2,000 a year, Lane would do the same. Incensed that he, 'a salaried book-trade administrator', should be expected to match Lane, a multi-million-aire, Jack stormed out of the restaurant. 'To hell with you both,' he cried, 'and to the lowest circle in hell with Allen Lane.' Jack Morpurgo and Allen Lane never spoke again.

On 27 January 1964, Sebastian Michael Morpurgo arrived in the darkness just before dawn. 'He was very thin, and very quiet,' Michael remembers, 'and he seemed almost weightless in my arms. I felt incredibly proud.' Kippe came down to stay at Wyndham Cottage after the birth. She lit the fire, cleaned the grate, cooked, and cuddled her grandson. She was, Clare remembers, 'very loving'.

In Canada, news of Sebastian's birth reached Tony Bridge. It was nearly twenty years since his divorce, and he had remarried. The time had come, he decided, for him to meet his sons and grandson. He wrote to Kippe to say that he was travelling to England, and a tea party was arranged at Oxhey Hall. It was a tense afternoon. Kay, on

Canon Shirley with Michael and Clare at Sebastian's
christening, 1 April 1964.

being told who was coming to tea, threw a hysterical fit and had to
be removed from the house. Nobody had ever explained to her that
Pieter and Michael were not her full brothers, she screamed; she
could not bear to think that this was true. And when Tony arrived
he was, not surprisingly, almost speechless with nerves. But Michael
was delighted by his visit. He was fascinated to find that he and
Pieter shared mannerisms – movements of the mouth and hands –
with the father who had been absent from their lives; and he was
thrilled by Kay's outburst. 'I was aware that this was a spanner in the
works as far as the "Morpurgo" family was concerned, and I liked
that. This unspoken thing was now out in the open, and I remember
thinking, "It's about bloody time."'

*   *   *

117

Less than two years before Sebastian's birth Michael had been a schoolboy; now he was a father. He found this hard to comprehend. 'I used to look at myself in the mirror and think, "This can't be true. This can't have happened. I am too young."' And young he seemed, even for his age, when he arrived at King's College in October. Jane Batterham, a fellow undergraduate who was to become a lifelong friend, remembers meeting Michael for the first time in a French class. The students had been asked to introduce themselves, and, oozing public-school confidence, Michael announced, '*Je suis Michael Morpurgo. J'étais à l'école du Roi à Canterbury.*' 'He was just a schoolboy,' says Jane, 'with a whiff of Sandhurst about him.' He had driven metal studs into the soles of his shoes, so his footsteps echoed with a military ring as he strode down the corridors.

There was no regular student life for Michael, no hanging out in bars or joining protests. His relationship to King's was that of a none-too-keen businessman to his office. He took the underground to Charing Cross every morning, and walked up the Strand to the college; he headed home as soon as possible at the end of the afternoon.

He and Clare were renting, for £5 a week, a basement and ground-floor flat in Well Road near Hampstead Heath, and on the face of it their life was enviable. 'Basty' was a sweet, easy-going baby, and Clare loved being a mother. She was so protective of her son that she would not allow anyone else to carry him up the stairs, and at the slightest cry in the night she shot out of bed and gathered him into her arms. Thanks to a trust set up by Allen Lane for his children, she had a regular income. To their contemporaries, Michael and Clare appeared to be very comfortably off.

But for Michael things were less rosy than they looked. He was not, he thinks, a natural father. 'I was more impatient than Clare, and I was too young to deal with it all. Small children have big egos, and I don't think I had really grown out of being a child myself.' Looking back, he gives Clare ten out of ten as a mother, but himself just 'six on good days, four on bad ones'. He disliked being dependent on Allen Lane, and continued to feel slighted by him. When Michael and Clare needed money, Clare was required to go and see Lane's trustees alone. Michael had to wait outside. Clare, meantime, was required to send her father regular letters detailing every penny she and Michael had paid the fishmonger, the newsagent, the dry-cleaner and the babysitter, and even how much they had spent on each other's Christmas presents. 'The difficulties in married life are many as you know,' Clare writes in an undated letter to Lane. 'But where ours is so simple in a lot of ways, we do have one very big one – that Mike is living on your money.' This, she explains, makes Michael feel 'guilty and useless'.

Because Michael had never had much money, he was far more interested in it, and more extravagant, than Clare. Fast cars were his particular weakness. It thrilled him to drive around London at speed, roof down, wind in his hair. Husband and father he might be, but he was still young, and a part of him still yearned to be carefree. In the summer of 1965, in a bid to be alone together once more, he and Clare headed off to the South of France in their British Racing Green MG Midget, leaving eighteen-month-old Basty to be looked after by a series of friends and relations.

Jane Batterham's overriding memory of visits to Well Road is of solid, settled family life. But she remembers also that, no matter what the conversation, it tended eventually to revert to the vexed question of Michael's future. King's had enabled him to play for time, but it had made him no clearer about what he might do in the longer term, and, if anything, his intellectual confidence had diminished rather than grown during his time there. Philosophy baffled him. And though the English teaching brought occasional stirrings of excitement – most notably when Professor Garmondsway read the students *Sir Gawain and the Green Knight*, awakening in Michael for the first time in years memories of Kippe's bedtime stories – critical analysis floored him. 'There was,' Jane Batterham says, 'something bemused and bewildered about Michael. He was quite needy.'

In the summer of 1967 Michael sat his finals. A few weeks later the results were posted up on the college noticeboard. He looked hopefully down the short list of Firsts, and then, with increasing dread, through the mass of Seconds. Finally, he found his name among the Thirds. When he rang to tell Clare, she was unmoved. 'Nobody in my family had ever been to university,' she says, 'and my father had left school at sixteen. What did it matter?' Checking her diary for that time, she finds she did not even mention Michael's degree – 'It's all about babies.' But Kippe and Jack were flabbergasted and appalled, and Michael at a very low ebb indeed.

Want of an alternative, rather than any positive desire to work with children, drove Michael back into teaching, and he thinks of the years that followed as a hopeless wilderness of floundering, disappointment and failure to settle. A précis of his CV goes some way to telling the story:

Autumn 1967–Summer 1968: junior master, Westbury House, Hampshire, friendly, eccentric prep school run by ex-naval officer for sixty-odd pupils. Michael not unhappy, but bored and unchallenged.
Autumn 1968–Easter 1970: housemaster, St Faith's, slightly larger prep school near Cambridge. Relentless clashes with headmaster and staff – 'a disaster'.

Summer 1970: Westbury House again.

Autumn 1970–Summer 1972: Milner Court, Kent, junior school for King's Canterbury. Further clashes with staff, particularly headmaster.

Autumn 1972: unemployed.

Michael (second from left, staff row) at St Faith's, summer 1969.

It was while Michael was teaching near Cambridge that Mark Morpurgo's future wife, Linda, met him for the first time. In appearance, she remembers, he was every inch the schoolmaster, dressed in a shabby leather-patched corduroy jacket, and scruffy suede shoes. But, though he looked the part, he struck her as 'incredibly unhappy, lost'.

Her impressions are confirmed by a photograph of the staff and pupils of St Faith's taken in the summer of 1969. Squeezed on to a trestle bench between two beaming, bosomy female teachers, Michael stares at the camera with an expression of smouldering resentment and discontent. It is not only his youth that marks him out from the other staff. Patricia Owens, whose son Simon was taught by Michael at St Faith's, remembers meeting him with Clare at a school function in 1969. 'Simon had gone on and on about his *amazing* new teacher, Mr Morpurgo,' she says, 'and as soon as I saw this young, handsome man across the room, I knew it must be him.' Clare was by his side, glamorous in a maxi leather coat and white fur hat. 'They just didn't fit with the rest of the staff at all.'

Nor, despite Michael's patched jackets and scuffed shoes, were they living the kind of life that one might expect of a young prep-school master and his wife. Handouts from the Allen Lane Children's Trust had become progressively more generous, and, alongside his fast cars, Michael had developed a taste for furniture, paintings, foreign holidays, houses. After accepting the job at Milner Court, they had bought a rambling Georgian house, Newnham Farmhouse, near the village of Wickhambreaux. It was surrounded by fields, outbuildings and several acres of garden, in a corner of which they built a swimming pool. 'We were living about twenty years beyond ourselves,' Michael says.

By this time the family had grown. In January 1967, Clare had given birth to a second son, Horatio. The following year, longing for a girl, but feeling it would be wrong to bring another child into an overpopulated world, they had adopted a seven-week-old baby, Ros, half Asian Indian, half Caucasian American. It was exciting to watch the children growing up in what Michael remembers as 'a little Camelot of happiness'. It dawned on him only gradually that the price of financial freedom was a kind of psychological imprisonment – that '"things" were becoming far too important to us, and money was undermining my will to take life by the scruff of the neck and move forward'. More and more, as the school terms rolled by, he was troubled by a sense of frustration and impasse. His life was drifting.

None of this conveyed itself to his pupils, who remember only the excitement and energy of his teaching. Forty years on, they all tell the same tale. Mr Morpurgo was inspirational; he knew how to get into the minds of children, to make them think for themselves, to believe in themselves. As, one after another, they offer their particular memories of being taught by him, a picture emerges of a man who made learning an empowering adventure.

Simon Owens was just seven when Michael arrived at St Faith's, and the first thing they embarked on together was *The Canterbury Tales*. Michael warmed the boys to the concept of pilgrimage, and then helped them to explore what it might mean for a band of twentieth-century pilgrims – a rally driver, a coastguard, a poet. Stephen Webster, who was in Michael's house, Firwood, remembers lessons being disrupted one evening by the sound of sawing and hammering. On Michael's instructions, the caretaker, Jack Staden, was rigging up a Heath Robinson sound system that ran to every room in the house. From that day on the boys were woken in the morning by music ('it might be Mozart's clarinet concerto, it might be "Sgt Pepper"') rather than an electric bell. At Milner Court Michael taught Guy Norrish a special 'scissor move' in rugby. When Norrish employed this to score the winning try against a hitherto unbeaten neighbouring prep school, Wellesley House, Michael 'leapt incredibly high in the air'.

Of all the schools where Michael taught Milner Court was, perhaps, the most bizarre and alarming. 'It operated in a kind of bubble, insulated from the world,' says Adam Finn, who was sent there in 1966. 'It had got stuck somewhere in the Fifties.' Michael's arrival on the staff was as explosive as the arrival of Mr Keating at Welton Academy in the film *Dead Poets Society*. Finn remembers him striding into the classroom one morning, switching on the record player, putting on Simon & Garfunkel's 'The Boxer' and asking the boys to listen really carefully to the lyrics.

I am just a poor boy
Though my story's seldom told …

'In that school,' Finn says, 'the only music we had ever heard was either choral or classical. You cannot imagine how odd it was for a master to be playing something like this.'

Yet none of Michael's former pupils remembers him as soft or even particularly warm. 'I can be very nasty,' he warned one class in his first lesson with them, 'and I can be very nice. It entirely depends on *you*.' He was fierce and commanding. He did not care whether the boys liked him, any more than he cared about school rules.

Next to St Faith's, and separated from it by a high wall, was an old people's home, Meadowcroft, with a large garden. One of the ways that the boys liked to prove their courage was to creep out of their dormitories at night, climb over the Meadowcroft wall, and go for what they called 'a midnight walk'. This, needless to say, was strictly forbidden, and the standard punishment was a beating. But for the boys in Firwood Michael introduced a new rule. 'I don't mind if you go for a midnight walk,' he told them. 'But, if you do, you must write a poem about it.'

His belief in the value of creative writing had begun to take root in his first term at St Faith's, when he had been invited to edit the school magazine. He was amazed by the poems and stories the children offered him for publication, by their 'wonderfully fresh take on the world'. Yet, rather than encourage this, it seemed to him that the thrust of most of the teaching in the school was to browbeat the children into uniformity, so that they could jump through the hoops required by public-school entrance exams. 'Their individual genius,' he says, 'was being throttled.' Encouraging them to write, to find their own voices, was one way to reverse this process.

His own memories of creative writing were not happy. At St Matthias the class had been asked one day to write about 'A Funfair'. Michael had never been to a funfair, and a cold paralysis crept over him as he watched his classmates bend over their desks and begin to scribble. At the Abbey stories were written against the clock, and the titles set were impossibly large and vague – 'Autumn', 'Fear'. Without anything precise to work on, Michael's mind had become a baffled void. Mindful of this, he tried to show his pupils paintings, or take them to look at a stream or a tree before they began to write. And, while they wrote, he wrote too, and found that he enjoyed it.

He was by no means alone, of course, in believing in the benefits of 'free expression'. All over the country, anthologies of children's work were being published and competitions for younger writers established. Michael encouraged his pupils to enter these, and took groups of them up to London to have their work recorded for the BBC radio programme *Living Language*. And he accepted a commission from the National Book League (Jack Morpurgo had by this time moved on) to collect and edit an anthology of writing by seven- to fifteen-year-olds from 'a broad social background'.

'Children's Words', which includes a poem by thirteen-year-old Daniel Day-Lewis, was published as a special issue of the NBL's periodical *Books* (Winter 1971). It opens with a fiery introduction from Michael himself, attacking politicians for exploiting education for their own ends; championing children and their 'freshness of approach'. It was the first time his name had appeared in print, and it sowed in his mind a seed of hope that there might be a life for him beyond the school gates.

He needed this hope, because at Milner Court his hatred of the teaching profession was becoming overwhelming. It was, says Adam Finn, a school 'governed by fear'. The headmaster, the Reverend John Edmunds, relentlessly humiliated pupils in lessons. Finn remembers with particular distaste Edmunds's habit of putting his face up very close to a boy's, and then hammering his fist on their desk. When anger got the better of him, he became violent, and chalk and blackboard rubbers flew.

The staff, on the whole, took their cue from Edmunds, and it was clear to Adam Finn even as a schoolboy that Michael was 'completely out of place'. It was not just the teaching methods of this young, rather flash, sports-car-driving master that set him apart, but the fearlessness with which he delivered his views and criticisms in the staff-room. As Robin Edmonds, who taught with Michael, puts it, he was 'not always most tactful' – and Michael himself admits that he was 'probably horribly arrogant'. The other masters were completely dependent on their jobs; but Michael had Clare's money to fall back on and could afford to be awkward. As the staff grew increasingly wary of him, he became, Finn remembers, 'more and more stratospherically popular' among the boys. It was a dangerous combination.

One afternoon in the summer term of 1972 Michael was told that, in a fit of anger, the headmaster had thrashed one of his pupils with a dog chain. He reported the incident to the school governors; but the governors, and even the parents of the boy concerned, closed ranks. Edmunds's actions had been justified, they insisted, and Michael's disloyalty was not. He was given notice to leave the school. Enraged, he took the matter to the Association of Assistant Masters, and his dismissal was revoked. He then resigned. At Speech Day, on 18 July, Michael made a point of sitting not on the dais with the rest of the staff, but among the boys.

It was an important moment for him. Everything in his upbringing had taught him to stand on the side of authority. He had flourished, as a schoolboy, on conventional recognition and success – and to some extent he continues to do so even now. But, on that Speech Day, he discovered in himself a new urge to express outrage, to expose wrongdoing, and to fight for the rights of his pupils. The path that would eventually lead him to become an ambassador for children not just in Britain but all over the world began here, at Milner Court. When, at the end of the afternoon, the time came for him to drive away from the school for the last time, he found that the boys had filled his car with cards and presents.

Relief at leaving Milner Court was tempered by anger, sadness and unease about the future. 'Even with Clare,' Michael says, 'everything began to feel unsettled and tense.' He needed time to recover and reflect. When the autumn came, and the children went back to school, he started work on a series of stories about three children, and their adventures in the countryside around their home. He also made a decision, crucial to his future, that he was so thoroughly disenchanted with private schools that he would never work in one again. His own children were by now at the local state school,

Wickhambreaux Primary, and in January 1973 Michael accepted an offer to go and teach there, as one of a staff of three.

This was a bigger step than it might sound. Ever since his days in Bradwell, when the village boys had poked their heads over the garden wall and teased him about being 'posh', he had felt nervous of children from different backgrounds. 'The moment an Englishman opens his mouth,' says Henry Higgins in *Pygmalion*, 'another Englishman despises him.' This was exactly what Michael feared – not that he would despise the pupils, but that, as soon as they heard his voice, they would despise him.

So it was a relief and revelation to find that the Wickhambreaux pupils responded to him as warmly as any of the children he had ever taught. It was a relief, too, to discover as he drank his coffee in

Michael reading to Ros and Horatio, 1973.

the staff-room at break time that 'this was a school in which the teachers smiled and laughed. They were happy!'

Mrs Skiffington, the headmistress, ran Wickhambreaux Primary with enlightened eccentricity. She was firm, and stood for no nonsense, but she also encouraged her small staff to teach in whatever way they found most effective. She was quite happy when Michael began regularly to walk groups of children out of the school gates and down the road to the nature reserve at Stodmarsh. 'On the way, they were allowed to talk,' he says. 'But once we got there, they had to be silent, and they had to remain silent until we had got back to school, and they had written a poem or story about what we had seen.'

By three o'clock, Mrs Skiffington believed, primary-school children were too tired to take in anything new. For the last half-hour of the school day, therefore, she asked the teachers to read them stories. As the weeks went by Michael found that he looked forward to this half-hour. Drawing on his memories of Kippe reading to him as a child he found that, if he could himself enter into a story, he could hold the children's attention perfectly until the bell went. But some stories worked better than others, and one February afternoon, reading Year 6 the first chapter of *Stig of the Dump*, he realised he had lost them.

That evening, after talking to Clare, he decided to tell the children a story of his own – one of the ones he had made up during the autumn term. 'The beginning,' he remembers, 'was awful. There were sighs and groans. Then they got into it, and I got into it, and ten minutes later they were completely absorbed. When the bell went, they begged me to carry on.' And so he did, telling the class a series of related tales that lasted until the end of the week.

Though he did not recognise it at the time, this was a turning-point in Michael's life. The frustrations he had suffered since leaving school had been rooted, in part, in his inability to find a way of life that could exercise all his gifts at once. Now, four at least of his 'six selfs' – the leader, the teacher, the writer and the storyteller – were working in harmony.

Mrs Skiffington got wind of the fact that something exciting was happening in the Year 6 classroom. On Friday afternoon, she slipped in to listen to Michael, and was impressed. She asked him to write down his stories over the weekend and, the following Monday, she posted them to a friend at Macmillan Education. Looking back at the stories now Michael is dismissive: 'the characters have no depth at all, there's no sense of their motivation'. But Aidan Chambers, who read them for Macmillan, liked them very much. 'They have a gentle but not at all sentimentalised style,' he wrote, 'and it is such a relief to find some stories that have realistic and not at all rosy-spectacled plots and narratives, but which belong to the country and are smooth and pleasant to read.'

Michael had called his collection of stories *It Never Rained*, and in July he signed a contract for their publication. He was to be paid royalties, but no advance. The following month Chambers wrote again. He wondered whether Michael might like to write for the Macmillan Topliner series – a collection of fiction 'for 11–16 year olds, and especially those who aren't overly literary in their tastes'. This time, he was offering an advance of £150 on royalties of 7.5 per cent of the sale price, which was 25p. On average, Chambers mentioned, books in this series sold 'about 10,000' copies a year. But Michael was already hoping to do a great deal better than average. At the top of the letter, in red biro, he calculated the royalties on sales of 20,000 books. '£400 *if lucky*,' he concluded.

It Never Rained was published in the summer of 1974. By the time it appeared, Michael had sold Newnham Farmhouse, left Kent and given up teaching. Writing to Clare shortly after they got engaged, he had looked forward to their learning together 'why we're both on this earth', and to 'doing our utmost … to fulfil any vocation'. Ten years into their marriage they were about to discover what their true vocation was.

How wonderful it is, all these years on, to hear about my old pupils Simon, Stephen, Guy and Adam! Fascinating to know all they have done, who they've turned out to be. I've often wondered how it must have been to be taught by me – I haven't asked them, maybe I don't dare. I certainly tried my best to be inspiring, but I'm not sure how effective this was. I do know that it got me into trouble from time to time. I tended to be rather enthusiastic, over the top probably. It's a tendency I have to this day.

Littleton 12–Wickhamstead 0

I'm sure it was him that I saw, but the strange thing was that I couldn't remember his name – his proper name I mean.

To us he was always Mr Flamingo. We settled for Mr Flamingo, but it could have been Mr Pongo, Mr Morpingo, or even Mr Montypergo. Mr Flamingo suited him best. It went with his pinkish complexion as he bounded into class after his bike ride from home, and with the red jacket he used to wear. There was a sense about him too that he might just take off and fly at any moment.

I suppose you'd call him a maverick. He taught only what he liked to teach: creative writing, history and drama were very strong in our class. He wasn't at all interested in keeping to the curriculum. Maths or Science hardly got a look in – which was fine with me then, but I've missed them ever since. I still don't know how an electric light bulb works. That's Mr Flamingo's fault.

Mr Flamingo particularly liked trips out of school, and so did we. He coached the school football team, not because he liked football or knew anything about it – as we very soon discovered – but because more often than not it meant a trip in the minibus to play our matches in a nearby village.

I was in the school team. Actually, almost everyone who was in the senior class was in the school team. Competition for places was not that fierce, because it was a very small school, only about sixty of us all together. Our worst defeat, the worst defeat the school team had ever suffered, was when Mr Flamingo took us to play Littleton. Littleton was a bigger village than ours, with a proper-sized football pitch, freshly painted white lines and real nets in their goals, which looked as wide as they are at Wembley. At Wickhamstead we had a little patch of grass for a playing field and a bundled-up coat for each of the goal posts.

Mr Flamingo was very keen on coach talks and game plans. Whenever he was coaching us he'd put on his New York Yankees baseball cap. We'd all crouch down in a serious semicircle around him before each match, and he'd talk to us very confidentially. His game plan was always the same, whoever we were playing, home or away. 'Don't try to do anything too fancy,' he'd say. 'Keep it simple. Just chase the ball, lads. When you get it, kick it. Hard. And if they've got it, tackle them. Hard!'

We had plenty of enthusiasm, but no skill – rather like Mr Flamingo when it came to football. We lost pretty well every match we played. Afterwards, he'd always say much the same thing, 'Bad luck, lads. Don't worry, you can't win every time. You did yourselves proud.'

But that rainy afternoon, after the match against Littleton, even Mr Flamingo was lost for words. We had chased the ball all over the pitch, hard, tackled, hard. I was in goal that day, so I'm not likely to forget the score: Littleton 12–Wickhamstead 0.

I wasn't the most popular boy on the pitch that day, and Mr Flamingo wasn't the most popular coach, either. But the next day, how did our coach respond to this debacle? First thing in the morning he sat us down and said simply: 'About yesterday's match. I want you to write about it. But it's not the football I want you to write about. It's not the football that matters, it's the disappointment we're all feeling. So think about a time, another time, away from the football pitch, when you've disappointed yourself, or others. Close your eyes and think. Then write it as you mean it, as you feel it.'

That day the writing came quite easily to all of us. We read our pieces out aloud, those of us who wanted to. When we'd finished Mr Flamingo decided we'd done enough work inside the classroom; as it was a lovely day, he took us on a walk to the nature reserve – a favourite haunt of his and by now a favourite haunt of ours too.

When we arrived back he got us painting herons and moorhens and ducks. That was when the head teacher, Miss Effingham, came storming in. She did not look happy. She ticked him off right there in front of us.

'I've told you time and again to ask me before you take the children out of school,' she told him, her fury thinly disguised.

'I'm really sorry, Miss Effingham,' he replied. 'It's such a supreme and wonderful day. I thought, let's go for a walk on the wild side – it'll cheer us all up after yesterday's match. Sorry.'

We loved these spats between Miss Effingham and Mr Flamingo. She went very pale and thin-lipped and Mr Flamingo turned even pinker than usual. But he kept smiling, which only infuriated her more.

'A round dozen this time, I hear,' she said acidly. 'That's a school record I'd say.'

'Everyone did their best, Miss Effingham,' Mr Flamingo said, still smiling. 'You can't ask for more than that.'

Without another word, Miss Effingham stomped off.

She was still in a stomping mood the next day when she came into our classroom again, and called Mr Flamingo to the door. 'A word in your ear, if I may,' she began, in a voice that was hushed, but quite audible.

'It's about the school trip to the Tower at the end of term,' she went on. 'As you know, Mrs Merton was going to take the children. But I'll have to ask you to take the trip instead – I've just learned that Mrs Merton will be taking maternity leave.'

'That's not my fault,' quipped Mr Flamingo.

The Effingham lips thinned visibly. 'I've no one else available to do it, otherwise I wouldn't have asked,' she said. 'It's in three months. Make sure you prepare them properly. No point in going all that way to the Tower, unless they know what they are going for.'

So that winter term at Wickhamstead School Mr Flamingo took over all the responsibility for our school trip. Half of us in the school, the senior half, a coach load, would be going off to the Tower of London, and every one of us was more than pleased with the news that Mr Flamingo was taking us. Not that we weren't looking forward to going with Mrs Merton. We were. A school trip was a day out of school, and that was always a great day, even with Mrs Merton. But with Mr Flamingo, anything could happen, and often did.

We had already done some project work on William the Conqueror and the Normans with Mrs Merton. We had learned about how the Normans had built the Tower of London, and about the Crown Jewels, which were always kept there. All quite interesting, but Mr Flamingo, we soon learned, had a rather different approach.

He wasted no time. The next day he gathered us all together in the hall and told us straight that we were going to have the most supreme school trip ever – *supreme* was his favourite word.

'And do you know what's going to make it supreme, children?' he went on. 'The Bloody Tower.'

We looked at one another, amazed.

When teachers swore, even Mr Flamingo, it was truly shocking. I mean, they shouldn't, they didn't, and he just had.

'No, no, no,' he said. 'Bloody, in this instance, children, means what it says, the red, dribbly stuff. It's not a rude word when it's the real thing, real blood. There's this place in the Tower of London called the "Bloody Tower" – it's what they call it, that's all.' We still didn't believe him.

'Honestly it is. And we'll be going there, visiting it. But before we do, you need to learn what happened there, how people lived then, how they died. So twice a week from now until we go on our trip in November, we're going to make things and do things, all to do with the Bloody Tower. We'll be doing drama and dressing up, and dancing, and even cooking! By the time we go off to the Tower, you'll be completely soaked in the history of the place, and a pretty bloody history it is too.'

We now knew for certain that whatever Mr Flamingo had in store for us was going to be a lot better than Mrs Merton's projects on nasty Normans or jangling jewels – Mrs Merton liked us to put lots of adjectives into our writing. We had no idea then just how far Mr Flamingo would go with all his ideas, only that it sounded as if it was going to be a lot of fun.

We began the next day. Mr Flamingo got us to make six standing figures from chicken wire and coat hangers, some of them representing taller people, some shorter, all of them life-sized. He sent us away that same afternoon with lists of dressing-up clothes to bring from home.

'And I don't want just dressing gowns,' he told us. 'Remember these are Tudors, Elizabethans.'

He'd shown us pictures of how they had looked in those days. 'So we need lots of old curtains, for ruffs, and doublets and hoses, and beads so we can make necklaces and earrings (they were big on jewellery).'

It took another few weeks, and lots of parent and teacher volunteers, to get all the costumes just right. Like a lot of the mothers, my mum entered into the spirit of the whole thing and got busy with her old Singer sewing machine. Meanwhile, this is what we did: we learned to dance like Henry VIII and all his six wives – quite a few of whom we learned had ended up in the Tower of London with their heads chopped off; we listened to Mr Flamingo playing music on his guitar that Henry VIII had written; and we made pasties with the school cook from an old sixteenth-century recipe Mr Flamingo had found – 'Elizabethan hotdogs' he called them.

Soon all the figures in the school hall were dressed and bejewelled and Mr Flamingo gathered us together to admire our handiwork.

'Like the ending to a good story, the best bit is yet to come,' he said. 'Look at our figures and tell me what's missing.'

Well it was obvious, so we all said it together.

'Heads, sir.'

'Such observant children. We're going to make their heads now, out of papier mâché.' So that's what we did, all twelve of them. We needed some spares, Mr Flamingo told us. And did we have fun doing it! By the time we had finished we were scuffling ankle deep through drifts of shredded newspaper, and all our hands and hair were sticky with glue. We went home reeking of marzipan that day – school glue always smelled of marzipan.

When the papier-mâché heads had hardened at last, and were dry, we painted them – eyes, noses, lips, ears, some smiling faces, some sad. We boys painted the heads of the lords, and kings and princes; and the girls did the ladies, queens and princesses.

Everyone seemed to be lords and ladies in those days! True, some of them did look a bit of a mess – too much dribbled paint, not enough care. But it was the hair that made them come truly alive – hair made from wool and string, some from straw. There were even a couple of real wigs; goodness knows where they came from.

By now, everyone had either seen or heard about the statues in the hall. Parents came in to see how they were coming on and were very impressed, which was probably why Miss Effingham suddenly became very enthusiastic about them, too. She was always popping in to see how we were getting on.

Each of our figures had to be someone who had been in the Tower of London and come out alive, Mr Flamingo said. So these weren't just any old historical characters. Among them was Queen Elizabeth I herself, with her bright red hair. She had more jewels than all the others put together. Each statue had its name printed out on a card and pinned to the wall, along with birth and death dates, and beneath there was the story of each life in a few lines. 'Information cards', Mr Flamingo called them.

There they all stood, completely finished now, along one side of the school hall, and we thought that was that. We were very proud of them and so, it seemed, was Miss Effingham. She even had the press come in to take a group photograph of us crouching down in front of our 'historical creations', as the newspaper called them the next day.

But Mr Flamingo hadn't finished. He had a surprise in store for us – for everyone.

'Those six extra heads you made are not just spares, children,' he told us. 'Watch, and all will be revealed.'

From behind the cupboard in the corner he then produced six broomsticks, each of them sharpened to a point. He had made a wooden base for every one of them, a block with a hole drilled through. We looked on in silence as he placed these blocks along the opposite side of the school hall, and then stuck a broomstick into each one, point uppermost. Then, very solemnly, he took the spare papier-mâché heads we'd made, one by one, and stuck them firmly, crunchily, on the poles. Beside each head he put up more information cards. Among them were Sir Walter Raleigh, Sir Thomas More, the Earl of Essex, and Lady Jane Grey. I can't remember the other two, probably two of Henry VIII's wives. Once he'd finished Mr Flamingo turned to us all with a satisfied smile on his face.

'So now, children, we have on one side six famous people who went into the Tower and came out alive; and on the other side, stuck on the poles, we have six of those unfortunates who went into the Tower and never came out at all, which is why they are represented just by their heads.'

We gaped at him.

'Well, don't look so shocked,' he said. 'That's what kings and queens did in those days – they chopped off the heads of anyone they didn't like. I told you about Henry VIII, didn't I? And remember the Queen of Hearts in *Alice in Wonderland*? "Off with her head! Off with her head!" What you might not know is that when kings and queens chopped off heads, they stuck them on spikes to show everyone what happened to people who displeased them.'

A few of us said, 'Yuck!' But just as many said, 'Brill!'

That was the moment Miss Effingham came into the classroom.

'What are you up to now?' she asked. 'More heads?'

As Mr Flamingo explained, Miss Effingham paled.

'It's all about bringing history to life, Miss Effingham. When we go to the Tower next week, I'll be taking the children up into the Bloody Tower, where' – he pointed to one of the severed heads –

'that one on the end there, Sir Walter Raleigh, was imprisoned for the last thirteen years of his life, before they chopped off his head.'

None of us had ever seen Miss Effingham speechless before.

It was the following week, the last time we all met as a group before the school trip, that I had my great moment. Mr Flamingo was up to something: there was a mischievous smile playing on his lips as he came bounding into the classroom.

'Drama!' he said. 'I love drama! I'll need a volunteer.'

I don't know why I put up my hand – probably because everyone else did.

'Me! Me, sir. Me!' I cried.

To my amazement he was pointing at me. 'Up here,' he said, suddenly stern. The smile was gone. I was at his side now, looking up into his face. He reached into his pocket slowly and took something out. A mask, just like the Lone Ranger on the TV! A gasp filled the classroom as he put it on.

'I am the executioner,' he announced in an overly sonorous voice, hamming it up. 'And you are about to have your head cut off, like Sir Walter Raleigh. First you have to give me some money.' He held out his hand. 'I'll need some money if I'm to do the job properly – that's what always happened on the scaffold. A kind of tip.'

I pretended to put some money into his hand.

'Kneel!' he commanded me. I did exactly as he said. 'Close your eyes now, say your prayers. And when you are ready put your head on the chair, and hold out your arms behind you like a swallow. That will be the sign that you are ready. Then I shall strike your head from your shoulders.'

I closed my eyes, and I did say my prayers, because I was a bit nervous, if I'm honest. I wanted to get it over with. There was no axe, I knew that. He was just Mr Flamingo, but I heard his legs shift, heard what sounded like the blade slicing the air. It was done.

'Behold the head of a traitor!' he shouted, pretending to hold up my severed head and showing it to everyone. There was a moment or two of silence. Mr Flamingo looked down at me. 'Don't worry, Michael,' he said. 'Shake your head, and you'll find it's still there.' That's when everyone started laughing and clapping. Now they all wanted a turn. But the school bell went and the lesson was over. I was the only one to have my head chopped off and I was so proud of that. I was quite the hero of the day at playtime.

At last the day of the school trip arrived. In the half-light of an early morning, all the parents and teachers were there to see us off on the coach. Flakes of snow were falling. Mr Flamingo was checking us all on to the coach. 'I'll try to bring all thirty-five of them back in once piece,' he quipped to Miss Effingham, who looked more frosty than ever. Mr Flamingo never could say the right thing.

There were two mothers with us on the coach, and Ken, the school caretaker. It was a long way to London but we were far too excited to sleep. The snow was falling harder all the time. By the time we got there it was settling on the roofs of houses and on the ground, swirling all around us as we stepped down from the coach.

'We've got to keep them warm,' Ken told Mr Flamingo. 'Keep them moving, that's what I say. They'll be fruzzed to death else.'

So we tramped through the snow into the Tower of London, Mr Flamingo spurring us on. The Beefeaters had icing on their hats. We didn't dawdle, Mr Flamingo didn't let us. We went into the

White Tower and saw all the armour and the swords; we went to see the Crown Jewels, glittering and gleaming in their glass cases. Outside, we counted six black ravens, hopping about on Tower Green. Mr Flamingo warned us that kidnapping the ravens and taking them home wasn't allowed, because if we did so – according to the legend – the whole country would collapse. By this time, anyway, we were exhausted and our feet and noses numb with cold. But Mr Flamingo, his face a beacon of enthusiasm, was still in full flow.

'Picnic time, children,' he announced. 'We'll have it in the warm, up in the Bloody Tower. Remember what I said, "the best till last". This will be supreme, I promise. Follow me!' So we climbed the stone staircase up into the Bloody Tower and had our picnic there. There was hardly anyone else about by now, so we had the place almost to ourselves. We ate our picnics, our 'Elizabethan hotdogs', and afterwards we wandered up and down the ramparts outside – Raleigh's Walk it was called – and looked out over the Thames. After a while Mr Flamingo called us all back in. We gathered round him to listen.

'Well, children,' he began, 'here we are in Sir Walter Raleigh's bedroom. Poet, soldier, sailor, explorer, adventurer, lover – he was the one who first brought back tobacco and potatoes to this country. Here in this tower he lived for thirteen years. He wrote his history of the world in that little room through the door behind you, and his poems too. He wrote one the night before he was executed.' Mr Flamingo closed his eyes and began to recite.

Even such is time, that takes in trust
Our youth, our joys, our all we have,
And pays us but with earth and dust;
Who, in the dark and silent grave,

When we have wandered all our ways,
Shuts up the story of our days:
But from this earth, this grave, this dust,
My God shall raise me up, I trust.

When he had finished it seemed to me the whole world had fallen still and silent.

'The next morning, children,' he went on, his eyes open now, 'they came for him. He got dressed, all in black. He was an old man by now and frail, but brave, very brave. He went out of that door, his bible in his hand, down those steps and they took him off to the scaffold. The executioner was waiting for him there in his mask. Sir Walter Raleigh gave him some money. Remember?' Mr Flamingo was looking directly at me. 'Then he knelt down, said his prayers, laid his head on the block, held out his hands behind him, and whoosh! Down came the axe. The end of a great man, one of our greatest.'

None of us said a word. That had really happened! Here, in this very place! Mr Flamingo paused for a long while before he spoke again, his voice no more than a whisper now.

'And do you know, children? At two o'clock' – he looked at his watch – 'and it is exactly two now – every Thursday (and today is Thursday), the ghost of Walter Raleigh comes up those steps, through that door and into this room … with his head under his arm.'

All of us turned at that moment and looked towards the door. I wasn't the only one who was quite sure that any moment now, we'd see a ghost coming up those steps. We hardly dared breathe. Then came Mr Flamingo's voice again, breaking the silence and the expectation. 'Oh, sorry, children, my mistake. It's Friday. It's all right. He won't be coming today.' He laughed then and we all did, out of relief. It wasn't that funny at the time because, by then, most of us were frightened out of our wits. But when he laughed, we had to, just to show we hadn't believed it in the first place.

On the way back to school most of us slept, a few of us were sick. I thought we'd all recovered from the incident in the Bloody Tower – by now it had become a really good joke, the highlight of the day. We got off the coach and there was a whole crowd of mums and dads and teachers waiting for us in the playground. All we could talk about was Mr Flamingo's story: the ghost of Walter Raleigh up in the Bloody Tower. My mum thought it was funny, but I could see that some of the mums of the younger children weren't so happy about what they were hearing.

Next morning we were in the playground when Mr Flamingo came riding in on his bicycle, hands free, arms folded, showing off as he often did. Miss Effingham's window opened, and we heard her calling out to him across the playground, 'In my office, if you please. Now.'

We watched him walk slowly across the playground like a man going to the scaffold. She didn't chop his head off, but it wasn't long after that we heard he was going to be leaving at the end of term. On the day he left we gave him a present, a tie dotted with tiny pink flamingoes, which my mum had found in a shop in town.

And then only last week, nearly forty years later, I thought I saw Mr Flamingo again. I was in Starbucks. I looked up and there he was. He was sitting at the table right next to mine, on his own, reading a newspaper. He was fuller in the face, with less hair, but ruddier than ever, and still wearing a red jacket. It was only when he looked up and caught my eye that I knew for sure that it was him. I think maybe he recognised me too. There was just a flicker around his eyes before he went back to his paper.

I wanted to lean across and tell him there and then that I was the one he'd chosen that day, whose head he'd chopped off. Did he remember taking us to the Bloody Tower? And did he remember, I wondered, that terrible afternoon in the rain: Littleton 12–Wickhamstead 0? But I didn't ask him, so I don't suppose I'll ever know.

4

A Winning Formula

One Saturday afternoon during his early days as a teacher at Great Ballard Michael had been asked to referee a rugby match. When Clare said she would stay at home she was struck by the force and firmness of his response. 'You are my wife,' he said. 'I need you to be with me.'

Frustrated though Michael was taking orders from a head teacher and operating as part of a staff, he was not someone who could work alone. 'Whatever happens, and whatever you do,' Clare had promised in a letter written just after their engagement, 'I will always, always love you.' Friends who have known them both over nearly fifty years of marriage confirm that she has been true to her word. 'It is Clare who has kept Michael focused,' says Peter Campbell. 'He could not have achieved all he has achieved without her.'

Very early in their marriage Clare had hoped that she might find some way in which she and Michael could work together. The obvious thing was for them to teach on the staff of the same school. With this in mind, when they moved to Kent, she had embarked on a teacher-training course in Canterbury. But as events at Milner Court unfolded she began to wonder whether they might build a future for themselves outside the classroom.

Clare had always been acutely aware of those less fortunate than herself. In early childhood she had a strong religious streak. Her sister Christine remembers her, as a small girl, 'staring out of the window one Christmas Eve, hoping to see God and his angels', and 'taking her role as Mary in the school nativity play extraordinarily seriously'. At eleven she was sent to a Quaker boarding school, The Hall, near Wincanton in Somerset. Influenced by the formidable but inspiring headmistress, Monica Brooks, she developed a lifelong passion for the countryside, for the poetry of A. E. Housman, and for reaching out to those on the margins of society. Girls at the Hall learned to think of service to others as far more important than any kind of academic success. In their free time they knitted blanket squares for a village in Switzerland, set up after the war to offer refugee children an education of 'head, heart, and hands'. 'We felt really close to those children,' Clare says; and though, after leaving school, her life appeared to unfold like that of any other carefree, middle-class girl of the time – a few months in Paris, secretarial training, a Cordon Bleu cookery course – she continued to feel close to them in spirit, and to hold as her heroes Joan of Arc, St Francis and Albert Schweitzer, the German theologian, philosopher and medical missionary who had won the Nobel Peace Prize in 1952.

Now, with her own children at school, she began to think hard about whether there might be some enterprise into which she and Michael could pour their joint energies, giving something back to the world which had given them so much.

During Michael's time at Milner Court, they had suddenly become very rich indeed. In 1968 Sir Allen Lane had been diagnosed with cancer of the colon. He was only sixty-six and, unable to contemplate letting go either of life or of Penguin Books, he fought against it. Even in his last illness, propped up in bed, he continued to scrutinise the Penguin ledgers every evening. Finally, towards the end of June 1970, he slipped into a coma, and on 7 July he died. Penguin Books had been one of the most phenomenal business successes of the century. When the long process of winding up

Lane's estate was complete, his daughters came into a substantial inheritance.

Michael had visited Sir Allen regularly in hospital over the last few months of his life, and they had grown finally to like and respect one another. But, to the end, Lane remained dominant – 'like a great oak tree, taking up all the light'. Both Michael and Clare wonder whether, if he had not died when he did, they would ever really have grown up, or have dared to contemplate throwing in the comfortable life they had established for themselves in Kent, uprooting their family for the fifth time in ten years, and embarking on an enterprise which Kippe, Jack and many of their friends considered at best idealistic, at worst foolhardy.

One of Clare's closest friends at the Hall was a girl called Judith Keenlyside, two years her senior. Judith was beautiful and self-assured, but she was also kind and intuitive. When Allen and Lettice Lane's marriage ran into difficulties, Clare turned to her for comfort and counsel. They stayed in close touch after Judith left school, became a debutante, and married, very young, Tom Rees, an Oxford graduate with a First from Christ Church and a fast-track career in the Civil Service. Clare's letters to Michael at Sandhurst make frequent reference to visiting Tom and Judith, and to dinner parties at their house in Markham Street, off the King's Road.

Despite her sophisticated Chelsea lifestyle, Judith, like Clare, had emerged from the Hall with a social conscience. After working as a nurse she retrained as a teacher, and took a job in a state primary school, The Hague, in Bethnal Green. She loved her work, but over time she began to feel unsettled. Too many of her pupils, she believed, were simply passing through the system, without their lives being enriched or their potential realised. They needed something that classroom teaching was not able to deliver.

Judith's feelings struck a chord with Michael. Even at Wickhambreaux Primary, where he was happier as a teacher than in any other school, he felt that not more than half his pupils were gaining anything significant from his lessons. The children who thrived almost invariably came from stable, supportive homes; but the ones whose lives he longed to touch were those from tougher backgrounds, whose experiences were often distressingly narrow and bleak.

When, in the summer of 1965, he and Clare had driven down to the South of France in their MG, they had stopped one hot midday in a medieval town with a moated château at its centre. As nobody seemed to be about, they wandered across the drawbridge. It was only when they were in the shady courtyard that they noticed towels and clothes draped from the windows. On enquiring in the town, they discovered that this was a *colonie de vacances*, where working-class urban children could escape the city for a week or so and get a taste of outdoor life – canoeing, walking in the forests, cooking on campfires. It was the first time Michael or Clare had come across such a scheme, and they were moved by it.

When Tom and Judith mooted the notion of their embarking together on some enterprise to give city children a break from the classroom, and offer them a taste of rural life, they were immediately enthusiastic. On long walks across the Kent marshes, the two couples tossed ideas back and forth. As Tom was to continue his career in the Civil Service, it was essential that they stayed within commuting distance of London. The ideal, they agreed, would be to find a house sufficiently large to accommodate themselves and their families, as well as groups of visiting children from inner-London state schools. They would need outbuildings, and a few fields in which they could keep livestock. Michael and Clare already had a horse, chickens and ducks at Newnham Farmhouse. Now they added two Jersey calves, Poogly and Emma, and two donkeys, Effie and Duncan, to their menagerie. At weekends they drove with Tom and Judith around the home counties inspecting properties. But the market was against them; prices were rising steeply and gazumping was rife. And, as the months passed, both sides began to have misgivings about working together so closely. Even then, decades before he developed a public persona, Michael was, Judith remembers, a powerful and rather controlling character. Judith had always enjoyed working as part of a team. She began to suspect that Michael would not.

Their plans and dreams might have petered out entirely had not fate, at this juncture, taken the reins. Michael is a believer in fate. Looking back over his life he feels certain that there has been 'someone conducting things', introducing opportunities 'beyond anything I could have dreamed of, or could have used my own will to effect'. Providence, good fortune, serendipity – call it what you will – now propelled him forward in a completely unexpected direction.

It started with a telephone call. On leaving university, Mark Morpurgo had taken a job in insurance, and in 1972 had been appointed broker consultant for Hambro Life in the West Country. He rang one day to say that while house-hunting to the north of Dartmoor he had come across a tumbledown, thatched farm-worker's cottage. Langlands was on sale for £6,000, and it was just outside the village of Iddesleigh.

Mark knew that Iddesleigh had a special place in Clare's heart. At its centre was a pub, the Duke of York, whose feisty landlady, Peggy Rafferty, had been one of Allen Lane's dearest friends. They had met in London in the early Thirties, when Peggy was working for the Windmill Theatre, and Lane was a young man about town, living high on the hog, out every night. Peggy was no beauty, but she was a match for Lane in vivacity, humour and appetite for life, and friends suspected that at some point they had become lovers. When, after the war, Peggy married a widower poet and playwright, Seán Rafferty, and moved from Soho to the depths of north Devon to run a pub, Lane remained in close touch.

Allen Lane had a sentimental attachment to Devon, as well as to Peggy. His cousin John Lane, who had first introduced him to publishing, had come from farming stock in Weare Giffard, near Bideford, and in middle age Lane developed a longing to return to the West Country, his fortune made, to serve some small community as a benevolent squire.

He realised this dream through his frequent visits to Peggy Rafferty and the Duke of York. At Priory Farm, as Jack Morpurgo notes in *Allen Lane: King Penguin*, Lane had had 'little hope of being anything but a businessman in gumboots'. But in Iddesleigh, as in no other environment, he found 'relaxation and acceptance that was touched neither by envy nor by obsequiousness'. In the Duke of York today, Lane smiles out from black-and-white photographs, silver-haired and spruce, chatting to local people at the bar, and presenting trophies to the champions of what is known still as the Allen Lane Darts League. The personality he projected here – generous, modest, eager, involved with the community – was, Jack Morpurgo notes sardonically, 'almost unrecognisable to those who knew him only in London or New York'.

When Clare was eight, Lane decided that it was time she too was introduced to Iddesleigh. Putting her, alone, on to a train at Paddington, he arranged for Peggy to meet her at Okehampton and to take her back to spend her Easter holidays at the Duke of York. It was to become, over the next few years, a second home to her. At night, she slept in a bedroom over the bar, falling asleep to the clink of glasses, the murmur of pub chat, and the thud of darts on the board. But, as soon as breakfast was over, Peggy expected her to make her own entertainment, and to make it out of doors.

In Iddesleigh itself there was plenty to keep her occupied. Opposite the pub was a bric-a-brac shop run by a First World War veteran, Wilf Ellis, and filled with treasures – china fairings, candlesticks, Bulgarian poker-worked ornaments. In the sloping churchyard, looking out towards Dartmoor, slow-worms, snails and lizards slithered across the gravestones. Clare liked to trap them, and take them back to the pub to keep in a shoe box under her bed. But what she loved most of all was to wander out of the village, and into the deep green hills and valleys that lay beyond. The land round Iddesleigh, some of it listed in the Domesday Book, had been worked by the same families for generations. They are a tough, circumspect people – 'quick to show some warmth', Michael says, 'slow to show much warmth'. But to a child these distinctions meant nothing. Clare had always found it easy to get on with people. She took it for granted that, when she knocked on the doors of thatched, cob-walled farmhouses, she would be welcomed in. It became a game with her to see how many different drinks she could be offered in the course of an afternoon.

One farmer, Thatcher Jones, became her particular friend. Living alone, eating fish pie for breakfast, lunch and supper, he found Clare's company a tonic. He had an old pony, Captain, which he encouraged her to ride. On Captain's back, she clopped around the narrow lanes – lanes bordered by hedgerows so dense and deep that in summer, when they were covered by canopies of elm and beech, riding down them was like wandering through a green labyrinth.

Just before Christmas 1963, when Clare was heavily pregnant with Sebastian, she had arranged to spend a weekend at the Duke of York so that she could share her Iddesleigh idyll with Michael.

Clare with Captain.

Since her first visit the village had made two significant advances: mains water had been installed, and then electricity. But to Michael it seemed, none the less, the strangest, most backward place he had ever encountered. There were so few cars that shaggy manes of grass sprouted down the centre of the roads; and the people spoke with accents so thick he could barely understand them. And, though everybody was friendly enough, he was aware of being sized up. Word had got about that he had recently come out of the army, and this caused some ribaldry around the bar.

He might never have wanted to return had it not been for the kindness of the barman, Seán Rafferty, who, like Michael, felt himself something of an outsider. A Dumfriesshire schoolmaster's son, allegedly descended from Rob Roy, Seán was by nature a poet, not a publican. When he was a child, it had become clear that he had a gift with words – 'hares grow merry and by night / leap the long furrows in delight', he wrote one bitterly cold night, aged nine, watching a jack hare from his bedroom window. In the Twenties Edwin Muir had tried to encourage and promote his work, but Seán was determinedly unambitious, and gently perverse. In 1932 he had moved to London – 'To get lost'. It was here, shortly after the death of his first wife (they had married at the start of the war; she died within days of the declaration of peace), that he had met Peggy. They were unalike in almost every way – she strident, forceful, snobbish; he quiet, melancholy, drawn to the lost and the down-trodden. But Seán was pragmatic. His only daughter, Christian, needed a mother, and Peggy would look after them both. If Peggy wanted to move to Devon, and to run a pub, so be it.

It was Peggy, always, who wore the trousers. The Duke of York was known as 'Peggy Rafferty's pub', and became famous for 'Peggy Rafferty's cooking'. It was Peggy who lured visitors down from Bristol and London; Peggy who kept up her friendship with Allen Lane, so that when she ran into financial difficulties he was on hand to help. Seán just served behind the bar, assuming what he called 'the role of father confessor'. People needed somebody to confide in; everybody knew he was discreet.

But at night, after the pub closed, Seán remained behind his bar. By candle-light, he wrote poems drenched in grief, and the despair he felt at having squandered his poetic gift:

The candles yawning and the fire gone out.
Silence, your sin; let silence make amends.
You will not write a line and if you wrote
what could you write but epitaphs and ends?

How much Michael learned of Seán's story that first weekend in Iddesleigh, he cannot now remember. But he does remember feeling that here was a man of sympathy and depth whom he would like to know better.

So, when Mark Morpurgo rang to tell them about Langlands, both Michael and Clare were intrigued. Bundling the children into the Land Rover, they drove to Devon. It was getting late when they reached the cottage, and all they could see in the dusk was that its roof was collapsing and its garden overgrown. But when they returned next morning, after spending the night at the Duke of York, a perfect rainbow appeared in the sky. It was a sign, Clare decided. Langlands was meant for them.

Seán Rafferty.

From that moment things moved quickly. On a visit to oversee the renovation of the cottage, Michael drove the Land Rover, all the children aboard, into a deep ditch. A local farmer, John Ward, with his tractor and two teenage sons, Graham and David, came to the rescue. The Wards lived at Parsonage Farm, just down the lane from Langlands, and had been farming in north Devon for generations. Clare and Michael seemed to them about as convincing as country people as Felicity Kendal and Richard Briers. But they liked one another. Suppose, John Ward suggested, the Morpurgos came and stayed at Parsonage Farm until the renovation was complete?

It was while staying with the Wards that Michael's eyes were first opened to what living on a farm really involved – not the Petit Trianon life he and Clare had established in Kent, but an endless, arduous round of toil and reward. The Wards were canny: they knew when to sell their livestock for the highest price; whether to take them to market at Hatherleigh, or at Holsworthy; how to feed their cattle to make them happy, but not fat. But they also knew, instinctively, when to infuse science with magic. When their cows had ringworm, they sent for the 'blessing man' from the next village. When a dog fox attacked their chickens, David was able to 'sing' to him to lure him to his gun. 'They could read the signs of the moon,' says Michael, 'and the wind in the trees.' Watching them at work, Michael found himself filled with wonder, humility, and excitement.

Then, flicking through *Country Life* one weekend just as the building work at the cottage was coming to an end, Michael noticed an advertisement for Nethercott House, a rambling Victorian pile a few minutes' walk from Langlands, with extensive outbuildings, a cottage, a milking parlour, a barn, a cider-press and fifty acres of land. Not only did the Nethercott fields march with those of Parsonage Farm; they had actually been rented for some years by the Ward family, who had used them to graze their beef cattle. If he and

Nethercott House.

Clare could convert Nethercott into a place where groups of school-children could come and stay, Michael thought, perhaps the Ward family might agree to let the children work alongside them at Parsonage Farm, in exchange for rent-free grazing.

It was 'utter insanity', Michael thinks, looking back. Neither he nor Clare had any idea how the finances would be organised, whether schools could be persuaded to visit, or quite how children might be occupied if and when they came. But, driven by an over-whelming need for radical change in their lives, they were deter-mined to make the project work. By Christmas 1974, Nethercott was theirs, and the Charity Commission had registered 'Farms for City Children': a charity whose purpose was 'to advance the education of boys and girls from urban areas by the establishment of suitable educational study centres in the countryside of England and Wales'. Early in 1975 Michael and Clare sold up in Kent and, with Sebastian, Horatio and Ros, Poogly and Emma, Effie and Duncan, moved lock, stock and barrel to Devon.

After some negotiation the Ward family had accepted Michael's invitation to play a part in Farms for City Children. Neighbouring farmers considered them foolish – 'but to be honest', says David Ward, 'we never thought of this as a long-term thing'. Michael and Clare were 'city types'; this was a temporary whim. The Wards had not reckoned on Michael's stamina and resolve. While Clare settled the children into new schools, and organised the conversion of Nethercott, he threw himself into learning how to be a farmer. Volunteering as a farmhand alongside John, Graham and David, he got up at cockcrow to help with the milking, and worked until the last cow had been bedded down and the last chicken shut up in its coop. 'The effort he put in was amazing,' says David. 'After a few months, we had come to trust him in everything – everything except tractor work.'

The diary that Michael kept over these months is a record of gruelling and often solitary labour. During lambing, he battles with a combination of sub-zero temperatures and a severe shortage of sleep: 'When you turn out yet again at 3 in the morning on a freezing windy night,' he notes on 3 January, 'it is a little difficult to be even-tempered with the milking cows 4 hours later down in the dairy.' Three months on, in late March, the temperatures have barely risen, and it is time for ploughing in gale-force winds and lashing, horizontal rain.

Every season brings its own challenges. In the summer, the milk overheats in its churns awaiting collection. In the autumn, lured by apples and acorns, the pigs break out of their pens, wreaking havoc in the orchard. And constantly, all through the year, the Wards watch their livestock for a seemingly endless catalogue of maladies: milk fever, warble fly, wooden tongue, foot rot, fluke, staggers, bloat.

Yet what the reader feels on every page of Michael's diary is his appetite for his new surroundings and his new life. He relishes the names of the fields he is helping to work around Parsonage Farm – Burrow Brimclose, Ferny Piece, Little Rat's Hill, Watercress Meadow. Between tasks he observes the behaviour of sun and rain, herons, larks and cuckoos; he watches salmon rising in the river Torridge and deer stepping through the shadows in the woods; and he describes everything he sees and feels in language that comes closer to poetry than anything he has ever written. 'A white, hard frost this morning with mists filling the valleys,' he notes on 4 December. 'Cows were gliding legless over the fields.' On 2 March, as the sun shines warm for the first time in months, all the farm smells take on 'the mustiness of summer'. By November, 'both the Okement and the Torridge are in full flood, great swirling brown gashes in the valleys'. This is 'the dead season', he notes towards the end of the month. 'Everything seems to be ending and nothing beginning.' For Michael personally, the opposite was true. He felt intoxicated, filled with a new sense of purpose. 'I was high on it.'

There was a great deal to be done before Farms for City Children could really take off – Nethercott House needed furniture, and a staff to run it – but fate, again, was on Michael's side. At about the time he and Clare acquired Nethercott, Seán and Peggy Rafferty were preparing to retire from the Duke of York, and were looking for a cottage. Nethercott had come with Burrow Cottage, and Clare suggested that they might live here, rent free, if Seán would take on the running of the large, walled vegetable garden ('I like vegetables,' he told an interviewer some years later. 'You can eat them, and they don't talk to you').

Joan Weeks, who had worked with Peggy at the Duke of York, agreed to come as cook. She had cooked at Nethercott for the Budgett family just after the war, and had always loved the atmosphere of the house. She would come for just two years, she said, to help get the charity going. She stayed, in the end, for twenty-one.

'Most people in the village were a bit sceptical about the whole thing,' says Joan, now in her eighties, and living in retirement in Iddesleigh. But because of their affection for Clare, she and the Raffertys were determined to give Farms for City Children their support. 'We begged and borrowed,' she says – furniture, kitchen equipment, garden tools. Clare, meanwhile, was busy writing to schools, inviting them to come and stay. During the summer of 1975, with their first few bookings in place, she and Michael drove to London and, in Brixton High Road, bought bundles of bed linen from a defunct Greek shipping company, and a job-lot of ex-army bunk-beds. These were iron-framed, and severe-looking: they would not, Clare thought, appeal to children. Visiting friends from Hampshire helped to paint them in rainbow colours.

Monday 26 January 1976 was a bright, icy day on which the thermometer never rose above freezing. As darkness fell, twenty-six nine- and ten-year-olds from Chivenor School on the Castle Vale estate, north-east of Birmingham, marched in red bobble hats down the drive of Nethercott House. Castle Vale was one of the most infamous examples of the failure of post-war overspill estates: a sprawl of pre-fabricated tower blocks, where nearly half the residents were unemployed and muggings, drug dealing, joyriding and fly-tipping all part of daily life. It was a place even the police felt afraid to enter; but this had not daunted the young teacher who now led her children down the drive, suitcase in one hand, guitar in the other.

Joy Palmer was just twenty-four, a Julie Andrews figure, with boundless energy, a Girl Guide qualification, a passion for nature and the open air, and a determination to help her pupils discover their gifts and realise their potential. In the weeks leading up to that first Nethercott visit she had organised musical evenings and sponsored silences to help buy the children wellington boots and warm clothes. Looking back, Michael and Clare do not believe that there could have been a teacher in England better suited or more eager to help them get Farms for City Children off to a good start.

Together, that first week, they devised the routine that has remained in place at Nethercott ever since. The children woke at 6.30 a.m., and by seven o'clock were assembled in the dark yard – 'the moon still in the sky,' one of them noted in a poem, 'the water frozen in the bucket'. They divided into three groups. One walked with Graham Ward to the milking parlour, to help milk the cows and feed the calves. Another piled into the back of David Ward's trailer, and bumped down the lane to see to the pigs, sheep and beef cattle. A third stayed with Clare to look after the animals close to the house: the horses and donkeys, ducks, geese and chickens.

After a large cooked breakfast at nine o'clock, there were all manner of farm tasks to tackle: mucking out stables, cleaning the hen-houses, collecting eggs, helping with the lambing. On Tuesday morning Michael walked the children over the moor to Hatherleigh to see the livestock market. On Thursday afternoon he took them to Iddesleigh to visit the village hall, with its photographs of turn-of-the-century children in hobnailed boots; and to wander round the church, and read the headstones in the graveyard. It was a learning experience for the villagers as well as the children: 'We had none of us ever seen a black child,' says Joan Weeks.

In the evening they gathered in front of the great log fire in the Nethercott drawing room, shared their memories of the day, sang to Joy's guitar, acted out plays, told stories.

Routine was vital, Joy insisted – but it must be flexible. That first week, Poogly began to calve. All twenty-six children dropped their tasks and were led into the barn. Many of them, at school, found concentration near impossible: they could 'scarcely sit through one lesson', Joy remembers. But a photograph of them watching the birth of Poogly's calf has the stillness of a nativity. They are lost in wonder.

Thirty-five years on, one of Joy Palmer's pupils, David Kelly, tracked her down on the internet, and sent her an email. He is now living in Portland, Oregon, father to four boys, and he wanted to thank her for her devotion to her work in Castle Vale, and especially for taking his class to Nethercott. His memories of the place remain vivid. He had lived in Castle Vale since his parents' marriage broke down when he was six, and he had never been into real countryside

*Children from Chivenor School, Castle Vale, watch the birth of
Poogly's calf, January 1976.*

before. He remembers feeling, as he stepped off the coach, that he had 'walked into paradise'. He was amazed by 'the sheer size and grandeur' of Nethercott House; by 'how clean the air smelled – how fresh everything seemed'; and by 'how the farmer really cared for his animals: this affected me a lot'. As the week drew to a close, he felt desperately sad: 'Don't get me wrong, I missed my family a lot, but this place was just so beautiful – so different from life in Castle Vale. I didn't want to leave.'

He was not alone. As one of his schoolmates wrote:

Oh my beautiful memorys of Sweet Devon
Are like the one's I have of heaven,
…
each minute felt like a secound each day like an hour
and how that country air gave me phsical power!
but we had to leave devon –
my pardise like heaven.

On the Saturday evening, before the children headed home, there was a disco. Flushed with joy at the success of the week Michael leapt and whooped among them in something resembling a Highland fling.

If the children had been enriched by their week, so too had everyone involved. Joy Palmer returned often in the years that followed, and what she calls her 'Nethercott days' instilled in her 'a very deep sense of the significance of children's experiences in the natural world', propelling her from teaching into educational research, and leading, ultimately, to her appointment as Pro Vice-Chancellor of Durham University. The Ward boys – Graham quiet, intelligent, reserved; David an extrovert and a joker – found themselves, as time went by, wanting to share more with the children than just the essential farm tasks. They took them out in the darkness to look at the stars; they played football with them after tea; they encouraged them to stop talking and listen carefully to the sounds of the river, the birds, the wind in the crops. Joan Weeks not only cooked, meanwhile, but invited the children to cook with her. Some of them, she discovered, had never had a birthday cake. For children whose birthdays fell during a visit to Nethercott, she made sure there was always a huge iced sponge, and candles.

And at the centre of them all, like the hub holding the spokes of a wheel, were Michael and Clare. They were, Joy Palmer remembers, always open, keen to listen and learn, to ensure a 'return flow of benefit' for children, teachers, farmers and staff. 'It was,' says Joy, 'a winning formula.'

Those early days of Farms for City Children were exhausting. Eight schools made bookings during 1976, but Michael and Clare's ultimate aim was to get four times that number – about a thousand children – to Nethercott each year. On top of their farm work, they were busy writing to state primary schools in west London, Bristol and Birmingham, and following up their letters with visits to those schools that expressed interest.

Then there was their own children's education to think of. They were twelve, nine and eight when they arrived in Devon, and they had all moved house, and therefore school, several times. Michael and Clare hoped that, by putting down roots, they would provide the children with stability at last – and, as far as education went, they hoped that they might find this in the local state schools. Sebastian was sent to Chulmleigh Community College; the younger two to Hatherleigh Primary. But Chulmleigh proved unsuitable, and Hatherleigh unchallenging, and before long all three children were moving schools again – and not for the last time. 'As parents,' Michael reflects, 'this was not our finest hour.'

With so much to preoccupy him, one might imagine that Michael, for a time at least, would have ceased to think about producing books. But Aidan Chambers's encouragement had planted a seed of hope and ambition; and, soon after moving to Devon, a new friendship had made him more determined than ever to keep writing, and to write better.

One July evening during their first summer at Langlands, Michael and Clare had taken visiting friends for a walk down to the Torridge, Tarka the Otter's river which runs through the fields of Parsonage Farm. The light was fading – it was becoming what Devonians call 'dimpsey' – when a great figure clad in river green loomed up, dragged himself in his waders out of the water, and strode towards them. Michael recognised him immediately as Ted Hughes. His voice, if not his physical presence, had been familiar for years.

In the late Sixties, Hughes had broadcast a number of talks for a BBC Radio Schools programme, *Listening and Writing*. Michael had been thrilled by them. They took the form not so much of instruction as of invitation: 'What Ted Hughes seemed to be saying was that writing is a mystery, but that we can become part of that mystery – that, if we just keep our minds and hearts open, we *all* can do this.'

Standing face to face with Hughes on the river bank, Michael found himself lost for words – fortunate, perhaps, because Hughes was fishing, and in no mood for chatter. But Hughes, too, was struck by the encounter. He had met a beautiful woman by the Torridge, he told his wife, Carol, that evening. She and her husband were doing amazing work with children from inner cities. He wanted to see more of them.

Before long, Michael and Clare and Ted and Carol Hughes were meeting regularly for dinner, either at Langlands or at Court Green, the low-roofed, hobbity rectory that Hughes had bought with his first wife, Sylvia Plath, in 1961. Often, Seán and Peggy Rafferty made up the party. All six loved good food and wine, and for Michael and Clare the memory of these evenings continues to glow. 'Everything about them was intense,' says Michael. 'Even the laughter was intense.'

Ted Hughes, they quickly learned, was a man of many moods, and of some contradictions. He radiated warmth and camaraderie, and was insatiably fascinated by other human beings; yet Michael

Carol and Ted Hughes.

was aware that he was, privately, 'a man in pain'. Sometimes, at the start of an evening, he would emerge from his study with 'a hooded expression', as if haunted by demons of which he never spoke. But in the company of friends, his mood would lift. He had a gift for making those around him feel at ease, but he could be sharp. 'He tended to put you on your back foot. You had to really think when you were with him.' Neither patronising nor manipulative, he was, none the less, authoritative. 'He told you what to do,' says Michael, 'and you did what you were told.'

It was Ted Hughes who, shortly after their first meeting, had instructed Michael to keep a diary. The excitement he felt about all he was seeing and learning as he worked with the Wards on Parsonage Farm would not last, Hughes warned – 'So write it down! While it's fresh!' He dangled a carrot. If Michael kept a diary, he promised to write a poem for every month of the year. Perhaps they might make a book of it.

And perhaps, Michael reflected, the book might be illustrated by another of their new friends, the photographer James Ravilious, whom they had met one morning in the Duke of York. A dark, handsome man, quiet and intuitive, James was the son of the great painter and wood engraver Eric Ravilious. He and his artist wife, Robin, lived in a tiny cottage in the village of Dolton, four miles from Iddesleigh, and he was employed by the Beaford Archive taking photographs to document the land and people of this pocket of north Devon as the twentieth century moved into its final decades. Bicycling from village to village, he had become so completely engrossed in his work that what was to have been a short-term commission had grown into a labour of love that was to occupy most of the rest of his life.

Michael was impressed and moved by Ravilious's work. Sympathetic, but never sentimental, his black-and-white photographs captured the humour, the love, and the hard graft that went to make up a kind of English rural life that was fast disappearing. 'If Samuel Palmer had been a photographer,' Michael says, 'these are the kinds of pictures he might have taken.'

All Around the Year, Michael's diary of twelve months on Parsonage Farm, interleaved with Ted Hughes's calendar poems and illustrated with James Ravilious's photographs and Robin Ravilious's line drawings, was published by John Murray in the spring of 1979. If sales were disappointing, the critical response was gratifying. Patricia Beer, in the *Listener*, praised 'the welcome straightforwardness' of Michael's style. 'I have the feeling,' wrote Martin Booth in *Tribune*, 'that, had Pepys been a twentieth-century farmer, he'd have done a similar book, and no better.'

Now long out of print, *All Around the Year* has a special place in Michael's heart. It was, he says, his 'learning book', carrying him out to a new circle of readers and reviewers, helping him to raise his sights as a writer. In Iddesleigh, and the countryside surrounding it, he had found a corner of rural England that he loved, and that he knew he could write well about. And having written about it in a diary, he found himself drawn to write about it in a novel, and to explore its past.

In the attic at Nethercott one afternoon, rummaging through a tea chest of Allen Lane's belongings, Michael found four framed paintings of cavalry horses in the First World War. By the artist F. W. Reed, they transported him straight back to the Abbey, and to its bound volumes of the *Illustrated London News*. In one of them, British horses were shown charging up a snowy slope towards the German line, and becoming entangled in barbed wire. Without knowing quite why, Michael dusted it down, brought it home to Langlands, and propped it up in his study.

The painting began to preoccupy him. He had never much liked horses – 'I'd always thought of them as beautiful, but stupid' – but soon after moving to Devon Clare had bought a Haflinger mare, Hebe. Hebe was loved by the Morpurgo children, by the children visiting Nethercott, and, eventually, by Michael too. His affection for her made Reed's painting very real to him, and prompted him one morning to telephone the Imperial War Museum to ask how many British horses had died in the First World War. The answer was that, of roughly a million sent out to France, only about 65,000 had returned home. The rest had either died in battle or been sold off to French butchers.

Then, sitting by the fire in the Duke of York one evening, Michael fell into conversation with Wilf Ellis, owner of the bric-a-brac shop that Clare had loved as a child. He asked which regiment Wilf had served in in the First World War. 'The Norfolk Regiment,' came the reply. Ellis invited Michael to his cottage, where he showed him some of the mementoes he had brought back from the Western Front – his trenching tool, a button, some medals.

Michael felt moved to find out more. Close to Langlands lived Captain Budgett, former owner of Nethercott House. Budgett had also fought on the Western Front, in the Berkshire Yeomanry, and he described to Michael how, because it was taboo to express emotion to fellow soldiers, he had walked up and down the horse lines at night, sharing his hopes and fears with the horses. He felt sure that they had, in their own way, understood.

As he listened to Captain Budgett, the outline of a story began to form in Michael's mind. It centred on a Devon farm horse sold to a British cavalry regiment and shipped over to France in 1914. The horse would be captured in a cavalry charge, and then used by the Germans to pull ambulances and guns, and it would winter on a French farm. It would get to know and love both German and French soldiers, and endure with them the horror, pity and futility of war. In his mind, Michael christened the horse Joey, after a foal born to Hebe. Joey, he decided, would tell his own story.

But here was the rub. If readers were to be lured into believing a story told by a horse, Michael himself needed to feel convinced that there could be real empathy between horses and humans. Captain Budgett's reminiscences had suggested that there could; but it was a nine-year-old boy who finally persuaded him.

In the autumn of 1980 a group of children from Pegasus School on the Castle Vale estate came to stay at Nethercott. Among them was a boy with a severe stammer. He was withdrawn and almost silent and, on his teacher's firm instructions, Michael avoided asking him questions or engaging him in conversation. 'Force him to speak,' the teacher had warned, 'and he will do a runner.'

Towards the end of the week, walking up to Nethercott one evening, Michael noticed a light on in Hebe's stable. The boy was leaning on the stable door in his slippers, stroking Hebe's nose and speaking to her without any hint of a stammer. Hebe, in response, was standing still, ears pricked forward. 'She may not have understood the words,' Michael says, 'but I felt sure that she understood that this boy was a friend, and was in need.' It was the final spur he needed to get to work on *War Horse*.

Some books, Michael finds, seem almost to write themselves; others prove more troublesome. This one was difficult. Horatio Morpurgo has written of the summer holidays of 1981, through which his father struggled with it: 'He sat sullenly at meals, answering in monosyllables.' Ted Hughes, in an effort to cheer him along, arrived one moonless night to take him eel fishing. They hooked five fat eels from the Torridge; but Michael's spirits did not lift.

Having been rejected by a number of publishers, *War Horse* was finally published by Kaye & Ward in the spring of 1982. The reviews were mixed. Jilly Cooper, in the *TLS*, wrote that, although the book owed a large debt to *Black Beauty*, it was 'very moving, sparely and beautifully written and well researched'. In the *TES* Fred Urquhart predicted, with prescience, that 'Joey's marvellous horse's eye view of the 1914–18 holocaust may remain a favourite long after other runners … have been retired'. But David A. Lindsey, writing in the *School Library Journal*, found the notion of a tale told by 'an anthropomorphic, trilingual, half-thoroughbred farm horse' risible. 'Morpurgo's effort,' he wrote, 'strains for pathos, descends into bathos, and overworks its cliché-ridden plot.'

Despite this, Rosemary Debnam at Kaye & Ward was quietly confident that the novel was outstanding, and her confidence seemed justified when news came through that *War Horse* had been shortlisted for the Whitbread Children's Book Award.

On the evening of the prize-giving, a black limousine was laid on to whisk Michael and Clare from Paddington Station to the ceremony at the Whitbread headquarters in the City, where proceedings were filmed by Channel 4. Cameras whirred; excitement ran high. Michael had been assured that he was the favourite for the children's award. So when Roald Dahl, head of the judges, rose to give his speech and announced that the award was in fact to be presented to W. J. Corbett for *The Song of Pentecost*, it came as a crushing disappointment. After stepping down from the podium, Dahl sought Michael out. Next time, he counselled, stick to the present: 'Children don't like books about history.'

Like Cinderella's carriage, the limousine had disappeared by the end of the evening. Michael and Clare returned to Paddington by tube, caught the night train home, and by seven o'clock the following morning were getting ready to set off for work at Nethercott. Then the telephone rang. It was Ted Hughes, suggesting that he and Michael go out and spend the day together. They did a bit of fishing, then poked about in bookshops and antique shops in Bideford –

'Ted loved pottering'. The Whitbread was not mentioned until, over tea in a café, Ted leaned forwards. He and Carol had watched the award ceremony on television. Michael must understand that these things did not matter: they were all a lot of nonsense. 'You wrote a fine book,' he said. 'And you'll write a finer one.'

At Nethercott, working so closely alongside the teachers, Clare and I got to know them pretty well. Some, like Joy Palmer, have remained lifelong friends. Of all the strange and wonderful things we witnessed together, the sight of that little boy from Castle Vale talking to Hebe over her stable door remains, for me, the most extraordinary. I have re-imagined it here.

Didn't We Have a Lovely Time?

I have been teaching for over twenty years now, mostly around Hoxton, in north London. After all that time I am no longer at all sentimental about children. I don't think you could be. Twenty years at the chalk face of education gives you a big dose of reality.

I was sentimental to start with, I'm sure. I am still an idealist, though not as zealous perhaps as I used to be, but the fire's still there. You could say that I have given my life to it – I've never had children of my own. I'm headmistress at the school now and I believe more than ever we should be creating the best of all possible worlds for our children, giving every one of them the best possible chance to thrive. That's why every year for at least the past ten years I've been taking the children down to a farm in Devon, a place called Nethercott.

It takes six long hours by coach from London and there, in a large Victorian manor-house with views over to distant Dartmoor, we all live together, all forty of us, teachers and children. We eat three good hot meals a day, sing songs and tell stories around the fire at night, and we sleep like logs. By day we work. And that's the joy of it, to see the children working hard and purposefully out on the farm, feeding calves, moving sheep, grooming Hebe the Haflinger horse who everyone loves, mucking out stables and sheds, collecting eggs and logs, and apples too. The children do it all, and they love it – mostly, anyway. They work alongside real farmers, get to feel like real farmers, know that everything they are doing is useful and important to the farm, that they and their work are appreciated.

Every year we come back to school and the whole place is buzzing. In the playground and in the staff-room all the different stories of our week down on the farm are told again and again. The magic moments – a calf being born, the glimpse of a fox or a deer in Bluebell Wood; the little disasters – Mandy's welly sucked off in the mud, Jemal being chased by the goose. The children write a lot about it, paint pictures of it, and I know they dream about it too, as I do.

But something so extraordinary happened on one of these visits that I too felt compelled to write it down, just as it happened, so that I should never forget it – and because I know that in years to come, as memory fades, it is going to be difficult to believe. I've always found miracles hard to believe, and this really was a kind of miracle.

The boys and girls at our school, St Francis, come from every corner of the earth, so we are quite used to children who can speak little or no English. But until Ho arrived we never had a child who didn't speak at all – he'd have been about seven when he joined us. In the three years he'd been with us he had never uttered a word. As a result he had few friends, and spent much of his time on his own. We would see him sitting by himself reading. He read and he wrote in correct and fluent English, more fluent than many of his classmates who'd been born just down the street. He excelled in maths too, but never put his hand up in class, was never able to volunteer an answer or ask a question. He just put it all down on paper, and it was usually right. None of us ever saw him smile at school, not once. His expression seemed set in stone, fixed in a permanent frown.

We had all given up trying to get him to talk. Any effort to do so had only one effect – he'd simply run off, out into the playground, or all the way home if he could. The educational psychologist, who had not got a word out of him either, told us it was best simply to let him be, and do whatever we could to encourage him, to give him confidence, but without making demands on him to speak. He wasn't sure whether Ho was choosing not to speak, or whether he simply couldn't.

All we knew about him was that ever since he'd arrived in England he'd been living with his adoptive parents. In all that time he hadn't spoken to them either, not a word. We knew from them that Ho was one of the Boat People, that as the war in Vietnam was coming to an end he had managed to escape somehow. There were a lot of Boat People coming to England in those days, mostly via refugee camps in Hong Kong, which was still British then. Other than that, he was a mystery to us all.

When we arrived at the farm I asked Michael – he was the farm school manager at Nethercott and, after all these years, an old friend – to be a little bit careful how he treated Ho, to go easy on him. Michael could be blunt with the children, pointing at them, firing direct questions in a way that demanded answers. Michael was fine about it. The truth was that everyone down there on the farm was fascinated by this silent little boy from Vietnam, mostly because they'd all heard about the suffering of the Vietnamese Boat People and this was the first time they'd ever met one of them.

Ho had an aura of stillness about him that set him apart. Even sweeping down the parlour after milking, he would be working alone, intent on the task in hand – methodically, seriously, never satisfied until the job was done perfectly.

He particularly loved to touch the animals, I remember that. Looking wasn't enough. He showed no fear as he eased his hand under a sitting hen to find a new-laid egg. When she pecked at him he didn't mind. He just stroked her, calmed her down. Moving the cows out after milking he showed no sign of fear, as many of the other children did. He stomped about in his wellies, clapping his hands at them, driving them on as if he'd been doing it all his life. He seemed to have an easiness around the animals, an affinity with the cows in particular, I noticed. I could see that he was totally immersed in this new life in the country, loving every moment of every day. The shadow that seemed to hang over him back at school was lifting; the frown had gone.

On the Sunday afternoon walk along the river Okement I felt him tugging suddenly at my arm and pointing. I looked up just in time to see the flashing brilliance of a kingfisher flying straight as an arrow down the middle of the river. He and I were the only ones to see it. He so nearly smiled then. There was a new light in his eyes that I had not seen before. He was so observant and fascinated, so confident around the animals, I began to wonder about his past – maybe he'd been a country boy back in Vietnam when he was little. I longed to ask him, particularly when he came running up to walk alongside me again. I felt his cold hand creep into mine. That had certainly never happened before. I squeezed it gently and he squeezed back. It was every bit as good as talking, I thought.

At some point during our week-long visit, Michael comes up in the evening to read a story to the children. He's a bit of a writer, as well as a performer. He likes to test his stories out on the children, and we like listening to them too. He never seems to get offended if someone nods off – and they're so tired, they often do. We have all the children washed and ready in their dressing gowns (not easy, I can tell you, when there are nearly forty of them!), hands round mugs of steaming hot chocolate, and gather them in the sitting room round the fire for Michael's story.

On this particular evening, the children were noisy and all over the place, high with excitement. They were often like that when it was windy outside, and there'd been a gale blowing all day. It was a bit like rounding up cats. We thought we'd just about managed it, and were doing a final count of heads, when I noticed that Ho was missing. Had anyone seen him? No. The teachers and I searched for him all over the house. No one could find him anywhere. Long minutes passed and still no sign of Ho. I was becoming more than a little worried. It occurred to me that someone might have upset him, causing Ho to run off, just as he had a few times back at school. Out there in the dark he could have got himself lost and frightened all too easily. He had been in his dressing gown and slippers the last time anyone saw him, that much we had established. But it was a very cold night outside. I was trying to control my panic when Michael walked in, manuscript in hand.

'I need to speak to you,' he said. 'It's Ho.' My heart missed a beat. I followed him out of the room.

'Listen,' he said, 'before I read to the children, there's something I have to show you.'

'What?' I asked. 'What's happened? Is he all right?'

'He's fine,' Michael replied. 'In fact, I'd say he's happy as Larry. He's outside. Come and have a look.' He put his fingers to his lips. 'We need to be quiet. I don't want him to hear us.'

And so it was that the two of us found ourselves, minutes later, tiptoeing through the darkness of the walled vegetable garden. It was so quiet, I remember hearing a fox barking down in the valley.

There was a light on over the stable door. Michael put his hand on my arm.

'Look,' he whispered. 'Listen. That's Ho, isn't it?'

Ho was standing there under the light stroking Hebe and talking to her softly. He was talking! Ho was talking, but not in English – in Vietnamese, I supposed. I wanted so much to be able to understand what he was saying. As though he were reading my thoughts, at that very moment he switched to English, speaking without hesitation, the words flowing out of him.

'It's no good if I speak to you in Vietnamese, Hebe, is it? Because you are English. Well, I know really you are from Austria, that's what Michael told us, but everyone speaks to you in English.' Ho was almost nose to nose with Hebe now. 'Michael says you're twenty-five years old. What's that in human years? Fifty? Sixty? I wish you could tell me what it's like to be a horse. But you can't talk out loud, can you? You're like me. You talk inside your head. I wish you could talk to me, because then you could tell me who your mother was, who your father was, how you learned to be a riding horse. And you can pull carts too, Michael says. And you could tell me what you dream about. You could tell me everything about your life, couldn't you?

'I'm only ten, but I've got a story I could tell you. D'you want to hear it? Your ears are twitching. I think you understand every word I'm saying, don't you? Do you know, we both begin with "H", don't we? Ho. Hebe. No one else in my school is called Ho, only me. And I like that. I like to be like no one else. The other kids have a go at me sometimes, call me Ho Ho Ho – because that's how Father Christmas talks. Not very funny, is it?

'Anyway, where I come from in Vietnam, we never had Father Christmas. I lived in a village. My mum and dad worked in the rice fields, but then the war came and there were soldiers everywhere

and aeroplanes. Lots of bombs falling. So then we moved to the
city, to Saigon. I hated the city. I had two little sisters. They hated
the city too. No cows and no hens. The city was so crowded. But
not as crowded as the boat. I wish we had never got on that boat
but Mum said it would be much safer for us to leave. On the boat
there were hundreds of us, and there wasn't enough food and
water. And there were storms and I thought we were all going to
die. And lots of us did die too, Mum and Dad, and my two sisters. I
was the only one in the family left.

'A big ship came along and picked us up one day, me and a few
others. I remember someone asked me my name, and I couldn't
speak. I was too sad to speak. That's why I haven't spoken to
anyone since then – only in my head like I said. I talk to myself in
my head all the time, like you do. They put me in a camp in Hong
Kong, which was horrible. I could not sleep. I kept thinking of my
family, all dead in the boat. I kept seeing them again and again. I
couldn't help myself. After a while I was adopted by Aunty Joy and
Uncle Max and came to London – that's a long way from here. It's
all right in London, but there are no cows or hens. I like it here. I
want to stay here all my life. Sometimes at home, and at school,
I'm so sad that I feel like running away. But with you and all the
animals I don't feel sad any more.'

All the time Ho was talking I had the strangest feeling that Hebe
was not only listening to every single word he said, but that she
understood his sadness, and was feeling for him, as much as we
did, as we stood there listening in the darkness.

Ho hadn't finished yet. 'I've got to go now, Hebe,' he said.
'Michael's reading us a story. But I'll come back tomorrow
evening, shall I? When no one else is about. *Night night. Sleep tight.*

Don't let the bedbugs bite.' And he ran into the house then, almost tripping over the doorstep as he went.

Michael and I were so overwhelmed that for a minute we couldn't speak. We decided not to talk about it to anyone else. It would seem somehow like breaking a confidence.

For the rest of the week down on the farm Ho remained as silent and uncommunicative as before. But I noticed now that he would spend every moment he could in the stable yard with Hebe. The two had become quite inseparable. As the coach drove off on the Friday morning I sat down in the empty seat next to Ho. He was looking steadfastly, too steadfastly, out of the window. I could tell he was trying his best to hide his tears. I didn't really intend to say anything, and certainly not to ask him a question. It just popped out. I think I was trying to cheer him up.

'Well, Ho, didn't we have a lovely time?'

Ho didn't turn round.

'Yes, Miss,' he said, soft and clear. 'I had a lovely time.'

5

The Heat o' the Sun

When Ros Morpurgo looks back on her family's early days in Devon, one memory remains vivid. 'It's of my mother,' she says, 'walking down the lane surrounded by Nethercott children, and they are not just holding her hands but hanging off her coat sleeves. If you can love someone you've known for less than a week, they loved her. I wonder now how my brothers felt about this.' Her brothers chose not to be involved in this book; their stories are their own. Yet one

Clare surrounded by children at Nethercott.

cannot understand Michael without knowing that his relationship with them has been troubled, and that this is a source of bitter regret – 'and regret', he says, 'lasts longer than any kind of pleasure that comes from success'.

The best children's writers are not necessarily – not often, in fact – the best parents. It is as hard to believe that Michael was a monstrous father as it would be easy to understand if, given his own background, he was less than perfect. Jack Morpurgo – distant, ambitious and lacking in affection – provided him with no good model of how to nurture and encourage children. Kippe, subsumed by sadness and then by alcoholism, left him feeling, often, 'very alone'. 'I write,' Michael says, 'for the child inside myself that I still partly am.' His books spring, to some extent, from a need to confront the boyhood loneliness that continues to nag at him.

He is more than lucky to have found Clare. Yet it was not easy, so soon and so young, to have to share her love with children of his own. He was catapulted into fatherhood before he had any clear sense of his own identity. 'I was still finding my feet, still trying to discover who I was,' he has written. 'I was too full of self perhaps to be a great father.' And while he had abundant energy – the thing for which most parents long – he had, maybe, almost too much of it. 'After being with Michael,' one of his editors, Gill Evans, remarks, 'I feel charged and super-charged.' Anyone who has spent time with him will know what she means. But it is possible to imagine that, for his children, this perception may have been reversed; that, growing up in a smallish cottage with a character so powerful and full of drive, they may sometimes have felt squashed and super-squashed, without sufficient space to breathe or to flourish.

In moving to Devon, Michael and Clare had been so preoccupied with the ultimate goals of Farms for City Children that they had barely considered its practical implications, either for themselves or for the family. It was not until the day before the first school party arrived that Clare realised with a jolt 'that all these hours were about to disappear out of our lives'. Time that she had hitherto lavished on her own children was about to be parcelled up and given out to hordes of total strangers.

In 1977, the number of bookings at Nethercott jumped from eight to sixteen; in 1978, it reached capacity at thirty-two, and Clare had to start turning schools away. She and Michael, meantime, had established the schedule to which they would keep for the next twenty-five years. In term-time, they worked three seven-day weeks in a row before taking a weekend off, allowing themselves just five hours' turnaround between visits. Yet Neil Warrington, who brought successive parties of children to Nethercott from Turves Green School in Birmingham, remembers how quick they were to learn new names, and to make each group of children feel 'that this lovely old house, with its cobbled yard, and horses leaning over stable doors, really was their home; that they were the only people who mattered'.

Having got her own children off to school, Clare supervised the Nethercott children in the lighter jobs – fruit picking, tree planting, egg collecting, grooming the horses. From Langlands she also, single-handedly, managed the administration, liaising with schools about bookings, keeping the accounts, fund-raising. For the first twenty years there was no proper office, and all this had simply to be done at the kitchen table. Mark and Linda Morpurgo remember that when they came to stay the telephone rang constantly, and, no matter how inconvenient, Clare insisted on answering it.

By 7 a.m. Michael was in the yard at Nethercott, ready to head off to the milking parlour. Apart from a quick break for lunch, he then worked alongside the children – mucking out cowsheds, washing down the dairy, stacking logs, clearing ditches – until they went back to Nethercott House for high tea at five o'clock. From 6 to 7 p.m. he was out with them again, milking, and feeding the pigs, lambs and calves. Then, once the children were ready for bed, he sat with them in the drawing room and told them stories by the fire.

David Hicks, a teacher at The Oaks Primary School in Birmingham, brought pupils on no fewer than eighteen visits to Nethercott, and he has compiled a video giving glimpses of every season of the year, and every moment of the farming day. It shows Michael pointing out and naming wild flowers as he leads children through the fields, inviting them to smell lumps of otter spraint by the Torridge ('Come *on*! It won't hurt you!'), explaining why cows have four stomachs. Both his theatrical genes and his Sandhurst training are constantly in evidence. 'How many of you feel *angry*?' he demands, as the children stagger, panting, to the top of a steep hill. 'Me!' they chorus. '*Good!*' he bellows. 'The angrier you feel, the warmer you'll keep!' Between farm tasks, he does not chat to the

Michael working with children at Nethercott.

teachers, but involves himself in the children's moments of pure pleasure – tobogganing with them down the hill behind Nethercott on a snowy afternoon, skimming stones across the river on a summer's evening.

'Sharing these things was no effort,' he says now, 'because I was so caught up in it all. I was like a wide-eyed child myself.' But it took its toll. By the end of the working day, Michael admits, he had 'precious little to give'; and by the end of the week, when he and Clare drove into Hatherleigh to buy fish and chips, they were often 'so knackered we couldn't speak'. Many children see their parents exhausted by work – and, as Michael says, 'it's no bad thing'. What was perhaps unusual for the Morpurgo children was to have parents engaged together on such an intense working life so close to home. Langlands is less than a quarter of a mile from Nethercott. If problems occurred, day or night, it was easy for the staff to nip round and offload them. And the lack of a proper journey between work and home – a luxury in many ways – meant, for Michael, that there was no period of adjustment and decompression between work and family life. Dealing with the children at Nethercott, he assumed a robust persona. 'If you are trying to engage with forty-odd kids,' he says, 'you can't just stand there like a lemon and talk flatly about what they are going to be doing and why. You have to talk in a way that's quite heightened, to persuade them by force of personality.' But difficulties arose when he carried this rather domineering persona from Nethercott into Langlands. The split between his public and his private self is, he says, his 'fault line'. It upsets Clare, and it used to upset the children. 'For a time, after I arrived home in the evening,' he admits, 'I was perhaps rather boisterous.'

*   *   *

Michael is visibly uncomfortable thinking himself back into moments of tension. What he remembers with ease are 'the glowing times' at Langlands, with the Beatles' 'Here Comes the Sun' thrumming through the cottage like a theme tune. Pushed a bit, however, he accepts that he spent too little time with his children, and that he could be difficult to live with – not only due to exhaustion.

For all the demands that Farms for City Children put on him, he was determined to pursue his writing. It was an uphill struggle. Even after his Whitbread shortlisting, Puffin declined to buy the paperback rights to *War Horse*, stating baldly that they were waiting for him 'to do something better', and many of the leading publishers continued to turn down his work. A sheaf of rejection letters is preserved at Langlands, and it makes disheartening reading. The Bodley Head finds Michael's stories lacking in both 'logical development' and 'a sense of humour'. Victor Gollancz criticises his failure to fuse 'fantasy and reality into an acceptable whole'. For Macmillan he is simply 'too prosaic'.

Reading these comments, and knowing he persevered, one might guess that Michael was extraordinarily thick-skinned. He is not. He is determined, but he is also, as Ros says, 'psychologically delicate, just as Kippe was'. The rejection letters, many of which are laced with Michael's frantic financial calculations, hit him in a number of weak spots. He was tilting not only with the ghost of Allen Lane, on whose money he and Clare were still dependent, but with the fear of failure planted in him by his stepfather. 'Jack left us all,' says Mark Morpurgo, 'with an insecurity about success, but Michael's has gone on a long time.' There is a reason for this. Mark did extremely well in the world of insurance. He made a great deal of money. Pieter Morpurgo, in his twenties, moved on from the theatre to the BBC, where he became a highly respected studio director. Both these careers Jack Morpurgo understood and purred over. But Farms for

City Children baffled him. It did not help that he disliked the countryside. On his rare visits to Langlands, he and Kippe sat at the kitchen table, filling the cottage with cigarette smoke. He refused to go outside.

Michael would not have dreamed of talking to Jack about his writing. In his heart of hearts, he suspected that the publishers might be right; that he was no good. 'The making of stories did not come easily. I didn't have enough self-confidence to be sure that I was managing it well.' When he was struggling with a book, he became silent, brooding and snappy in a way that his family could not ignore. 'They'd all have to walk on eggshells.'

Often, especially in the early days, he wove his family's experiences into his books – opening himself, later, to accusations of exploitation. But, perhaps because they had been too close to them in the making, he hardly ever read his stories to his own children. Instead, he took them down the road to read to the children at Nethercott.

To begin with, both Michael and Clare had hoped that their children might join in with Nethercott life; and in the early days the younger ones sometimes went over there for breakfast before school. But Ros remembers that no sooner had she made new friends than they disappeared; and it was not long before she was too old to want to play with nine- and ten-year-olds anyway. Yet the Nethercott children remained an inescapable presence. When Ros got a pony, she was not allowed to mount or ride it in sight of Nethercott in case the visiting children felt jealous; and her toys were often taken for them, without consultation. Did she mind? 'I didn't *mind*, but I noticed.'

In an early piece of literature about Farms for City Children Michael had written boldly about the ill-effects on a child's security of having two employed parents. 'Any parent knows,' he wrote, 'how important is that hour after the return from school when all the problems and triumphs of the day need a sympathetic hearing.' It was not long, however, before the local schools proved so unsatisfactory that all three Morpurgo children were sent away. It was a painful decision all round. Remembering the homesick letters that the children sent back from boarding school, Clare looks stricken. 'Awful,' she says, 'really awful. It was a really horrible time.'

If one was to tell this story from the point of view of the teachers and children visiting Nethercott, of course, it would read very differently. Farms for City Children was achieving more than Michael and Clare had ever dared hope. There were the obvious benefits: boys and girls who had only known life on an inner-city estate were learning where their food came from, what mud looked like, how to pick out Orion in the night sky. They travelled home pink-cheeked from a week of fresh air and exercise. But Nethercott was also changing lives in ways that Michael and Clare had not foreseen. Farm work proved a great leveller. Children who lacked self-confidence, who struggled in the classroom, or whose grasp of English was poor, often turned out to be heroes when it came to shovelling dung, delivering lambs, or reaching under tetchy hens to gather eggs. Working in teams, they not only came to accept and understand one another better, but also saw their teachers in a new light. 'One of the hardest things for a boy to learn,' Mrs Lintott tells Irwin in *The History Boys*, 'is that a teacher is human.' Living and working for a week on a farm with their teachers taught the children this lesson.

Removed from television, meanwhile, many of them discovered a new appetite for reading, a capacity for reflection, and a desire to express their feelings in words. 'As I sat in total silence in the wood,' wrote one boy on his last afternoon at Nethercott,

I looked at the sky and thought.
I thought about the Nethercott cows, donkeys
    and Quest, the great horse.
I thought about the cool running river, passing
    at the bottom of the woods.
I wished I lived in this place, where the water
    runs and everyone is safe.

Yet life at Nethercott, as at Langlands, was not perfect. Michael never waved off a party of children without feeling that at least some lives had changed for the better, but there were times when it was a relief to watch a coach disappear down the drive, and there were moments of crisis, frustration and near-collapse, when he and Clare asked themselves whether the whole venture had been a terrible mistake. Not all teachers were like Joy Palmer or Neil Warrington or David Hicks. Some made it clear that they disliked the countryside, found watching the birth of farm animals revolting, and objected to getting up early to go out in the rain or snow. Others regarded Michael and Clare, with their plummy accents and nice manners, as do-gooders with no real grasp of working-class children's lives. 'Sometimes,' says Michael, 'we felt that they were actively working against us.' He remembers trying to restrain a boy who was hurling stones at a horse. The boy's teacher turned on Michael, shouting that this was an experiment to see how the horse would react, and that it must be allowed to continue.

More than once, a teacher had to be sent home, either for improper behaviour – one was discovered encouraging a group of children to undress slowly to music – or because they had lost control of their pupils. 'You brought with you a group of children who were quite clearly not manageable,' Michael writes to one such teacher after her mid-week departure in June 1978. 'I do not consider

Children from Hoxton swimming in the Torridge during a week at Nethercott, 1976.

it my business to interfere with the way teachers treat their children, or are treated by them, but I will not stand idly by when children swear at their teachers, at Mrs Weeks, at David [Ward], and are allowed to get away with it.' The headmaster's reply is blistering: 'You have no direct first-hand experience of the home circumstances of many of our children. Nor have you … any conception of the kinds of difficulty they can and do lead to.' His was one of a number of schools that had to be told that they would never be welcome at Nethercott again.

While, on the whole, Michael and Clare could see that their work was having a palliative effect on children whose home lives were painful – removing them from deprivation and abuse, offering 'a huge deep breath of something different' – there were some children for whom staying at Nethercott simply heightened a sense of despair. The day before one London school party was due to leave, an eleven-year-old girl from a troubled background went missing. She was eventually discovered semi-comatose, having taken an overdose, and rushed to hospital in Exeter. When she came round she confessed that she had not been able to face the thought of going home.

At the end of weeks like these, Michael and Clare turned for comfort to Seán and Peggy Rafferty, and Ted and Carol Hughes. Sometimes they offered gentle teasing, sometimes wise counsel. From the start, Michael had had a sense that Ted Hughes understood more deeply than he did himself why Farms for City Children mattered. 'I knew,' says Michael, 'that by bringing children to Nethercott we could offer them an educational experience that could broaden their outlook. Ted understood something more profound: that being close to nature was part of our elemental being, and that it should be a part of every child's heritage.'

From time to time Hughes came to read at Nethercott. He was apprehensive to begin with, Michael remembers, and he addressed the children 'in exactly the same tone he used when speaking to six hundred people at Hay: a hushed voice with a nervous tremor'. Then he relaxed – 'and I think,' says Michael, 'he loved it. Here was an audience with no baggage. Nobody was about to bowl a googly about Sylvia Plath.' It was Ted Hughes who, in time, helped to secure Farms for City Children a royal patron, Princess Anne – and she, in turn, encouraged the charity to grow, opening new farms first in Wales and then in Gloucestershire.

But Hughes was also protective of Michael and Clare. 'He worried about us crucifying ourselves with overwork,' says Michael, 'and he knew how important it was to remove us mentally from Nethercott and the milking parlour.' With Seán Rafferty, Hughes would gently guide the conversation away from the troubles of the week and on to books and poetry, and in their company Michael delighted in feeling out of his depth. 'I loved just to listen to them, to lose myself in their discussions of Yeats, or Eliot, or Rimbaud. And often I would come away and look out the works they had been talking about, and try to understand them for myself.' Literature, which had for so much of Michael's life been a source of boredom and humiliation, became a treasure house to be plundered.

It was not only dead writers he was getting to know. Ted and Carol Hughes were legendary hosts, and in the dining room at Court Green, eating salmon that Ted had caught in the Torridge, he and Clare found themselves chatting to some of the great figures in contemporary literature: Seamus Heaney, Stephen Spender, Basil Bunting, Alan Sillitoe, Yehuda Amichai. 'When I grow up,' Michael sometimes quips, 'I'll be a poet.' He envied the 'extraordinary, miraculous gift' of these men; he knew it was something to which he could never aspire. Yet when he speaks publicly now about the importance of children meeting great writers, he is thinking of the evenings at Court Green. 'I caught something from being with these people,' he says. 'It gave me self-confidence to be near them.'

At the centre of the poets, Ted Hughes sat like some rugged Prospero, fascinated to see how his guests got on with one another, mischievously delighted when they did not. He cast a sort of magic over them all. 'Pretty well everyone, male or female, was in love with Ted,' says Michael. 'I think you can definitely call it love. He was our king – though there was no sense of subservience. Each of us felt this strong connection to him, and probably each of us overestimated how strong it really was. Each of us, individually, wanted to be in his glow.'

When he had writers staying with him, Hughes often turned up with them at Langlands, unannounced. Ros remembers her grave disappointment when he arrived one morning with Charles Causley. 'I'd been studying Causley's poetry at school, and I thought it was great, and then there was this *tiny* man in the kitchen.' Michael and Clare would never have dreamed of dropping in unexpectedly at Court Green, but when Ted arrived it was an unwritten rule of their friendship that they would stop whatever they were doing and give him their undivided attention. How did he hold them in such thrall? Everyone who knew him attests to his charisma. One editor remembers that, when he walked into the offices of Faber & Faber, 'you could feel him in the building, even if he was on the floor below'. And Emma Chichester Clark, the morning after watching Michael Fassbender in *Jane Eyre*, comments that if you ever met Ted Hughes 'then no other Rochester quite cuts the mustard'. In all the years of their friendship, Michael 'never got over a feeling of awe in Ted's presence'. For his children, he acknowledges, this must sometimes have been irksome. 'It was not easy to balance the intensity of that friendship with our family life.'

*   *   *

'More life may trickle out of men through thought than through a gaping wound,' wrote Thomas Hardy. The mistakes and regrets that Michael and Clare now dwell on so painfully in relation to their family life should not be allowed entirely to distort the past. Ros, for example, has no memory of her parents' friendship with Ted and Carol Hughes causing tension. 'We got a lot of our entertainment from Mum and Dad knowing them. They were always there for our birthdays – a really happy presence.' And if Farms for City Children was all-consuming during the school terms, there were always the holidays.

Looking through photographs of the school holidays in the albums kept by Clare is, for an outsider, like entering an idyll of family life – page after page of picnics and expeditions, laughing children and almost absurdly youthful-looking parents. 'No young lady will remain for ever young and maidenly,' Canon Shirley had warned Michael in a letter when he and Clare got engaged. 'She will be middle-aged one day, and middle-spreaded.' But as the mother of teenage children Clare continued to look just like a teenager herself. In August the family headed abroad, sometimes to Greece, more often to France. In the shorter holidays, and at half-term, they packed up the car and shot down the A30 to their bolt-hole in Cornwall.

In the late Seventies, Clare had spotted in the Classified section of the *Sunday Times* an advertisement for Tower House, once home to Katherine Mansfield and the writer John Middleton Murry, near the village of Zennor, five miles south-west of St Ives. A square-built, granite cottage, tucked away down an overgrown lane, it looks out across a rugged patchwork of Iron Age fields to the sea. Above it, rocky, windswept moors offer wide views across the Atlantic as it crashes into the cliffs, jewel green over white sand. Visiting on a warm, bright day in May, the hedgerows filled with campion, bluebells, trefoil, stitchwort and baby fists of new bracken, it is not hard to see why the Morpurgo family loved the place. But Michael remembers Zennor as magical in all weathers: 'In there,' he says, peering through the picture-window into the living room of Tower House, 'we played chess and Scrabble for hours and hours, with rain and snow lashing against the windows.'

In that room too was a wide, low window-seat looking out towards the sea. When the children were playing in the garden, or had gone into Penzance with Clare to shop, Michael, armed with a biro and a school exercise-book, liked to wedge himself in here with cushions. He had once come across a picture of Robert Louis Stevenson in Samoa, leaning back against a mountain of pillows, knees up, notebook before him, and had since tried to ease himself into the same position before beginning to write. Even so, the blank page alarmed him, and over time he developed the psychological tricks he employs to this day to get the words flowing. 'I'm nervous of writing,' he confessed in a recent email to a nine-year-old. 'I keep worrying it's no good – always been like that. So I find it's better if I just pretend I'm not writing at all. Instead, I tell the story from my head, down my arms, through my fingers, and on to the page. I'm good at kidding myself, but whatever works, eh?'

If the writing was slow in coming he could comfort himself that this was just a hobby: Farms for City Children was his *real* work. But in Zennor it came easily. Often he produced 2,000 words in just a couple of hours, his handwriting getting faster and faster, and smaller and smaller, until he was cramming up to forty words on a line.

Nethercott proved a rich seam. Working with the children there, watching them interact and listening to their conversations, Michael found stories constantly suggesting themselves. Before going to bed, he jotted down in a notebook incidents and phrases that had struck him during the day, and he then brought his notebooks with him to Cornwall. There is not space here to give more than a handful of examples of the many reworkings of Nethercott experiences in Michael's stories. *The Ghost of Grania O'Malley* opens with little Jessie Parsons struggling, despite her cerebral palsy, to reach the top of Big Hill. It was inspired by a girl with cerebral palsy who came to Nethercott one spring and, against her teachers' wishes, insisted on taking part in a two-mile race around the village. *Sam's Duck* is based on the true story, told to Michael by a teacher who came to Nethercott, of a little boy who stole a penguin from Dudley Zoo and brought it home on the coach hidden in his duffel bag. And *Little Foxes*, the tale of a miserable foster-child on a bleak inner-city estate who befriends a fox and escapes with him to find a better life, took shape in Michael's mind after he went to see for himself what life was like in Castle Vale.

Sometimes, visiting children unwittingly put Michael in touch with boyhood feelings, long buried. Sitting in Langlands one morning, he heard a child crying in the field outside. Her classmates were herding sheep, but this little girl was sobbing uncontrollably. 'Suddenly I knew from the tone of that sobbing that it was homesickness, and that terrible feeling of being completely separate from the world, of wanting to die, flooded back to me.' *The Butterfly Lion*, the story of a little boy found running away from school by an elderly lady who takes him home and tells him an extraordinary tale, flowed from that moment. It remains one of Michael's best-loved books.

In Zennor, too, stories suggested themselves to Michael almost wherever he turned. It is a place where history shades into prehistory, and reality into fable. Legend has it that, in the 'silent' years before the start of his public ministry, Jesus came to this part of Cornwall, travelling the trade-routes between the Mediterranean and the tin mines that provided the chief source of income until the early twentieth century. Today the landscape remains dotted with tumbledown smelting chimneys and counting houses, and in the churchyard at Zennor, among the graves of nameless, shipwrecked sailors, are those of miners who lost their lives to landslides and rockfalls. It is said that the ghosts of trapped miners continue to knock at the walls of underground chambers, begging to be released. Michael was fascinated by the 'knockers', and by tales of wreckers and smugglers, spriggans and boggarts and mermaids. They became the inspiration for one of his finest collections, *The White Horse of Zennor* – the title story inspired by his meeting, when rambling one day by the ancient burial chamber Zennor Quoit, a grey stallion which appeared before him out of the mist.

But Tower House, fruitful though it was both for family life and for writing, was a practical nightmare. It was impossibly damp; and the water supply, shared with a neighbouring farm, very often ran dry. After five years Michael decided that it was time to sell up.

The loss of Zennor proved a blessing in disguise, opening the way to the discovery of a corner of the British Isles that was to become even more precious to Michael. Just as Tower House was being sold, one of the boys went on a school trip to Scilly, and came home thrilled by the islands. Clare too had happy memories of Scilly. In her early teens she had spent a number of weeks with her father on the island of Tresco. But by the time she had persuaded Michael that they should have a holiday there the accommodation on Tresco was all taken. They booked, instead, rooms in a B&B on the much smaller, more rugged, less fashionable island of Bryher. From the moment they arrived, Michael felt he had 'entered another world' – a world he has since revisited every summer.

For an island just two miles long, and less than half a mile wide, Bryher offers an extraordinary variety of atmospheres. On a Sunday morning, sitting in its little church, All Saints, with the sun slanting through the stained-glass windows and the organ playing 'The King of Love My Shepherd Is', one might be in deep rural England. But, outside the church, the sandy paths (Bryher has no real roads) are selvaged with wild crimson gladioli and bright red and yellow mesembryanthemums – plasticky-looking flowers, like the ones used to decorate ladies' swimming caps in the Fifties. Giant green houseleeks sprout from the masonry of Bryher cottages, twisting about in such outlandish shapes that one feels one has stepped into a Maurice Sendak illustration. On Rushy Bay, to the south of the island, the sea laps gently on to a beach of fine, white, icing-sugar sand, and when the sun shines, as it does in Scilly more than in any other part of Britain, one might be in the Caribbean. But in Hell Bay, to the north, the Atlantic seems to rage and boil, crashing relentlessly against dizzying cliffs.

This variety of sights and moods, encompassed in a small, traffic-free space, makes for a child's paradise – and a paradise for anyone inclined to see the world through a child's eyes. For Michael, the sense that he has put a stretch of sea between himself and his 'real' life brings a feeling of release. Sitting with him over scones and jam at the start of his summer holidays, one can feel his mood lightening, and as he putters between the islands in his miniature blue-and-white catamaran, *Léa Eloïse*, it is as if he is becoming a boy again. Walking round the island before supper, he whistles to the seals across the sea. 'Just look at that!' he exclaims, lying on the grass above Hell Bay, eyes fixed on an enormous seagull as it rides the wind above him. 'I mean, how much fun must that be?'

Animals and human beings live in unusual harmony on Bryher. As Michael writes at a table in the garden of Veronica Farm, little

Michael in Scilly.

birds hop up so close to his exercise-book that it seems they are stealing a first glimpse at a new story, and a starling confounds him by imitating precisely the ring tone of his mobile phone. But it is the history of Scilly, as much as the landscape and wildlife, that draws him back year after year. The islands have been continually inhabited since the Bronze Age, and in the little museum on St Mary's it feels as if a great wave has crashed across two floors, leaving behind the flotsam and jetsam of centuries. Roman coins are displayed alongside Victorian 'Karmit' seasick pills. There are stuffed sea birds and treasures from the 400-odd wrecks that lie submerged around the islands, the giant shell of a leatherback turtle, and the Gannex mac bequeathed by Harold Wilson, who had a house on St Mary's, where he is buried. The entire archipelago fits into a stretch of the Atlantic just seven miles by five. 'I have never been anywhere so small,' says Michael, 'where so much has happened.'

The past breeds stories. South of Bryher is the twin-hilled island of Samson, honeycombed with Bronze Age burial chambers. Legend has it that in 1540 Samson was overrun by giant plague-carrying rats, and that in the early years of the nineteenth century all the men of the island were shipwrecked off Wolf Rock, leaving their women and children to starve. What is certain is that, by the middle of the nineteenth century, Samson's well had run dry, and the last few islanders were forced to abandon their granite cottages and move across the water to Tresco.

One wet summer's evening during his first holiday on Bryher, Michael asked a boatman to row him out to Samson, and leave him to explore. Sheltering from the rain in the hearth of one of the ruined cottages he felt he was not alone, that the ghosts of Samson were gathering about him. *Why the Whales Came* began to form itself in his mind. Opening just before the outbreak of the First World War, it is the tale of two Bryher children, Daniel and Gracie, who befriend 'the Birdman', a loner shunned and feared by the other islanders – and based, in part, on Seán Rafferty. Through the Birdman, the children learn about the curse put on the island of Samson during his boyhood, and with his help they overcome it. It is a tale that tackles huge themes – shame and redemption, ignorance and prejudice – but they are enfolded in such a page-turning adventure that a child can absorb them almost without noticing.

Even now, with more than a hundred books to his name, Michael is sometimes seized by anxiety that his gift will desert him, or that his ideas will run dry. There are times when he feels 'becalmed, waiting for another wave, not knowing whether it will ever come'. But on Bryher stories have never ceased to shuttle through his mind, and *Why the Whales Came* has been followed by a string of further 'Scilly' novels including *The Wreck of the Zanzibar* and *The Sleeping Sword*. 'This place imposes stories on you,' he says. 'You just can't get away from them.'

By the time Michael first visited Scilly in April 1982 family holidays with all three of his children were becoming a thing of the past. Sebastian was eighteen, and was about to go to Trinity College Dublin to study English. He had a French girlfriend, Olivia Stahly, whose aunt had once worked as an *au pair* for Kippe, helping to look after Mark and Kay. The two families were devoted to each other, and Michael and Clare were delighted when, despite the distance between Dublin and Paris, their relationship continued to flourish through Sebastian's university years. They were delighted too when, in the spring of 1986, Olivia told them that she was expecting their first grandchild.

Léa Pauline Clare Morpurgo was born in Rouen on 17 December 1986, and the following summer the Morpurgo and Stahly families gathered at her great-grandmother's ancient *manoir* in Salies-de-Béarn for Olivia and Sebastian's wedding. A priest close to the family blessed the couple and infant under a tree in the garden, and friends and family celebrated long into the night beneath a Tricolore and a Union Jack. Michael had brought a barrel of beer from England. He felt deeply contented. He loved the Stahly family, and he loved France.

As a small child, he had been used to hearing French spoken around him at the Eyrie, where Tita had sat him on her knee and sung him French nursery rhymes in her deep voice. His first

Continental holiday had been to Le Tréport in Normandy, and everything about it – the éclairs, the smell of fresh bread and coffee, the long empty beaches, the seaside architecture – had seemed so thrilling to him that France became his ideal of a foreign country.

Some time after the publication of *War Horse* it happened that Canon Shirley's granddaughter went to work for the French publisher Gallimard. She urged one of the children's editors, Christine Baker, to read the novel, and Christine did so – 'with some reluctance and anxiety, as one does when one is "made" to read a text by a friend'. She remembers the relief of realising, very quickly and 'with absolute certainty', that 'this was simply a perfect book'. *Cheval de guerre*, published in 1986, has never since been out of print. Gallimard Jeunesse has published nearly forty more of Michael's titles, of which two – *Le roi Arthur* (*Arthur, High King of Britain*) and *Le secret de grand-père* (*Farm Boy*) – are on the '*Liste de titres prescrits*' published by the Ministry of Education. Michael has been garlanded with French prizes, and is one of just a handful of children's authors to have been appointed Chevalier de l'Ordre des Arts et des Lettres. 'We French would do almost anything not to crown a British author,' says Christine. 'But Michael Morpurgo [which she pronounces *Meek-ay-el Mor-purr-goh*] is so well loved here he is perceived as an honorary Frenchman.'

For some time Michael had wanted to write a novel set in France. Then, during Sebastian's wedding celebrations, he fell into conversation with Olivia's grandmother, Séverine Puech. She talked at length about what it had been like to live in occupied France, and about how, when the Germans arrived, she had at first been dazzled by their impeccable uniforms and manners. She talked, too, about Gurs, a concentration camp near Salies-de-Béarn where Jews and '*indésirables*' had been held under the Vichy government, and she took Michael to visit the clearing in a forest where it had stood.

'There was nothing left of it,' he remembers, 'but it was dark and silent, and the atmosphere was heavy with sadness.'

Back in Devon Michael set to work on *Waiting for Anya*, the story of a dreamy shepherd boy, Jo, living in a village in the Pyrenees in the early Forties. Jo befriends Benjamin, who is engaged in smuggling Jewish children across the border to safety in Spain. For the actress Juliet Stevenson, who has read many of Michael's books aloud to her children, *Waiting for Anya* is 'my quiet favourite'. Even more than usual, she says, 'I feel that Michael was immersed and engaged in that story and that landscape. He brings the history alive.'

The novel is set in Lescun, a mountainside village frequently cut off by snow in the winter. Michael and Clare had spent a few days here after Sebastian's wedding, and on their way to it they had taken a wrong turning and got lost. They found themselves instead in Bource where, on the village green, they met a caged bear, pacing miserably. *The Dancing Bear*, which grew from that encounter, is perhaps the most irredeemably bleak of all Michael's stories. An orphaned girl, Roxanne, adopts an abandoned bear, which she christens Bruno. They form an extraordinary bond, news of which travels beyond the village, attracting the attentions of a film crew. Bruno is made to dance for the crew with a chain around his neck, and when Roxanne is seduced away to seek fame and riches in the city he dies of a broken heart.

Readers, over the years, have written to protest at the sadness of the story. Even Ted Hughes, who saw it in manuscript, suggested that the ending should be lightened. But Michael is unrepentant. In very early childhood, he believes, there should be a period of 'pure delight', when the world seems a bright, safe place, and stories can be relied upon to end happily. It was one of the joys of becoming a grandfather to experience this 'glowing' time with a new generation.

As children become aware that the world around them is more complex and disturbing, however, this should be reflected in what they read. 'One of the first lessons I learned as a teacher,' Michael says, 'is that children like to be talked to truthfully. And the truth is that we live in a slough of despond. You'd have to walk about with your eyes closed not to see all around you the effects of greed and selfishness on people's lives. The trick is to see the joy as well. But to understand joy, you have first to acknowledge suffering. They can't be separated.' Perhaps children have more instinct for the inter-dependence of pain and joy than grown-ups imagine. 'Michael Morpurgo's books have always enchanted me,' writes a London schoolgirl, Laura de Lisle, in her essay 'My Reading History'. 'His soft, sad style is perfect for sitting inside on a rainy afternoon with a cup of tea and a bun. I found *War Horse* and *Private Peaceful* heart-breakingly beautiful.'

Michael's homesick vigils at the Abbey set the pattern for a lifetime of insomnia; but while, as a schoolboy, his anxieties had focused on the next day, in middle age it was the next life that began to concern him. Would the God with whom he had pleaded and bargained so intimately in his teenage diaries be waiting to welcome him when the end came? Or would death open a door on to nothing but dark-ness and void? His questions both fuelled and fed on hypochondria. The slightest illness or physical weakness had him leaping to cata-strophic conclusions.

In fighting these night hauntings, stories became his best weapon. He found that, almost without fail, he could escape in his imagin-ation into whatever he was working on, involving himself with char-acters and situations, allowing them to 'weave' in his mind. Clare sleeps soundly, and in order not to disturb her Michael resists switching on the light or writing anything down. Sometimes, thoughts and images melt away with the dawn, but this 'dream time' is, he believes, an essential prelude to his writing with integrity – 'writing in such a way as to awake a sense of wonder, and truth, and joy'. When it has been squeezed out in the race to meet deadlines (and he is a stickler for these) his books have suffered.

Running a schoolmaster's eye down a list of his titles to date, Michael's verdict on roughly one in four is, 'Nice try. Could have done better.' But in the late Eighties and early Nineties, so gradually that he cannot be precise about the timing, publishers began to take his work more seriously. None would have spoken of him in the same breath as Roald Dahl or Alan Garner or Clive King; nor was he rising to fame like his near-contemporaries Anne Fine or Berlie Doherty. But he was, none the less, proving himself a solid, slow-burn seller. His Public Lending Right returns, creeping up year on year, showed that his books were in demand in public libraries; and he was in demand in schools. Children and teachers who had stayed at Nethercott regularly invited him to speak on prize days, or at the opening of libraries, and were gratified to find that, away from home, he communicated the same energy and charisma and ability to make individual children in a packed room feel that he was talk-ing directly to them. 'Everybody tells me when they've seen him,' says Christine Baker, '"Well, we've *never* had an experience like that!"'

Michael himself began to have a sense that he was 'on the circuit', and to build up relationships that were to be vital to his work. In a corridor at St Ives Primary School, for example, he fell into conver-sation with the illustrator and writer Michael Foreman. They took to each other immediately. 'It was,' says Foreman, 'as if we'd been friends a long time' – or more than friends. 'People say you can't choose your relations, but in Michael Morpurgo I have chosen a brother – a posh brother.' Despite a difference in background – Foreman's widowed mother kept a small shop in the seaside village of Pakefield in Suffolk, and he went on from the local primary to Notley Road Secondary Modern – both had grown up in the Forties, and felt moved to communicate the futility of war to succeeding generations. Both, too, had an almost insatiable appetite for work, and an openness to the other's ideas. 'There's a kind of cookery that goes on between us,' says Foreman. 'It sometimes feels like telepathy.' The first book they produced together was *Arthur, High King of Britain*, a retelling of the Arthurian legends, set in the Scilly Isles and opening memorably with a small boy's attempt to walk from Bryher to Tresco and from Tresco to Samson at low tide. Since then, they have collaborated on a book almost every year.

Professional relationships like this mean more to Michael Morpurgo than to most writers. Had he been brought up by his real father, he is confident that he would have made a professional life for himself on the stage, not the page. As it is, the theatrical genes he has inherited from both the Bridge and the Cammaerts families mean that he is happiest when he is involved with a team, or a cast. As he became gradually better known, his work, too, seemed to invite involvement and interpretation by other artists and art forms. In 1982 the Children's Film Foundation spotted the potential in *Friend or Foe*, Michael's story of two evacuees, David and Tucky, who meet and befriend a pair of German airmen whose plane has crashed on Dartmoor, and made 'a very good little film' for Saturday-morning viewing in cinemas. And, early in 1988, the producer Simon Channing Williams booked up every cottage, B&B and campsite on Bryher, and shipped in a star cast to make a film of *Why the Whales Came*.

It is a spring the older inhabitants of Bryher have never forgotten. For ten unseasonably cold weeks, the island was overrun with caterers, cameramen and make-up artists, not to mention troublesome fibreglass whales that had to be weighted down with rocks before they would swim beneath the surface of the sea. Locals were roped in as extras, or to help with administration. Marian Bennett, in charge of billeting the cast, kept a giant chart – 'like a patchwork quilt' – on which she moved Helen Mirren, Paul Scofield, David Suchet and David Threlfall from holiday cottage to sofa bed. If the resulting film was not such a critical success as Channing Williams's later productions, which were to include *The Constant Gardener* and *Vera Drake*, it provided a boost to the economy of the Scilly Isles, and to Michael's standing with his publishers. Here was an author whose potential lay not only in book sales.

Even Jack Morpurgo was impressed. 'I can but confess,' he writes in characteristically highfalutin fashion in his memoirs, 'that all my oft-boasted capacity for critical dispassion vanished, submerged by pride, even by a sort of personal vanity, when I sat in the audience at the Royal Première of the film-version of [Michael's] book, *Why the Whales Came.*' The première had been held at the Odeon, Leicester Square, with the Prince and Princess of Wales in the audience. As the film ended Kippe turned and smiled at Michael. 'It was a beautiful smile,' he says. 'She didn't care about success, or that this was a grand event. She was just very happy in her son.'

Kippe and Jack were now living in London, in a small house in Hammersmith bought on Jack's retirement. Both were ageing fast. Jack, suffering from glaucoma and cataracts, had all but lost his sight; Kippe spent long spells in hospital with angina, anxiety and depression. She was still drinking. Jack's way of coping with her problems had always been to pretend that they didn't exist, and he was now able, literally, to turn a blind eye on the empty bottles that piled up around the house. He continued to take on writing and editing commissions, to accept invitations to lecture abroad, and to shore up his self-regard by mixing, whenever possible, with the great and the good. 'Our social calendar,' he noted with pathetic pride shortly before his death, 'was brisk with names of men and women who were prime prey for zealous autograph-collectors. We knew socially Cabinet Ministers, an Archbishop, a couple of Bishops, a Judge, Ambassadors from many countries and one of our own, Generals, an Admiral, an Air Chief Marshal, several Peers of the Realm, some tycoons, a score of leading novelists, several eminent poets (including three successive Poets Laureate), a "procession" of learned Professors, and a galaxy of bright lights from the world of entertainment.'

Kippe, inwardly, shrank from social engagement. Even staying at Langlands, she chose to spend long spells in her room alone. But she remained steadfast in her loyalty to Jack. When, in the spring of 1993, he was invited to lecture in Washington, she insisted on going with him.

The day that they were due to leave, a small theatre company put on a production of *Jo-Jo the Melon Donkey*, Michael's tale of an ill-used Venetian donkey, in the foyer of the National Theatre. Jack and Kippe came to watch it, and afterwards had lunch with Michael before catching a taxi to the airport. It was to be the last time he saw his mother. A few evenings into their Washington visit, Kippe excused herself early from dinner. She went upstairs, laid Jack's pyjamas on his pillow, set out his shaving brush and razor in the bathroom, and climbed into her bed where, in the morning, Jack found her lying dead.

*   *   *

On hearing the news of his mother's death, Michael walked into Iddesleigh and sat alone for some hours in the village church. He felt 'exposed'. 'No matter how old you are,' he says, 'if you lose a parent, you feel like an orphan.' He also felt overcome with fresh grief at the needless wreckage of his parents' marriage fifty years earlier. 'Both of them would have had more fulfilled lives if they'd stayed together,' he says. 'I'm sure of that.' Three thousand miles away in Ontario, Tony Bridge received the news from Pieter. For years, he admitted in a letter to Michael, he had persuaded himself that '"all that" was behind us and forgotten'. Yet he was devastated to think he would never see Kippe again.

Since Tony's first meeting with Michael just after Sebastian's birth, they had stayed in touch, exchanging occasional letters, speaking sometimes on the telephone. Tony was endearingly vague about both geography and time zones. If there was a natural disaster anywhere in Britain – a blizzard in Inverness, a flood in Kent – he would ring, often in the middle of the night, to check that Michael was safe. Three or four times, he came to stay in Devon, and he got on well with Clare and the children, with Seán Rafferty, and with Ted and Carol Hughes. For Michael, however, his visits were complicated. Anyone could see that Tony was his father, but because he had been absent during Michael's formative years, and because he was a man who naturally kept his own counsel, it was hard to know quite how to pitch their relationship. 'I wanted to be close to him,' says Michael, 'but I wasn't.'

Kippe's death gave Tony an excuse to express for the first time not only his pride in his sons' achievements but also his belief that Jack Morpurgo had perhaps given them as fine an upbringing as he could have done himself. 'There is no proof that I would have been good for you,' he writes, 'and it has to be said that in the matter of the lives that you and Pieter have built around you, I could have done absolutely nothing that would have bettered that. So I suppose we grow up the way we are meant to. Fate? I don't know about Fate, but something in us makes us do what we do, regardless of what and who surround us.'

Kippe's was the first major death that Michael had had to face, and it was followed, within months, by a second. Soon after dawn on 4 December 1993 he was woken by a hammering on the door of Langlands. David Ward had found Seán Rafferty lying dead, face down, in Burrow Lane. Together, he and Michael hurried in the tractor to where Seán lay, outside his hen-house, his coat stiff with frost. 'There was a stillness about him,' Michael remembers. As he waited by Seán's body for the doctor to arrive, he wept. Peggy Rafferty had died five years earlier and, as a widower, Seán had become even more closely folded into Morpurgo family life, coming to Langlands always for Sunday lunch, and for Christmas and Easter. Yet even at his most convivial and open-hearted he remained, essentially, solitary. 'We were honoured,' Michael says, 'to have been allowed to interrupt that solitude.'

Ted Hughes, too, was deeply moved by Seán Rafferty's death. For years, Hughes wrote in a letter to Christopher Reid at Faber & Faber, Seán had appeared to be dragging out a 'frustrating seemingly wasted life', under the thumb of his 'powerful little wife', exhausted by the pub, toiling privately at poems that did not quite hit the mark. But, around his eightieth birthday, it seemed to Hughes that he had discovered 'a sudden really wonderful musical inspiration, what he'd been looking for all his life', and had begun to pour out work of rare quality. Carcanet had agreed to publish Seán Rafferty's *Collected Poems*, and three days before his death, when Ted Hughes called on him with the Israeli poet Yehuda Amichai, the kitchen table at Burrow Cottage was buried in typescripts. Perhaps, Hughes reflected, it was a blessing that Seán had not lived to see his work launched upon the world: 'Exit before one critical squeak can be raised against him. There he fell, dart-free, not an arrow. (And lay in the lane all night.) Sweetest fellow.'

Seán's absence, and a shared sense of loss, brought Michael and Ted Hughes even closer together. After dinner at Court Green, while Clare and Carol chatted together in the kitchen, they would sit and talk long into the night in front of the fire. Their conversation was not generally either profound or professional, but one evening it suddenly took a serious turn. 'It had been an evening of great cheer,' Michael remembers. 'None of us wanted it to end. We got talking of writing for children, how little it is valued, the whole issue of its status. It was a hobby horse we'd been on before, but that evening we began to gallop.' Michael had had an idea batting about in his head for some time, 'and in my cups I dared mention it to Ted. I said, "You know, there should be a Children's Laureate." And Ted said, "You're right, Michael. Let's make it happen."'

Fetching pen and paper, Hughes made a list of people whose help they would need to get the idea off the ground. He then swung into action. 'He masterminded a strategy,' says Michael. 'He canvassed support. He wrote letters no one else could write. He drove it on.' Together, Ted and Michael went to see Princess Anne, who gave the idea her formal endorsement. Lois Beeson, who had run the W. H. Smith Young Writers' Competition for seven years, was enlisted to manage the administration; and Ted arranged for Michael to see Tim Waterstone to ask whether Waterstone's might come on board as sponsors. Waterstone was impressed. 'He was such a courteous man, and very likeable,' he remembers. 'Totally admirable. Very comfortable in his own skin. Modest in manner, but with a most considerable drive.' There are always, Waterstone points out, hundreds of 'good' ideas floating around the book world at any one time. 'But the ones that get through are the ones whose champions are unrelentingly determined, first to get them to the starting block, and then to push them into proper life. Michael did all of that, and in spades.' Finally, Ted and Michael arranged to meet Chris Smith, newly appointed Secretary of State for Culture, Media and Sport, to secure ministerial support. But when Michael turned up at his offices on 28 May 1998, he was alone.

The previous spring Ted Hughes had sent Michael and Clare a letter, in which he had explained, 'with mighty reluctance', that he had been 'foolish enough to get ill'. 'I hate it being known,' Hughes writes. 'Instinct, I suppose. In the animal kingdom the injured one is abandoned or destroyed by its clan – and certainly marked down by the malicious predator. People forget that. I now feel like avoiding everybody who knows I've been ill – till I'm absolutely better.' He looked forward to celebrating over a 'jolly banquet' when he was fully recovered.

There was no recovery. Hughes had cancer of the colon, and in the autumn of 1998 he was admitted to London Bridge Hospital. On 29 October, driving home through the rain from Exeter station, Michael and Clare heard on the car radio that he had died. They made their way straight to North Tawton to be with Carol. It was a sobering moment. Ted Hughes was a greater man than any other Michael has known. 'He was a *mighty* person; an immensely kind, gifted human being, whose generosity when it came to the welfare of others knew no bounds.'

The following spring a service of thanksgiving for the life and work of Ted Hughes was held at Westminster Abbey. The Tallis Scholars sang the Miserere; Alfred Brendel played a Beethoven adagio; Seamus Heaney read Hughes's poem 'Anniversary'; the congregation sang 'Jerusalem'. Then Hughes's own gentle, granite voice filled the abbey, speaking lines from *Cymbeline*:

Fear no more the heat o' the sun,
Nor the furious winter's rages;
Thou thy worldly task hast done,
Home art gone, and ta'en thy wage:
Golden lads and girls all must,
As chimney-sweepers, come to dust.

For everyone in the abbey there was a sense that Hughes was still in their midst; and it was perhaps not altogether illusory. For Michael, he remains present to this day: 'He continues to enrich all that we do. We can't walk down the lane, or to the river, without thinking of him. His footsteps are everywhere.'

There comes a stage in our lives when we have to face the death of someone we love. It is always bewildering to me. I think a little piece of me dies each time. But I have the memories. Seán's death and Ted's were huge moments for me, but maybe I'd been prepared for them, in a way, by losing my mother. It's sometimes hard, even now, to accept that Kippe has gone. I think of her still every day, and of my childhood. This story is set in Bradwell, the home I loved best.

A Bit of a Daredevil

The problem with being thought of as a bit of a daredevil, a bit of
a Jack the Lad, was that I was continually having to live up to my
reputation. That, I discovered, can land you in all sorts of trouble.

We lived in a draughty rambling old house by the coast, full of
ghosts and spiders. Sometimes when the wind blew in off the sea
we could hear the whole house complaining, groaning and
creaking and sighing around us. On nights like this I knew for
certain that the ghosts had been woken up and were not at all
happy. I could hear their footsteps on the stairs, and their
whispering outside our bedroom door.

I slept with my older brother, Anthony, up at the top of the
house in the attic. Ant, I liked to call him, because even though he
was older than me, he was smaller. I could be a bit mean that way.
We felt very far away from the rest of the family, particularly on
windy nights when the ghosts were up and about. To keep my
courage up I'd often crawl into Ant's bed, where we'd tell each other
funny stories. I was always much more frightened than he was –
although I never told him that – so I did most of the talking, most
of the storytelling, anything to keep my mind off the whispering
ghosts outside the bedroom door. But sometimes even that didn't

work. And when I found I couldn't stand it any longer, I'd invent some excuse to switch on the light. I usually told him I wanted to read. I did a lot of pretending in those days, a lot of bluffing.

Anyway, one night I'd just switched the light on, and I was lying there beside him, book in hand, pretending to read, trying hard not to be frightened. I was listening out for ghosts when Ant said: 'Nothing out there, you know, Mikey. It's only the wind rattling the windows, only the floorboards creaking. And anyway, if there were ghosts, the light wouldn't keep them away.'

'Huh,' I said, 'I'm not frightened of ghosts. I can't sleep. Just wanted to read, that's all.'

'All right, so you're not frightened of ghosts. But maybe you're a bit frightened of the dark then,' he went on. 'Don't be, there's no need, honestly. I'll look after you.' He was like that, my brother, always kind – so kind sometimes, it drove me mad.

'I'm not frightened of the dark,' I said. 'I'm not frightened of anything. It was me who climbed that tree yesterday. Right to the very top. You didn't dare, did you? Scared of heights. I mean if I dared you, right now, to climb out of that window, sit on the ledge, and count to a hundred, I bet you wouldn't do it, would you?'

'I might,' he replied.

'Go on then,' I said. 'I dare you.'

'All right, I'll do it,' he said, getting out of bed, 'but on one condition. Afterwards, I can dare you back. And whatever I dare you, Mikey, you've got to do it. Deal?' He didn't seem at all nervous, and that worried me. But I couldn't back out now.

'Promise,' I said.

He didn't hesitate. He climbed up on to the window sill, opened the window, squeezed himself out, sat there on the ledge, folded his arms, and started counting. He was soon back in bed with me. 'Cold,' he said, snuggling down under the blankets. 'But anyway, while I was out there, I thought of a dare for you. Here's what you've got to do – and without turning any lights on, mind. Go downstairs to the larder, and get us a peppermint humbug each – y'know, from the sweet tin on the top shelf.'

'That's stealing,' I said.

'So?' my brother replied. 'We're always stealing stuff from the larder, what's the problem?' He knew my problem of course. The problem was that everywhere in the house it would be dark and full of ghosts. For me, that was just as terrifying as having to walk through a pit of snakes, or swim across a river full of crocodiles. But then I thought to myself, it's all right, you can turn on the lights, no one will see, you'll be fine.

'Easy peasy,' I said.

But, as if he'd read my mind, Ant immediately scotched my plan. 'You've got to promise, Mikey. No lights. You mustn't turn on any lights. Cross your heart and hope to die.'

I had no choice. I promised, crossed my heart. I had to. There was no way now that I could cheat – not that I was honourable, or anything like it, just deeply superstitious.

So there I was a few moment later, scared stiff, standing at the bottom of the attic staircase in pitch darkness. I tiptoed past my mother's room, felt my way down the winding stairs into the sitting room, past the armchairs towards the kitchen door. And all the while the ghosts were right there watching me – creaking, groaning, rattling. I was sure they were after me. It was all I could do to stop myself screaming. As I reached for the latch on the larder door I couldn't stand the darkness any longer. By now I didn't care about my promise to Ant. I didn't care about all that crossing my heart and dying. I reached for the light switch inside the door, and turned it on, my heart thumping in my ears. No ghosts. But there was something. And it was infinitely more terrible and terrifying than any ghost.

Dangling there, just above my head was a rabbit or a hare, dead. It was hanging by its feet from a hook, blood dripping from its nose, bulging eyes staring down at me. I couldn't move, I could only scream. The whole house came running. Within moments, it seemed, Ant was there, and then Mum and Dad. Prynne, our black-coated retriever, was barking from the laundry room where he slept. Dad was firing questions at me.

'What on earth are you doing down here in the middle of the night? Why aren't you in bed? Were you after the sweet tin again?'

Ant said nothing. I said nothing. That was one thing we were good at, not ratting on one another. I made up a story. I said I'd come down to get a drink of milk and that's why I'd gone into the larder. Mum had her arm around me, wiping away my tears.

'You poor boy, it must have been a terrible shock,' she said.

'Lot of fuss about nothing,' Dad said. 'It's only a hare for goodness sake. A bunch of sissies, you are.'

Mum explained all about the hare as she took us back up to bed. 'Mr Warren brought it in for us,' she said. 'You know, the farmer out by the sea wall, big fat chap with mutton-chop whiskers and a voice like a foghorn, the one you hear louder than anyone else in church. He shot it. It was a sort of present for your dad. He told us we've got to hang it for a day or two more before we cook it. And his wife has given me a recipe – jugged hare, she calls it. Dad says he'll skin it tomorrow, and then we can have it for Sunday lunch.'

'I'm not eating that,' I told her. 'It's disgusting.'

'Nor me,' said Ant.

'I'll make it delicious, don't you worry,' she said. 'You'll love it.'

* * *

Back in our beds, Ant and I couldn't sleep, but now it wasn't the wind or the ghosts that were keeping us awake – all that had been forgotten about. It was the hare. We couldn't stop thinking about him and talking about him, and the more we talked, the more we convinced ourselves that a murder had been committed. That hare had been a wild and beautiful creature and shot to death for no good reason. We were quite sure of one thing: that neither of us could ever bring ourselves to eat him.

It was Ant's brilliant idea. 'Why don't we cut him down?' he said. 'We can bury him in the orchard, put a cross over his grave. Let's do it now, while it's still dark, while everyone's asleep.'

So we stole down the stairs to the larder, avoiding all the creaking floorboards. Ant switched on the light. I didn't want to look, but somehow I couldn't stop myself. It made me sick to my stomach.

'I'll get him down,' Ant whispered. He did everything. I just stood there and watched, full of revulsion, as he got a chair and a knife from the kitchen, climbed up and cut the hare down.

'Here, Mikey, you take him,' he said, holding him out to me. I shook my head and backed away. 'He's dead,' Ant said. 'He can't hurt you. Take him for a minute, while I get down.'

So I held the dead hare in my arms, trying not to feel his deadness, the cold damp of his fur, the stiffness of him. The only way I could do it was to imagine what he'd been like when he was alive. I'd seen a hare only once, watched him out on a ploughed field near the sea wall. At first I'd thought he was a rabbit, but he was too brown, his ears were too long. When I clapped my hands, he ran off. He seemed to be flying over the ground, his feet barely touching it. I was breathless with admiration at his power and his speed and his grace.

*   *   *

It was this memory that made me want to go on holding him as we walked out through the laundry room to the back door. Prynne insisted on coming with us. He'd have barked his head off if we'd left him behind, and we didn't want that. He kept jumping up at me, and sniffing at the hare. As I walked out into the orchard that night, it occurred to me that this might be the very same hare I had seen that day by the sea wall. Ant was digging the hole, and I could feel the blood sticky on my fingers. It was heartbreak I was feeling now, not revulsion any more. When the time came I couldn't bring myself to lay him down. Ant did it for me. We covered him with the cold damp earth, folded the turf over, and pressed it down. I found a small twig on the ground that did for a cross. We stood for a moment over the place, and then left him there. Ant took my hand and we crept back to the house. Neither of us spoke a word to one another till we were back in bed, but all the while something was worrying me.

'What are we going to say, Ant, when they find out?'

'I've thought of that,' he replied. 'We'll blame it on Prynne. He jumped up and pulled him down. He's always thieving stuff out of the larder, isn't he? Remember that pork pie he ate?'

It was true. Prynne was a thief with a long criminal record. It was a good idea.

As it turned out we didn't need to say anything. When we came downstairs for breakfast the next morning we could hear Dad blowing his top about Prynne.

'No good as a gun dog, no good as a guard dog. He's just a lousy thief. I was looking forward to that jugged hare too. Ruddy dog.'

When we came into the kitchen Prynne was cowering in his basket, blinking with guilt and contrition at Dad's every word.

Mum, I noticed, was saying nothing, which was odd, because she was always getting furious with Prynne, for running off, for stealing, for making a mess. Ant asked innocently what was up, and Dad ranted on again about Prynne, while Mum just busied herself about the kitchen. Then suddenly Dad rounded on us.

'That dog didn't open the door by himself, did he? Which of you left the kitchen door open?' he demanded. 'One of you did.'

Mum spoke up for the first time. 'Don't blame them,' she said, 'it was probably me. Maybe I didn't latch it properly last night. It's easily done. It doesn't matter that much.'

'Doesn't matter?' Dad raged. But then he seemed lost for words. He stormed out, leaving the three of us alone. For a while Mum said nothing more. She brought us our porridge in silence, poured out our milk in silence. Then she sat down opposite us and sipped her tea, looking at us over the top of her cup.

'That Prynne,' she said, 'he's a mighty clever dog. Do you know what he must have done? The hare was still hanging in the larder when I went up to bed last night. I know he was. I saw him there. And I didn't leave the door open. Do you know, that dog must have opened the laundry-room door, then the larder door, jumped up, cut the string – I've had a good look and it was definitely cut. Then he must have carried the hare out of the house, unlocking the back door and opening it as he went. Now that is a clever dog, a very, very clever dog. Something wrong with your porridge this morning, boys? You're not eating.'

I didn't dare speak.

'We didn't want to eat it, Mum,' Ant said.

'I know, neither did I really,' she said, smiling at us. 'But don't tell your father. We'd just better hope he doesn't find out, eh?'

*   *   *

It must have been a week or so later. We were all of us out in the garden making a bonfire of branches and twigs from a tree that had come down in a storm, when Prynne came trotting across the lawn, tail high and wagging and proud, and dragging something heavy. It was the carcass of the hare – or what was left of it anyway. Dad hurled abuse at him, and a stick or two as well. Prynne dropped his prize and ran off, tail between his legs.

The hare ended up on the bonfire on the Fifth of November, which in a way wasn't so bad because, as Ant said in bed that night, at least he had a proper funeral – a funeral fit for a hero. We found two of the hare's teeth in the ashes later and kept them in the Cadbury's tin under Ant's bed with all our other secret treasures: a grass snake skin, a blackbird's skull and our most prized possession, a bright blue kingfisher's feather we'd found among the bullrushes out on the marshes. And that was the end of it. Mum kept our secret and Prynne did too of course. All was well that ended well – we thought.

But then one Sunday afternoon a few weeks later I saw Mr Warren's car pull up at our gate. With his loud booming voice, we heard very clearly what he was saying to Mum: 'Met your husband in the pub, and he told me what happened to that hare I gave him. Bally thief dog. Needs a good hiding. Anyway, got to put that right, I thought. Can't shoot the dog, more's the pity, but I can bring in another hare for you. Shot it a couple of days ago. Just hang it for a week till he's good and smelly. Jugged hare. Your husband says it's his favourite. Can't stand it myself, I just like shooting the beggars. Got it in the car. Shall I fetch it?'

There was a moment when Mum could have refused, but Dad came out of the house, and it was too late. For a week the poor creature hung in our larder. Neither Ant nor I went near the sweet tin.

Mum cooked him the next Sunday. A sickly smell wafted through the house all morning. Ant and I knew there was no way we could eat him. Strangely, we both caught the same sudden stomach bug, and lay on our beds, clutching our bellies and groaning in agony, until even Dad was convinced we were really ill. Mum made us have Milk of Magnesia, which was horrible, but not as horrible as jugged hare.

That afternoon, after their lunch was over, we told them we felt much better, that we wanted to go for a walk. We were tramping together along the sea wall. The late afternoon sun was shining through the clouds and lit up the ploughed field by the old Saxon chapel. And there, right beside it, we spotted two hares playing with one another, running around in crazy circles, up on their hind legs, boxing. We stood and watched. It was the finest sight I ever saw.

6

Better Answer – Might be Spielberg

'Sometimes, if you're lucky, you get lucky,' Michael writes in the *Mail on Sunday* in the spring of 2011. 'And I got lucky.' He is looking back on a decade that has brought him such a cornucopia of good fortune that he still sometimes wonders whether it is all quite real. And his sense of amazement is compounded when he remembers the first two years of the new millennium, when disaster struck and it seemed for a time that a great part of his life's work was about to unravel.

In February 2001 Michael and Clare went to spend half-term in a hotel in St Ives. Farms for City Children had just celebrated its silver jubilee. It was now welcoming parties of schoolchildren not only to Nethercott but also to Lower Treginnis on the Pembrokeshire coast, and to Wick Court, a moated manor-house in a bend of the river Severn in Gloucestershire, and both Michael and Clare had been appointed MBE for services to young people. There was much to be proud of, and they felt they deserved a treat. But, listening to the news in their hotel room, they heard something deeply unsettling: foot-and-mouth had been detected in pigs in an abattoir in Essex. Nobody in the farming community had ever forgotten how quickly the disease had spread when it struck in 1967, and how it had ravaged livestock all over the country. They packed their bags and drove straight home.

Within days, the countryside was shutting down. The outbreak of the disease had been traced to a farm in Northumberland where pigs

Michael and Clare after being invested as MBE,
12 November 1999.

had been fed 'untreated waste', and the European Union announced
a ban on all British exports of livestock, meat and animal products.
In late February, foot-and-mouth was found in animals on a farm
in Highampton, just six miles from Nethercott. By March there were
240 cases, and teams of soldiers, under Brigadier Alex Birtwistle, had
been called in to slaughter infected livestock.

In the lanes around Nethercott, dead sheep and cows lay piled up in the gateways of infected farms, and the smell of death was inescapable. The carcasses were incinerated on towering pyres, and the flames fed with car and tractor tyres to increase the heat. Black, foul-smelling smoke drifted across the valleys. 'If I could paint a picture of paradise,' Michael has sometimes said, 'it wouldn't be far off the countryside round Iddesleigh.' But now the place was turning into a vision of hell. In order to stop infection spreading, movement between farms was severely curtailed. 'Hatherleigh,' says Michael, 'became like a plague village.'

The moment the crisis broke, schools planning visits to Nethercott, Lower Treginnis and Wick Court cancelled their bookings. And when word reached sponsors and grant-making trusts that children were no longer visiting the farms they all took the line that this was a disaster the charity could never survive, and withdrew financial support. With Neil Warrington, now chairman of the board of Farms for City Children, Clare undertook the mournful task of visiting the three farms and laying off the staff. The charity had enough money to keep going until August; then it would be bankrupt. As spring turned into summer, with new cases of foot-and-mouth continuing to break out daily, Michael felt paralysed by a mixture of dread and irrational guilt.

Early that year he had received a letter from Marion Lloyd, an editor at Macmillan, inviting him to write a horror story. He was toying, in response, with a novel about vampires, and it was not going well. As a child, fantasy had never appealed to him – 'I never really felt at ease in other worlds, like Narnia' – and, as a writer, it has continued to leave him cold. 'I can do ghosts,' he says, 'though even then I have to have a historical reality from which to grow them, but pure fantasy I cannot manage.' Now, he realised, there was no need for fantasy. A real horror story was unfolding around him. In a fortnight, during May, he wrote the imaginary diary of a teenage girl, Becky Morley, growing up on a farm infected by foot-and-mouth. Becky's father owns a prize herd of Gloucester cows. When they are slaughtered he begins to lose his grip, and is eventually hospitalised with depression. 'And depression,' Becky's mother explains to her, 'isn't just sadness. It's an illness that makes you feel very bad about yourself, that makes you feel completely useless and lost, as if you're living at the bottom of a deep dark pit of hopelessness that you can see no way out of.'

Michael's description of Morley's depression came partly from personal experience. His impotence in the face of the crisis had driven him into a state of frozen despair from which, without Clare's calm and buoyancy, he feels it might have been hard to emerge. But his writing sprang also from his observation of anguish in the farmers living around him, in particular Graham and David Ward. 'I saw in them both,' he says, 'this enormous gathering of grief. There was no laughter, no smiling.' Michael had learned, over the years, that a farmer's greatest satisfaction comes from seeing his animals flourish. Instead, Graham and David were now going out every day looking for the tell-tale signs of disease: limping, listlessness, lesions on tongues and hooves. 'I felt they were barely coping with the trauma,' Michael says, and he was right. 'I'm not a religious man,' says David Ward. 'But I was praying then.'

Armed with the handwritten manuscript of Becky Morley's diary, Michael travelled up to Macmillan's offices in London, and invited Marion Lloyd and six of her staff to gather around the board table, as around a campfire, while he read it aloud. He is always happiest if he can present new work in this way. He began as a classroom storyteller, and he has remained much more confident about the spoken than the written word. His rough copy, editors agree, can be very rough indeed; 'but if I can *tell* people a story, I can usually convince them that it works'. The Macmillan team was convinced. Rushed through production in record time, and with a photograph of Léa Morpurgo on the cover, *Out of the Ashes* was published in July, and within weeks had sold 25,000 copies.

In early August, just in time to avert the closure of Farms for City Children, a Canadian trust stepped in with a grant sufficient to keep the charity going until Christmas; but foot-and-mouth continued to spread, and for the first time in years Michael found himself at a loose end. In the early afternoon of 11 September, when normally he would have been out working with children in the fields, he was lying on his bed half-watching the television when he witnessed something that at first seemed scarcely possible. An aeroplane rocketed into one of the twin towers of the World Trade Center in New York; the tower burst into flames. 'I thought it was some Hollywood movie. Then I read the news bar, and saw the second plane coming in, and I shouted downstairs to Clare to come and join me.' They watched together as events unfolded. Outside their bedroom window, black smoke was still drifting across the Okement Valley.

It was October before foot-and-mouth was brought under control and schools returned to Nethercott. Graham and David Ward were surprised how glad they felt to have the children back. 'We'd missed them,' says David. But in Michael and Clare the strain of the crisis had hardened feelings that had been nagging at them for some years. The time had come for a parting of the ways with Farms for City Children.

The reasons for this were both practical and personal. Michael and Clare had long been aware of the danger that, if they stayed too long at the heart of the charity, it might collapse when they were gone. Roughly seventy per cent of charities do not survive their founders, and they had before them the cautionary example of Sir Allen Lane, whose refusal to loosen his grip on Penguin had resulted in bitter wranglings after his death ('Penguin Now a Sitting Duck' was the *Daily Telegraph*'s headline as the big publishing conglomerates descended on the firm like a pack of wolves).

Physically, Michael was beginning to feel he was no longer up to the job. Farmers like Graham and David Ward who have grown up working long, heavy days, he says, can continue into late middle age 'heaving hay bales around in a way that looks so easy and natural it's almost balletic'. But Michael was struggling, and so, in a different way, was Clare. She had raised £1 million to get Lower Treginnis up and running and, hot on the heels of this, a further £2 million for Wick Court. Her appetite for badgering and cajoling trusts and individuals into opening their wallets for Farms for City Children was exhausted – 'the sparkle just wasn't there any more'. Both she and Michael had also become exasperated by intrusive health-and-safety legislation, whose tentacles now seemed to reach into almost every aspect of their work on the farm. At milking time, for example, children were no longer allowed to gather around the cows, but had to watch them from above, standing on a specially (and expensively) constructed gallery. 'In twenty-five years,' Michael fumes, 'no harm had come to a single child who came with us. So all this was hard to stomach.'

Underlying these concerns, and more pressing than any of them, were Michael's increasingly frequent absences from home, and the tension they were creating in the marriage. His books, which for years had been a kind of hinterland, were beginning to take up the foreground, and invitations to speak had him 'regularly flying the nest'. When he came back from his travels to schools or festivals, he and Clare found it difficult to readjust to one another. 'We didn't often argue,' Clare says, 'but there was a lot of silence; a sense of imbalance.' Clare, who was working a fourteen-hour day running Nethercott, Lower Treginnis and Wick Court, felt unable to tune in to Michael's excitement when he arrived home 'high as a kite'. But for Michael the thrill of holding audiences captive with stories was addictive. It was not something he could bear to relinquish.

One editor who worked with Michael on a number of books at this time sensed that, after years of relative obscurity, he was now becoming 'hungry for success'. But Michael considers 'hungry' the wrong word. For a quarter of a century, he had been sending his books out like messages in bottles, hoping they would wash up on friendly and receptive shores. Finally, this was beginning to happen. Children, who had previously looked quite blank when he visited their schools, were starting to tell him they had read his books and loved them. The knowledge that he was forming invisible bonds of connection through words and stories satisfied a deep need in him. 'We read to know we are not alone,' C. S. Lewis believed. Michael Morpurgo is slightly different. He *writes* to know he is not alone.

Michael never experienced what he calls 'a Harry Potter moment', but from the mid-Nineties onwards his books began to attract attention. *The Dancing Bear*, despite its sadness and bleak ending, sold well. 'People talked about it as a "bestseller",' Michael says. 'It was not – but it was the first time that word had been used in connection with my work.' The year after its publication, in 1995, *The Wreck of the Zanzibar* won the Whitbread Children's Book Award. The year after that, *The Butterfly Lion* scooped the Smarties Prize. Things were, as Michael puts it, 'gearing up'.

He was now on a virtuous circle: success bred confidence, and confidence enabled him to write with new ease and depth. Shortly after winning the Whitbread, Michael had chanced on a newspaper article about a Japanese soldier, Private Yokoi, who had chosen to remain hidden on a Pacific island, Guam, at the end of the Second

World War. At about the same time he read the article, a child sent him a letter begging him to write a story about a boy stranded on an island. Then, at a local party, he fell into conversation with a couple who had sailed round the world with their son and dog. The three things began to weave together in his mind. Larking about with a dog on deck, Michael imagined, a boy might fall overboard, and be washed up on the island where the Japanese soldier had created a private kingdom. 'Anyone got a good name for a dog?' he asked the children at Nethercott. 'Ours is called Stella Artois,' one boy volunteered. He now had everything he needed to set to work on *Kensuke's Kingdom*.

Many of Michael's books explore fruitful relationships between children and old people – a reflection, perhaps, of the fact that he himself has found it easier being a grandfather than a father. But the relationship that develops in *Kensuke's Kingdom* is more subtle and hard won than most. After the death of his wife and children at Nagasaki, Kensuke – proud, meticulous and fiercely independent – has learned to manage his grief by hiding on his island and shutting out the rest of the world. When a homesick, shipwrecked child, Michael, arrives to disturb his sanctuary, it takes him a long time to recognise that this is a blessing.

As she turned the last page of *Kensuke's Kingdom*, Carol Hughes found herself 'oddly overwhelmed, and yet with a strange feeling of peace'. 'It seems,' she wrote to Michael from Court Green, 'you have touched something, or tapped into something quite different within yourself ... it reads almost like some internal, yet necessary journey *you* have had to travel, confronting early crises, finding oneself in a situation requiring all one's inner and unknown reserves – and the "coming through" almost a spiritual journey, a "healing".'

The public, too, recognised this as Michael's greatest achievement yet. *Kensuke's Kingdom* flew off bookshop shelves. To date, it has sold close to a million copies in the United Kingdom alone – more than any of Michael's other titles. 'For the first time,' Michael remembers, 'people I met began to say, "Aren't you the man who wrote *Kensuke's Kingdom*?"' And at Farms for City Children, Wendy Cooling, one of the directors, spoke firmly to the rest of the board: 'We can't expect Michael to go on doing what he's been doing for us now. Not after *Kensuke's Kingdom*.'

Gradually, from then on, Michael began to delegate some of his work at Nethercott; and in the brown-carpeted offices of Faber & Faber in Bloomsbury – an unlikely hunting-ground – he discovered the ideal person to take over from Clare. Jane Feaver had been at Faber for more than ten years and had worked with Michael on an anthology of children's poetry, *Because a Fire was in My Head*. When she mentioned, one day, that she longed to move out of London with her small daughter, Michael invited her to Langlands for a weekend. 'It was deep summer,' she remembers, 'and there was this amazing, idyllic village shimmering in a heat haze.' In the autumn of 2001, as the foot-and-mouth crisis came to an end, she moved into Paradise Cottage, on the lane between Langlands and Parsonage Farm. She lives there still. 'She is a companion and confidante,' Michael says, 'who has helped to keep us young. A great grist to our mill.'

A few months after its British publication, *Kensuke's Kingdom* was published in Canada, and Michael went to help launch it in Toronto. From there he caught a night ferry across Lake Ontario. He was almost the only passenger on board as the ferry ploughed through the dark water, and when it arrived at Niagara-on-the-Lake at midnight his father was on the quayside to meet him. They had hardly ever spent time alone with each other, but now they had three days together – 'and they were quiet, gentle, good days'. They break-fasted in a diner; they pottered about the town, Tony Bridge pedal-ling a giant tricycle like Mr McHenry in *The Magic Roundabout*. Tony was acting in the evenings in Conan Doyle's *A Story of Waterloo*, and Michael saw how, like himself, his father was two people: a passionate, energetic man who strode and bellowed about the stage; a shy, sometimes painfully reticent man in private life. After one performance Tony threw a party so that Michael might meet the rest of the company at the Shaw Festival Theatre. The theatre had become his home, Michael saw, and his fellow actors his surrogate family.

There was unspoken sadness on both sides when the visit came to an end. Michael suspected he might never see his father again, and indeed, when next they met, Tony's health was declining rapidly. He died on 20 December 2004, leaving instructions that, while half his ashes were to be scattered on a beach in Bermuda where he had walked with his second wife, half should be reunited with his 'Kate'. Four years earlier, after a bleak final illness in Charing Cross Hospital, Jack Morpurgo had also died, and his ashes had been laid to rest with Kippe's. Feeling it unsuitable that all three should share the same spot, Michael planted an apple tree on the other side of the lawn, and prepared to scatter Tony's ashes there. But Sebastian's six-year-old daughter Alice protested that Tony would be lonely all by himself, and so, at the last moment, he joined Kippe and Jack beneath the hornbeam.

Kensuke's Kingdom was not long published when Michael received a letter with a Belgian postmark. It came from Piet Chielens, who had recently opened a museum of the First World War in the Cloth Hall in Ypres – a building left in ruins in 1918, but now perfectly restored.

Chielens was organising a conference on 'War and Peace in Youth Literature', and wanted Michael to speak.

Ypres is a city still haunted by the misery and slaughter it witnessed nearly a century ago. In hotel lobbies, where normally guests might expect to see flower arrangements or pieces of modern art, there are instead displays of helmets, buckles and bullets, encrusted with Flanders mud. Every spring, farmers ploughing their fields turn up more of this grim paraphernalia, and with it tons of unexploded shells, and human bones. A quarter of a million men died at Ypres; about 44,000 are still waiting to be unearthed and given a proper burial. 'They enter into your consciousness,' says Chielens.

Striking out from the city, Michael made a pilgrimage to De Kippe, the hamlet after which his mother had been named. He visited the field where, on Christmas Eve 1914, British and German troops laid down their weapons, ventured out of their trenches, and played football in No Man's Land. Returning to Ypres at dusk, he stood beneath the Menin Gate, on which are engraved the names of 54,896 men whose bodies have never been found, and stood to attention as the city buglers saluted them with the Last Post. There was enough of the soldier in Michael to make this not only moving, but profoundly thought-provoking.

Once Michael was back at home in Devon one small exhibit in Piet Chielens's museum began to gnaw at his imagination. It was a letter from a British army officer to a mother in the Midlands informing her that her son had been court-martialled, and was to be shot at dawn. Nearly 300 soldiers had been executed in this way, Michael learned, most for desertion or 'cowardice', two simply because they had fallen asleep at their posts. Many were known to be suffering from shell-shock, and a disproportionate number were Irish or black. As he began to study the records of their peremptory trials, it became clear that very often executions had taken place ahead of major attacks – *pour encourager les autres*. 'There was an agenda here,' Michael says. Yet, despite repeated pleas from soldiers' descendants, the British government had doggedly refused to grant retrospective pardons.

This was not just something Michael wanted to write about; he felt he *must*. 'There was a sense of compulsion, and that's always exciting.' He knew that the only way to help readers share his sorrow and outrage over the courts-martial was to tell the quiet, private tale of one victim of injustice. Wandering through the rows of bone-white Portland-bonnet headstones in the Bedford House Cemetery near Ypres, he had come across the grave of Private T.S.H. Peaceful. Around this soldier he began to weave what he feels to be his very best book.

Michael in Ypres.

Private Peaceful follows one long night in the life of a seventeen-year-old soldier, Thomas Peaceful, fighting near Ypres in 1915. His older brother Charlie, who has disobeyed orders in order to remain with him after he has been wounded, is to be executed at dawn. As 'Tommo' Peaceful keeps vigil with Charlie in spirit, counting down the hours, he is determined neither to sleep nor to dream:

> I have the whole night ahead of me, and I won't waste a
> single moment of it … I want to try to remember everything,
> just as it was, just as it happened. I've had nearly eighteen
> years of yesterdays and tomorrows, and tonight I must
> remember as many of them as I can … Tonight, more than
> any other night of my life, I want to feel alive.

In his memory, Tommo travels back to his boyhood in a Devon village, allowing Michael to pour into his writing his feelings for Iddesleigh. It had been his home now for a quarter of a century and, though he knew he could never belong to the place in the rare, deep sense that farmers like Graham and David Ward belonged, it had nevertheless taught him more about belonging than anywhere else. As he imagined the Peaceful boys growing up among its lanes, fields and rivers, the words flowed from his pen – 'the story seemed to tell itself'. And as the shadow of the First World War fell across the village, and Michael prepared to send Charlie and Tommo to the Western Front, 'the writing became very intense'.

Initially there were to have been just two Peaceful brothers; then a letter arrived from Scotland. It was from the mother of three sons, one of them, Joe, autistic. Joe had loved *The Butterfly Lion*; he had rocked with pleasure when his mother read it aloud to him. Michael was touched by this. He had learned over the years, first from his sister-in-law Anna Lane, who has Down's syndrome, then from children visiting Nethercott, that those who appear weak and broken often have gifts of the heart that many 'normal' people lack. In response to the letter he created a third brother, Big Joe, a gentle giant filled with affection, humour and intuitive wisdom, around whom the Peaceful family revolves. It is to Big Joe, and his favourite song, 'Oranges and Lemons', that Charlie Peaceful's thoughts turn for comfort when, at one minute to six, he walks out to face the firing squad.

Michael became more involved in *Private Peaceful* than in any book before or since, and when the reviews came out they confirmed his hunch that this was the finest thing he had ever written. It was, the *Observer* noted, a story that 'came from the heart with a passion and anger that pervades every page'. The *Guardian* called it 'humanising and humane', while the *Irish Times* likened Michael's lyrical evocation of a Devon childhood to Laurie Lee's *Cider with Rosie*. *Ink Pellet*, a magazine for teachers, suggested that 'a better novel ... for lower school English classes is hard to imagine'. But grown-ups were enjoying it too. Among *Private Peaceful*'s admirers was Jim Naughtie, who invited Michael to speak about and read from it on the *Today* programme.

Simon Reade, then director of the Bristol Old Vic, heard the reading in his bath, and was struck by the possibility that *Private Peaceful* might make a powerful one-man play. He got in touch with Michael; they arranged to have lunch. Reade had decided that, for theatrical purposes, the ending of the story would need to be changed: it was Tommo, and not Charlie, who must die on stage. He sensed that he would need to tread carefully in suggesting this. Behind all Michael's apparent confidence, Reade was aware of 'a kind of hubris' and a nagging sense of inferiority – 'I think he asks himself, "Am I a major minor writer, or a minor major one?"' He was also aware of an unusual warmth and generosity. That first lunch was the beginning of a close and enduring friendship. For Reade, whose own father died when he was very young, Michael has become 'a quasi father', who has nursed him through a time of great trauma. 'He doesn't drop you when things get tough,' Reade says. 'He's loyal.' It was the beginning, too, of a fruitful working relationship. The one-man play of *Private Peaceful*, after two sell-out seasons at the Bristol Old Vic, went on to tour the country to enormous acclaim.

And what of the true Private Peaceful? On a cold, bright morning in November 2010, Michael visits the Bedford House Cemetery and walks through the frosty grass to his grave. Many of the headstones he passes are engraved with messages from the families of the fallen: 'Ever in our hearts'; 'Thy will be done'; 'Gone'. This one is absolutely plain – 'Private T.S.H. Peaceful, 4 June 1915'. Michael has brought a poppy, but a school party has been here ahead of him. They have read his book, made a pilgrimage, and left a wreath of messages.

What had Michael and Clare imagined that their lives would be like once they had put Farms for City Children behind them? 'As usual,' Michael says, 'we really hadn't looked very far ahead.' Clare had thought that perhaps they would move away from Devon, to make things easier for their successors at Nethercott. 'But then there was my garden, and my plants,' she says. 'And all those dead relations,' Michael adds. In so far as they had envisaged the future at all, they had thought that Michael would devote himself to writing, and to speaking in schools and at festivals, and that Clare would spend more time in her garden, and with her grandchildren.

But by the time *Private Peaceful* was published Michael was already some months into a job more demanding than Farms for City Children had ever been. In the spring of 2003, he had been invited to become the third Children's Laureate, succeeding Quentin

Blake and Anne Fine. Clare's heart had sunk when the invitation came through, but she had realised, not for the first time, that there was no holding Michael back.

This two-year post is not one that every children's writer covets. 'If you want to celebrate someone's work,' Philip Pullman wrote when the idea of a Children's Laureate was first mooted, 'then give them a gold medal, give them a silver salver, give them a cheque, give them a vote of thanks – *but don't give them a job*.' It was a role, Pullman felt, that robbed a writer 'of those most precious things, time and silence'. But Michael is a very different kind of writer from Philip Pullman. He prefers, in fact, not to call himself a writer at all, but a 'storymaker' – 'because while I hope that I can turn a good phrase and weave a powerful tale I know that I am *not* a great writer'. Writing has remained a tortuous business for him, whereas engaging an audience comes naturally, and gives him energy. Alone in front of a blank page he can too easily find himself brooding on aspects of his life that make him sad. Up on a stage he can, temporarily, forget these, while affirmation and love roll over him in waves from audiences of strangers. Ahead of a performance, says Phil Perry, who manages Michael's publicity, 'I can sometimes feel the weight and sadness coming from him. But once he starts, I've never seen him off form.'

With public performances becoming a regular part of his life, Michael assumed a new costume – red linen suit, red-banded panama in summer, long, stripy scarf and black beret in winter. In late middle age a faint but unmistakable expression of sadness had crept into his face. He looked less the matinée idol now, more the tragic clown. It was in this mode that he became Children's Laureate, and he immediately staked out his goals: 'to put literature before literacy', and 'to take the fear out of reading, so that people feel it is for everyone, not just for clever people, and not just for learning'.

*Michael reads to children from St John the Baptist School,
Hoxton, spring 2003.*

These he summed up in one rallying cry: 'Let the joy of the book
come to the fore!'

As his predecessors had discovered, the title 'Children's Laureate'
commanded attention: 'I was saying exactly the same things I'd been
saying for years and years, but suddenly people were listening to me.'
His views and comments were constantly solicited by newspapers,
and on the radio and television. His diary became a cat's cradle of
appointments that had him travelling the length and breadth of
Britain. 'Like some superannuated strolling player,' he says, 'I set up
and performed wherever anyone let me' – village halls, concert halls,
tents, bookshops, libraries, school gyms. One week he was visiting a
school with just fourteen pupils on the Hebridean island of Jura; the

next addressing an audience of 2,500 in the Albert Hall. He and Clare spent not more than three or four nights a month at Langlands; and even when they were there Michael was regularly whisked off to Exeter to speak in the BBC studios.

A Children's Laureate, like a Booker Prize winner, enjoys a huge boost in book sales, and this, added to his speaker's fees, guaranteed Michael a substantial income. He suspected, however, that during his two years in the post he would have almost no time for writing, and was determined to ensure instead that he had a good store of ideas when the moment came to hand on the laureate's wreath. His most reliable stimulus for stories has always been travel. 'A new landscape,' he says, 'acts for me like the backdrop in a theatre – stories begin to take shape against it.' And so he accepted invitations to talk and perform not only all over Britain, but abroad. Twice, he made week-long trips to Scotland, touring the Highlands and Islands in a little yellow bus. He visited South Africa, where, in grilling heat, he was taken to a township in Soweto. The children in the ramshackle, tin-roofed school had done their research and discovered that Michael had spent his early childhood in London, and to make him feel at home they entertained him with a concert of cockney songs.

Most memorable of all is the journey he made to Moscow in the autumn of 2003 to attend a conference and celebration for 500 Russian librarians. Jointly organised by Lyudmila Putin and Barbara Bush, and with Cherie Blair a guest of honour, it opened with a dinner in the Kremlin, and culminated in a prize-giving ceremony. 'First there was a salacious floor show, during which the vodka flowed,' Michael remembers. 'Then came an announcement that a prize was to be presented to the most admirable librarian in all of Russia.' Drums rolled, and a diminutive man in an ill-fitting suit squeezed his way to the front through the tables and chairs. In his home town, 2,000 miles from Moscow, the library had recently caught fire. Repeatedly braving the flames, he had rescued nearly all the books.

This act of heroism prompted Michael to write a magical and inspiring short story, 'I Believe in Unicorns'. But by the time he wrote this he had, despite all the demands on his time, embarked on what was to be his longest and most ambitious novel to date. *Alone on a Wide Wide Sea* is a complex mariner's tale spanning two generations, opening in an orphanage in Australia in the late Forties, and ending in present-day London. In the early spring of 2005 Michael and Clare took a holiday in the Engadine Valley in Switzerland so that he could finish it. His term as laureate was nearly at an end, and both of them were exhausted. 'We had spent two years ricocheting around the world,' Clare says. 'Michael was absolutely rolled out; and I remember feeling I just didn't have much more to give.'

'We have just walked down to the river through banks of bluebells,' Clare emails after returning from a literary festival in Dubai. '*Bliss* to be home again.' Pottering about in Devon, she finds great happiness in small things: watching her tomatoes and her roses flourish, visiting Ros in Exeter, chatting to her granddaughters on the telephone. Michael is different. He cannot relax for long without taking on a project or a cause. During one cloudless week in May 2011, for example, he becomes concerned about the tadpoles burgeoning in the rutty puddles in a field across the lane. The puddles are drying out, and the tadpoles don't yet have legs, so he makes a series of journeys down to the field with a bucket, carries the tadpoles home and empties them into a granite trough in the garden. But the trough is three feet above the ground. For a baby frog to jump from it would mean certain death. So he constructs a broad wooden ramp, and when he leaves Devon for his annual holiday in Scilly he emails Jane Feaver to check that the frogs are using it.

Michael's drive, his almost missionary zeal, is fuelled by the need to fight what Clare calls 'his tendency to sink'. To keep his spirits up, she says, he requires 'big things, and strong emotions'; he needs 'to feel plugged into a wider world'. And, just as when he was a junior schoolmaster refereeing Saturday-afternoon rugby, he needs his wife at his side. Sometimes, when Michael introduces Clare to journalists or parents or children as they swarm around him after a talk, 'they look at me bewildered, as if to say, "What's she got to do with the price of eggs?"' But the truth, as he knows better than anyone, is that without Clare Morpurgo there would be no Michael Morpurgo. So when, just after Michael's retirement as laureate, fate dealt him a trump-card, it was, he says, 'our joint achievement and our joint reward'.

It began with a telephone call from Michael's theatrical agent, Marc Berlin. The National Theatre, Berlin explained, was thinking of making a play of *War Horse*. Images of pantomime nags galumphing across a stage set of trenches and Flanders mud drifted through Michael's mind. The whole notion seemed so far-fetched it might have been an April fool. But it was not April, and the National Theatre was not fooling.

Following the success of the stage production of Philip Pullman's trilogy *His Dark Materials*, the National's artistic director, Nicholas Hytner, had asked Associate Director Tom Morris to come up with another show that would play effectively both to older children and to grown-ups. In response Tom immersed himself in contemporary children's literature, and several novels – Cornelia Funke's *Inkheart*, Neil Gaiman's *Coraline*, Eoin Colfer's *Artemis Fowl* – fired his imagination. Then a friend gave him a copy of *Private Peaceful* and, intrigued by Michael's work, he went on to read *Kensuke's Kingdom*,

The White Horse of Zennor, This Morning I Met a Whale. 'It was my mum who said, "Have you read the one about the horse in the First World War?" She'd heard Michael talk about it on *Desert Island Discs.'*

Turning the pages of *War Horse*, Tom felt increasingly excited. The classic Orpheus structure of the story – 'the falling in love, the separation, the quest through hell to recover the love' – gave it clear theatrical potential. And the fact that one of the two central characters was a horse struck Tom as a positive advantage. Some years earlier he had seen *Tall Horse*, a retelling by the South-African-based Handspring Puppet Company of the true story of a giraffe caught in Sudan in the early nineteenth century, and shipped across the Mediterranean as a gift for the King of France. At its centre was a life-sized giraffe puppet made of a skeletal bamboo frame with internal hinges and articulated by a team of actors, and he'd been bowled over by it. 'I knew,' he says, 'that these people could create a life-sized animal puppet that could hold a big stage. And I wanted to work with them.'

Nick Hytner, once assured that no horse puppet would be given a speaking part, gave Tom his blessing to start 'playing around' with *War Horse* in the National Theatre Studio. He was not making a firm commitment to it – fewer than one in four ideas trialled in the Studio ever reaches the stage – but he had an inkling that it was 'mad enough to be something that just might work'. Handspring Puppeteers Basil Jones and Adrian Kohler were flown over from South Africa. Eventually, they would create horses on bamboo frames just as they had created their giraffe, but to begin with, using scissors, cardboard and old newspapers, they simply mocked up heads, and invited actors to try them on and experiment with being horses. Nick Hytner sat in on an early workshop. 'It was *weird*,' he says, 'but I thought, "OK, Tom, if you say so."' But Michael, also

*Toby Sedgwick (choreographer), Tom Morris and Adrian
Kohler in rehearsal.*

Puppeteer Tim Lewis with Topthorn.

invited to watch, was much less sceptical. Since Marc Berlin's initial call, he had been shown a DVD of Handspring's giraffe walking across a studio and had found it 'unbelievably, inexplicably moving'. Seeing the actors in their horses' heads in the Studio, Tom says, Michael became 'really quite emotional. It was a watershed moment. I felt we had his confidence.'

Tom Morris and his co-director, Marianne Elliott, then set to work in earnest. The production involved a vast team – 'and we were all', says Tom, 'well outside our comfort zone'. But from the start the wheels were oiled by Michael's enthusiasm and support. 'Graceful is the word that keeps coming to mind when I think of him,' says Tom. 'He was graceful in his involvement.' When it comes to adaptations and collaboration, Tom has learned, writers divide into two types: 'Some brilliant creative people become paranoid, fearful of competition or of someone else taking the credit for their work. Others understand that their skill as storytellers is enhanced, rather than threatened, by collective effort and enterprise. Michael was definitely in this second camp.' For Michael, meantime, 'the sheer enjoyment of watching this huge jigsaw come together, piece by piece, was mind-boggling'.

Not that all was plain sailing. There had never been any question of Michael's writing the script – 'We needed a level of detachment from the original source,' says Tom, 'we needed to be quite cold-blooded' – and at various stages he was unhappy with it. 'Then,' says Tom, 'we saw a fiery side to him.' And, though Philip Pullman had encouraged Michael to trust the National Theatre, and had assured him that all would be well if he did so, the first preview seemed such a disaster that Michael barely slept for several nights. With just a week to go before it opened to the public *War Horse* was diffuse, ill-focused, clumsy, and far too long. 'Michael was plainly alarmed,' Nick Hytner remembers. 'But I knew the difference between a show that's not a success and will never be a success, and one that will, with a bit of work, turn into something amazing. And I knew that *War Horse* was one of those.' By press night, on 17 October 2006, the play had been radically tweaked and tightened, the script altered, some whole parts removed, twenty minutes cut from the running time. Michael found himself sitting in the audience behind Mike Leigh and in front of Sir Peter Hall and it was clear, by the end, that both were as deeply moved as he was himself.

The reviews the following day were ecstatic: 'If ever a piece of theatre worked magic, then it must be War Horse' (*Evening Standard*), 'Genius isn't too strong a word to describe this astonishing performance' (*Daily Telegraph*), 'Extraordinarily fresh and moving' (*Independent*). Even critics such as Benedict Nightingale who felt that the story steered 'perilously close to sentimentality' were overcome by the brilliance of the puppets. 'Even "Equus",' wrote Nightingale in the *Guardian*, 'pales in comparison with the dazzling puppet design of Basil Jones and Adrian Kohler, who ultimately make you forget you are watching fabricated quadrupeds.'

Yet nobody dreamed of the scale of success that lay ahead of the show Tom Morris now calls 'the Beast': that its National Theatre run would be extended from one year to two; that it would transfer to the New London Theatre in Drury Lane and break the record for the highest weekly grossing play in the West End; that shortly after the millionth ticket had been sold in London it would open on Broadway and scoop five Tony Awards – including the award for best play. 'At every turn, it's amazed us,' says Nick Hytner. 'None of us can remember a play ever behaving in this way. It's unprecedented.'

What has all this meant for Michael? He has been to *War Horse* more than forty times now, and has become a familiar figure to the cast, rising to his feet at the end of performances and leading the applause. On a purely practical level, it has made him a very rich man and, though materially his life has changed little, this matters more to him than some might guess. After decades of hard slog, he has finally settled his debts with Allen Lane, and laid his ghost to rest. 'It's not that I feel I'm quits with the Lane family, exactly, because I will always owe them a huge amount. But not to have to worry about living off them any more is a relief to me – and to Clare. It makes her happy that things have come right financially through nobody's efforts but our own.'

More personally, the play has brought Michael a sense of late homecoming. 'When I'm in the theatre,' he says, 'I know that, but for the Second World War and Jack Morpurgo, this is where I would have made my life.' Every time the *War Horse* cast changes, he goes in to meet the new actors. He unrolls before them a map of Devon, and points out Iddesleigh. He talks a bit about the First World War and reads from the poetry of Edward Thomas. He tells the actors about how he met Wilf Ellis and Captain Budgett, how he watched a troubled child one evening confiding in a horse over a stable door, how *War Horse* took shape. It is as if he was once again taking a Year 6 class, and the lesson ends with 'show and tell'. From a deep jacket pocket, Michael produces one of the brass boxes sent by Princess Mary to soldiers on the Western Front, and it is passed round the cast. Originally it was filled with cigarettes, but Michael has crammed it full of Maltesers. The actors are allowed one each as a reward for attentiveness. 'I don't know whether it helps them,' he says when the session is over. 'But the truth is it does a lot for me. I'm a bit greedy about my involvement. I'm never quite satisfied.' Now that there are plans to take *War Horse* on a tour of American cities, and to Canada, Australia and Japan, he knows that he must loosen his grip, and this makes him anxious. 'My role diminishes as the thing widens,' he says. 'I don't want to lose it.'

*　　*　　*

In letters home from boarding school, Sebastian Morpurgo gently ribs Michael about the unlikelihood of any of his books ever selling really well, or being made into a film. 'I'm anxious to see Dad's completed "masterpiece", he writes in one. 'I'll knock off the inverted commas when it sells more than 150,000 copies, or when you sell the filming rights to MGM.' Clare joined in the teasing. To keep the atmosphere from turning sour when the telephone rang at awkward moments she often joked, 'Better answer – might be Spielberg.' So when, shortly after *War Horse* had transferred from the National Theatre to the West End, Marc Berlin rang to say that Kathleen Kennedy, an American producer who had worked with Steven Spielberg on *ET*, *Jurassic Park* and *Schindler's List*, was interested in making a film of the book, Michael wondered whether he was bluffing.

Berlin warned him not to get his hopes up – this was probably just a speculative enquiry. But then Spielberg came to London, saw the play, and invited Michael and Clare to lunch at Claridge's. Sitting with him on sofas around a low table, sharing a Mexican salad so beautiful that Spielberg insisted on photographing it before they started to eat, it became clear that he was as keen as a hound that had picked up a scent. He questioned them closely about the First World War, about horses, about Devon. 'For two and a half hours,' Michael says, 'I told him stories, and he told us stories. And I thought, "I am listening here to one of the great storytellers."'

Within months Michael and Clare were watching a $90 million film take shape on set. In the Wiltshire village of Castle Combe they joined a cast of 300 extras, Michael dressed as a whiskery squire, Clare as his glamorous lady. In the grounds of Stratfield Saye, home to the dukes of Wellington, they stood under an oak tree and observed the filming of a cavalry charge: 'one hundred and fifty horses galloping towards us, with soldiers on their backs, sabres drawn'. They watched the filming of a scene in which Benedict Cumberbatch and Tom Hiddleston, playing two army officers, pore over a battle plan. Spielberg filmed the scene again and again – 'teasing out of them their very best performance' – then turned to Michael and whispered, 'They're just like Ferraris.' They visited Spielberg in his director's tent, and noted, next to the banks of monitors and screens, a well-thumbed copy of *War Horse*. 'I kept thinking about how it had all begun,' says Michael. 'How a chance conversation in the pub had led to all this. I love the arc of that story.'

The arc of Michael's own story over the same period is just as remarkable. When first he fell into conversation with Wilf Ellis in the Duke of York, he was a would-be author touting his stories around publishers like a door-to-door salesman. Now, he sells well

Michael and Clare as extras in War Horse,
with Steven Spielberg.

over a million books a year, and it is not only publishers who beat a path to his door. One way to measure his success is to spend time with him at Langlands. Here, during one morning in the spring of 2011, emails arrive from Barnaby Spurrier, a producer, concerning the story Michael has been commissioned to write for Mandeville and Wenlock, the official mascots for the London 2012 Olympics; from HarperCollins about the deal they have struck with McDonald's, whereby 10 million copies of stories by Michael are to be given away with Happy Meals; from Michel Kains, a French producer with whom Michael is working on an animated version of his Holocaust novel *The Mozart Question*; and from Simon Reade, who is shortly to start work on a film of *Private Peaceful*. Another is to visit his agent, Veronique Baxter, in her book-lined cubicle at David Higham, off Golden Square in Soho. She has represented Michael since 2006. In that time, she says, his sales 'have gone *like this*', and she shoots her arm skywards. And sales are only part of the story. David Higham represents a number of bestselling children's authors, including Jacqueline Wilson. But the postbag that comes in for Michael every day is bigger than anyone else's 'by miles'. Letters that seem particularly touching, or interesting, are forwarded to Langlands. When at home, Clare reckons, Michael replies to between thirty and forty a day.

In some writers this level of attention and demand would breed arrogance, in others reclusiveness. In Michael, friends and relations agree, its effects have been mellowing and relaxing – so much so, says his brother-in-law David Teale, 'that it is hard to believe he is the same man we once knew'. For those who know Michael only through his stories it is easy to recognise what Philip Pullman describes as his 'deep, true decency' – and this, Pullman says, 'must be the man himself coming through, because all we can write, really, is ourselves, over and over. Michael is a truly good man.'

But for those who had to live close to him through his years of obscurity and struggle, this goodness was sometimes baffled by insecurity, moodiness, and ego. 'I wish,' Michael says, 'that my sons could have known me as a child.' It is as if they might have seen in him then an essential sweetness, which became buried along the way under frustration and stress and exhaustion, but which success has now restored to him.

Yet there is still, mixed in with this sweetness, a dash of anger. Quentin Blake, who has illustrated several of Michael's books, suspects that, if one could analyse him in terms of the four 'humours' believed in the ancient world to govern temperament, Michael would be 'mainly sanguine, but potentially choleric'. The conductor Stephen Barlow makes a similar observation. Working with Michael on a ballet of his story *The Rainbow Bear* he was aware of 'a darkness driving him forward – a kind of tempered irascibility'. Success has liberated him, allowing him to channel this anger outwards, and to positive ends. Michael has become, as Barlow says, 'a crusader'.

Early in 2011 Michael was invited to give the thirty-fifth Richard Dimbleby Lecture. Founded in memory of the BBC broadcaster, this has been delivered over the years by a formidable roll-call of speakers – Bill Clinton, Richard Dawkins, Stella Rimington and Rowan Williams among them. It had never before been given by a children's writer. Stepping up to the lectern in the Great Hall at King's College London – dressed not in his storytelling clothes, but in a sober statesman's suit and tie – Michael looked unaccustomedly nervous. What followed was an hour of oratory that nobody present that evening will ever forget.

His talk was entitled 'Set the Children Free', and his aim, he explained, was to carry the audience with him on 'a personal and sometimes uncomfortable journey' as he explored with them three of the basic ground rules laid down by the United Nations

Convention on the Rights of the Child: the rights to survival, to liberty and to education. 'We shall discover,' he warned, 'that even under our noses, these rights have been and still are woefully neglected.'

Three years earlier, Juliet Stevenson had invited Michael to come with her to the Young Vic to watch a play by Natasha Walter, *Motherland*. It had made him aware, for the first time, of the existence of Yarl's Wood in Bedfordshire, an immigration removal centre for asylum seekers – 'a kind of holding pen before deportation'. Families and children were imprisoned there, often for months, in conditions at best bleak, at worst brutal. Fired by indignation, Michael had visited Yarl's Wood with a film crew from the BBC *Politics Show*. Refused entry, they set up their cameras outside the barbed-wire fence, and Michael recited lines from William Blake:

A Robin Redbreast in a Cage
Puts all Heaven in a Rage.

He then poured his fury into the fictional tale of a young Afghan boy who, with his mother and a stray dog called Shadow, escapes from Afghanistan and makes his way to England, only to find himself, six years later, locked up in Yarl's Wood.

Writing *Shadow*, Michael told his Dimbleby audience, 'was my way of dealing with the feelings I had about such grave injustice'. Similarly, the anger that welled up in him as he watched a documentary about the wall that Israelis were building around Palestine had driven him to write a story about a Palestinian shepherd boy and an Israeli girl who learned to communicate with one another by writing messages of peace on kites, waiting for a good wind, and then flying them over the wall. 'Sentimental claptrap?' Michael challenged his Dimbleby audience. 'Maybe. Or rather a hope that a new generation will one day rise above the prejudice and suspicion, hurt and hatred – as has happened in Europe, in South Africa, in Ireland, and now, only days ago, in Egypt … It is the children of today, yesterday and tomorrow who will do this also in Israel and Palestine, given half a chance.'

He had the children's own word for this. After the publication of *The Kites are Flying!* Save the Children had invited Michael to become their Ambassador to the Middle East. They wanted him to visit children in Israel and Gaza, and to find out whether there was any real cause for hope. Both sides of the wall, he had sat and made kites with groups of children, and had asked them what they thought. Might their grandchildren make peace one day? 'I think it'll be my grandchildren's grandchildren,' one had replied. 'But there will be peace one day.'

Relating these experiences, Michael played his audience like a great fish. One moment he was the jocular scoutmaster, drawing them in with stories, eccentricities and jokes, the next he was the fiery evangelist roaring with wrath. Later that evening his performance was broadcast on television, and the following day Veronique Baxter and her team at David Higham were overwhelmed with emails from people who had switched on the television by chance, and had felt compelled to listen to Michael until he had finished speaking. For Richard Dimbleby's son Nicholas, it had been possibly the most memorable of all the lectures he had heard. 'Your deep concern came across, both emotional and practical,' he wrote to Michael. 'You took us on *your* journey.'

Sitting in the audience that evening, one person in particular had reason to feel moved. Few would have recognised the lady in the black hijab as Michael's half-sister, Kay. For nearly twenty years

Michael had not seen or spoken to her, and nor had Pieter or Mark. In 1976 she had married an Egyptian, converted to Islam and, not long afterwards, severed all ties with her blood relations, breaking her father's heart. 'If I knew how to pray,' Jack Morpurgo wrote towards the end of his life, 'there would be one prayer forever on my lips: that I be granted time and the capacity to recover … the affection of my daughter and my two Muslim grandchildren.'

Everyone believed that Kay had cut herself off of her own accord, but this was not the case. As a child she had felt outraged by Jack's controlling treatment of Kippe; as a married woman she learned very quickly that her own husband was a more extreme bully than Jack Morpurgo had ever been. He tried to poison her against her parents and siblings, and then, using threats, forbade her to have any contact with them. He kept her away from the funerals of both Kippe and Jack, and ripped up copies of Michael's books in front of their children. Occasionally, listening to the radio in their west London home, Kay caught snatches of Michael's voice. Sometimes, if she heard a car draw up by the house at night, she dreamed that he and Pieter and Mark had come to her rescue. When finally she broke free of her husband, her greatest fear was that her brothers would want nothing to do with her. She need not have worried. Within days of hearing from her, Michael and Clare had arranged to visit. 'We went for tea,' says Michael. 'It was very moving. We chatted and chatted for nearly three hours.' 'And there was Clare, as beautiful as ever,' says Kay. 'And when we talked about *War Horse* and all Michael's successes, he was just as full of awe and amazement as the rest of us.'

I hope I'll never get too old to travel. As you've read in this chapter, a new place usually means a new story. It doesn't always work. When we went down the Nile with Ted and Carol Hughes we laid bets as to whether Ted or I would be first to write an Egyptian story of some kind, a crocodile tale or a camel poem. Neither of us did, so far as I know. But a couple of years ago I went to Norway, to the fjords, to the mountains and valleys of Edvard Grieg, to the land of Beowulf, a country not so long ago living under the heel of a foreign occupier. Here I did write a story.

The Saga of Ragnar Erikson

From the ship's log:
14 July 1965

As I sailed into Arnefjord this morning, I was looking all around me, marvelling at the towering mountains, at the still dark waters, at the welcoming escort of porpoises, at the chattering oystercatchers, and I could not understand for the life of me why the Vikings ever left this land.

It was beautiful beyond belief. Why would you ever leave this paradise of a place, to face the heaving grey of the Norwegian Sea and a voyage into the unknown, when you had all this outside your door?

The little village at the end of the fjord looked at first too good to be true, a cluster of clapboard houses gathered around the quay, most painted ox-blood red. On top of the hill beyond them stood a simple wooden church, with an elegant pencil-sharp spire, and a well-tended graveyard, surrounded by a white picket fence. There seemed to be flowers on almost every grave. A stocky little Viking pony grazed the meadow below.

The fishing boat tied up at the quay had clearly seen better days. Now that I was closer I noticed that the village too wasn't as well kept as I had first thought. In places the paint was peeling off the houses. There were tiles missing from the rooftops and a few of the windows were boarded up. It wasn't abandoned, but the whole place looked neglected and sad somehow.

As I came in on the motor there was something about the village that began to make me feel uncomfortable. There was no one to be seen, not a soul. Only the horse. No smoke rose from the chimneys. There was no washing hanging out. No one was fishing from the shore, no children played in the street or around the houses.

I hailed the boat, hoping someone might be on board to tell me where I could tie up. There was no reply. So I tied up at the quay anyway and jumped out. I was looking for a café, somewhere I could get a drink or even a hot meal. And I needed a shop too. I was low on water and I had no beer left on board, and no coffee.

Almost immediately I came upon a place that looked as if it might be the village store. I peered through the window. Tables and chairs were set out. There was a bar to one side, and across the room I could see a small shop, the shelves stacked with tins. Things were looking up, I thought. But I couldn't see anyone inside. I tried the door and, to my surprise, it opened.

I'd never seen anything like it. This was shop, café, bar, post office, all in one. There was a Wurlitzer jukebox in the corner and then to one side, opposite the bar, a post office and shop. And there was a piano right next to the post-office counter, with sheet music open on the top – Beethoven sonatas.

I called out, but still no one emerged. So I went outside again and walked down the deserted village street, up the hill towards the church, stopping on the way to stroke the horse. I asked him if he was alone here, but he clearly thought that this was a stupid question and wandered off, whisking his tail as he went.

The church door was open, so I went in and sat down, breathing in the peace of the place and trying at the same time to suppress the thought that this might be some kind of ghost village. It was absurd, I knew it was, but all the same I could feel the fear rising inside me.

That was when the bell rang loud, right above my head, from the spire. Twelve times. My heart pounded in my ears. As the last echoes died away I could hear the sound of a man coughing and muttering to himself. It seemed to come from high up in the gallery behind me. I turned.

We stood looking at one another, not speaking for some time. I had the impression he was as surprised to see me as I was to see him. He made his way down the stairs and came slowly up the aisle towards me.

He had strange eyes, this man, unusually light, like his hair. He might have been fifty or sixty and was weathered, like the village.

'Looking at you,' he began, 'I would say you might be English.'

'You'd be right,' I told him.

'Thought so,' he said, nodding. Then he went on, 'I ring the bell every day at noon. I always have. It's to call them back. They will come one day. You will see, they will come.'

I didn't like to ask whom he was talking about. My first thought was that perhaps he was a little mad.

'You need some place to stay, young man? I have twelve houses you can choose from. You need to pray? I have a church. You need something to eat, something to drink? I can provide that too, and my prices are very reasonable. You're looking a little pale. I can tell you need a drink. Come along, follow me.'

Outside the church he stopped to shake my hand and to introduce himself: 'Ragnar Erikson.' As we walked down the hill he told me who lived in each of the houses we passed – a cousin here, an aunt there – who grew the best vegetables in the village, and

271

who was the best pianist. He spoke as if they were still there, and this was all very strange, because it was quite obvious to me by now that no one at all was living in any of these houses. Then I saw he was leading me back to where I'd been before, into the bar-cum-post-office-cum-village-store.

'You want some music on the Wurlitzer?' he asked me. 'Help yourself, whatever you like, "A Whiter Shade of Pale", "Sloop John B", "Rock Around the Clock". You choose. It's free, no coins needed.'

I chose 'A Whiter Shade of Pale' while he went behind the bar and poured me a beer.

'I don't get many people coming here these days,' he said, 'and there's only me living here now, so I don't keep much in the bar or the shop. But I caught a small salmon today. We shall have that for supper, and a little schnapps. You will stay for supper, won't you? Supper is free – you will be my guest. You must forgive me – I talk a lot, to myself mostly, so when I have someone else to talk to, I make up for lost talking time. You're the first person I've had in here for a month at least.'

I didn't know what to say. Too much was contradictory and strange. I longed to ask him why the place looked so empty and if there were people really living in those houses. And who was he ringing the church bell for? Nothing made any sense. But I couldn't bring myself to ask. Instead I made polite conversation.

'You speak good English,' I told him.

'This is because Father and I, we went a lot to Shetland in the old days. So we had to speak English. We were always going over there.'

'In that fishing boat down by the quay?' I asked him.

'It is not a fishing boat,' he said. 'It is a supply boat. I carry supplies to the villages up and down the fjords. There is no road, you see. Everything has to come by boat, the post as well. So I am the postman too.'

After a couple of beers he took me outside and back down to the quayside to show me his boat. Once on board, I could see it was the kind of boat that no storm could sink. It was made not for speed but for endurance, built to bob up and down like a cork and just keep going. The boat suited the man, I thought. We stood together in the wheelhouse, and I knew he wanted to talk.

'My family,' he said, 'we had two boats, this one and one other just the same. Father made one, I made the other. This is the old boat, my father's boat. He made it with his own hands before I was born, and we took it over to Shetland, like the Vikings did before us. But we were not on a raid like they were. It was during the wartime, when the Germans were occupying Norway.

'We were taking refugees across the Norwegian Sea to Shetland, often twenty of them at a time, hidden down below. Sometimes they were Jews escaping from the Nazis. Sometimes it was airmen who had been shot down, commandos we had been hiding, secret agents too. Fifteen times we went there and back and they didn't catch us. Lucky – we were very lucky. This is a lucky boat. The other one, the one I built, was not so lucky.'

Ragnar Erikson, I was discovering, wasn't the kind of man you could question or interrupt; but I did wonder, all through our excellent supper of herring and salmon, what had happened to the other boat. And I still hadn't dared to broach the subject that puzzled me most: why there seemed to be no one else living in the village but him. When he fell silent I felt he wanted to be lost in his thoughts. So the right moment never came.

But after supper by the fire he began to question me closely about why I had come sailing to Norway, about what I was doing with my life. He was easy to talk to because he seemed genuinely interested. So I found myself telling him everything: how at thirty-one I was suddenly alone in the world, that my mother had died when I was a child, and just a couple of months ago my father had too. I was a schoolteacher, but not at all sure I wanted to go on being one.

'But why did you come here?' he asked me. 'Why Norway?'

So I told him how, when I was a boy, I had been obsessed by the Vikings; I'd loved the ancient legends of Beowulf and Grendel. I'd even learned to read the runes. It had been a lifelong ambition of mine to come to Norway one day. But arriving here in this particular fjord, I explained, had been an accident. I was just looking for a good sheltered place to tie up for the night.

'I'm glad you came,' he said after a while. 'As I said, no one comes here much these days. But they will, they will.'

'Who will?' I asked him, rather abruptly and without thinking. At once I regretted it, for I could see he was frowning at me, looking at me quite hard. I feared I might have offended him.

'Whoever it is, they will be my family and my friends, that's all I know,' he said. 'They will live in the houses, where they all once lived, where their souls still live.'

I could tell from the tone of his voice that there was more to tell and that he might tell it, if I was patient and did not press him. So I kept quiet, and waited. I'm so pleased I did. When at last he began again, he told me the whole story, about the empty village, about the other boat, the unlucky boat.

'I think perhaps you would like to know why I'm all alone in this place?' he said, looking directly at me. It felt as if he was having to screw up all his courage before he could go on.

'I should have gone to her wedding myself,' he said, 'with everyone else in the village, but I did not want to. It was only in Flam, down the fjord just north of here, not that far. The thing was that, ever since I was a little boy, the bride had been my sweetheart, the love of my life, but I was always too timid to tell her. I looked for her every time I went to Flam to collect supplies, met her whenever I could, went swimming with her, picking berries, mountain climbing, but I never told her how I felt. Now she was marrying someone else. I didn't want to be there, that's all. So my father skippered my boat that day instead of me. There were fourteen people in the boat – everyone from the village except for me and two very old spinster sisters. They did everything together, those two. One of them was too sick to go, so the other insisted on staying behind to look after her. I watched the boat going off into the morning mist. I never saw it again, nor anyone on board.

'To this day, no one really knows what happened. But we do know that early in the evening, after the wedding was over, there was a rock-slide, a huge avalanche which swept down the mountainside into the fjord and set up a great tidal wave. People from miles around heard the roaring of it. No one saw the boat go down. But that's what must have happened.

'For a few years the two old sisters and I kept the village going. When they died, within days of one another, I buried them in the churchyard. After that I was alone. To start with, very often, I thought of leaving. But someone had to tend the graves, I thought, someone had to ring the church bell. So I stayed. I fished, I kept a few sheep in those days. I wasn't quite alone. I had my horse.

'I discovered there is one thing you have to do when you are on your own, and that is to keep busy. So every day I work on the houses, opening windows in the summers to air rooms, lighting fires in the winters to warm them through, painting windows and doors, fixing where I can, what I can, just keeping them ready for the day they return. There's always something. I know it's looking more and more untidy as the years go by, but I do my best. I have to. They're living here still, my family and friends. I can feel them all about me. They're waiting and I'm waiting, for the others to come and join them.'

'I'm not sure I understand,' I told him.

'I don't blame you, young man,' he said, laughing a little. 'I'm not off my head, not quite. Honestly I'm not. I know the dead cannot come back. But I do know their spirits live on, and I do know that one day, if I do not leave, if I keep ringing the bell, if I keep the houses dry, then people will find this place, will come and live here. In the villages nearby, they are still frightened of the place. They think it is cursed somehow. But they are wrong about that. It was the boat that was cursed, I tell them, not the village. Anyway, they do not come. Most of them are so frightened, they won't even come to visit me. They say it is a dying village and will soon be dead. But it is not, and it will not be, not so long as I stay. One day, people will come, and then the village will be alive once more. I know this for sure.'

Ragnar Erikson offered me a bed in his house that night, but I said I was fine in the boat. I am ashamed to admit it, but after hearing his story I just didn't want to stay there any longer. It was too easy to believe that the place – paradise that it looked – might be cursed. He did not try to persuade me. I am sure he knew instinctively what I was feeling. I told him that I had to be up early in the morning, thinking I might not see him again. But he said he would be sure to see me off. And he was as good as his word. At first light he was down on the quay. We shook hands warmly, friends for less than a day but, because he had told me his story, I felt that in a way we were friends for life. He told me to come back one day and see him again if ever I was passing. Although I said I would, I knew how unlikely it would be. But through all the things that have happened to me since, I never forgot the saga of Ragnar Erikson. It was a story that I liked to tell often to my family, to my friends.

From the ship's log:
1 August 2010, midnight

Today I came back to Arnefjord. It has been over forty years and I've often dreamed about it, wondering what happened to Ragnar Erikson and his dying village. This time I have brought my grandchildren too, because however often I tell them the story, they never quite seem to believe it.

I had my binoculars out at the mouth of the little fjord and saw the village at once. It was just as it had been. Even the boat was there at the quay, with no one on it, so far as I could see. There was no smoke rising from the chimneys; when we tied up, no one came to see us. I walked up towards the village shop, the grandchildren running off into the village, happy to be ashore, skipping about like goats, finding their land legs again.

Then, as I walked up towards the church, I saw a mother coming towards me with a pushchair.

'Do you live here?' I asked her.

'Yes,' she said, and pointed out her house. 'Over there.'

My granddaughter came running up to me.

'I knew it, Grandpa,' she cried, 'I always knew it was just a story. Of course there are people living here. I've seen lots and lots of them.'

And she was right. There was a toy tractor outside the back door of a newly painted house, and I could hear the sound of shrieking children coming from further away down by the seashore.

'What story does she mean?' the mother asked me.

So I told her how I'd come here forty years before and had met Ragnar Erikson, and how he was the only one living here then.

'Old Ragnar,' she said, smiling. 'He's up in the churchyard now.'

She must have seen the look on my face. 'No, no,' she said, 'I don't mean that. He's not dead. He's doing the flowers. We wouldn't be here if it wasn't for him. Ragnar saved this village, Ragnar and the road.'

'The road?' I asked.

'Fifteen years ago they built a road to the village, and suddenly it was a place people could come to and live in. But there would have been no village if Ragnar hadn't stayed and kept it going, we all know that. There are fifteen of us living here now – six families. He's old and does not hear so well, but he is strong enough to walk up the hill to ring the bell. It was the bell that brought us back, he says. And he still likes to go on ringing it every day. Habit, he says.'

I went up the hill with my granddaughter, who ran on ahead of me up the steps and into the church. When she came out there was an old man with her, and he was holding her hand.

'She has told me who you are,' he said. 'But I would have recognised you anyway. I knew you would come back, you know. You must have heard me ringing. If I remember rightly, you liked "Whiter Shade of Pale" on the Wurlitzer. And you liked a beer. Do you remember?'

'I remember,' I said. 'I remember everything.'

7

Still Seeking

On Christmas Day 2011 Steven Spielberg's *War Horse* opens in cinemas across America. In Britain, critics who have managed a sneak preview have been sharply divided. Writing in the *Daily Mail*, Christopher Tookey describes it as 'the most moving picture I have seen all year … a cinematic masterpiece', and awards it five stars. The *Guardian* gives it just two, and calls it 'lachrymose', 'buttery' and 'chocolate-boxy'. In America, however, there have been enough rave reviews – 'A rare and genuine movie masterpiece' (*New York Observer*), 'Heartfelt and marvelously crafted' (*Rolling Stone*), 'Heartbreaking understatement' (*New York Times*) – to guarantee huge ticket sales. Outside Clearview's Movie Theater on New York's 62nd Street queues have been snaking round the block for several days, and at the fourth showing, on Christmas evening, every seat is taken. As the film ends, the audience breaks into instant and rapturous applause.

A month earlier, on a damp, grey, November morning, Michael and Clare, with their eldest granddaughters, Léa and Eloïse, and Jane Feaver, have joined the cast and crew for a showing in London at the Odeon, Leicester Square. Clare wears a cameo brooch that once belonged to Kippe – 'I felt she should be here with us'. Michael looks exhausted. He has seen the trailer for the film, and one or two of the scenes have struck him as 'overly sentimental'. Anxiety about this has given him several sleepless nights. As the audience takes their seats,

John Williams's soundtrack sweeping through the cinema like the waves of a big sea, he is not in the mood for chatter. And two and a half hours on, as the credits begin to roll and before the lights go up, he slips quietly out. As so often when he was a schoolboy, he feels an urgent need to be alone.

It is only later, over Dover sole at Sheekey's in Covent Garden, that Michael reveals that his reactions to the film are overwhelmingly positive. The sentimentality of the trailer snippets has assumed a kind of integrity seen in context – 'because this is not meant to be an accurate portrayal of life, but an epic story which you have to embrace as a whole'. Spielberg's depictions of pre-war rural life in England and France may be rather rose-tinted, 'but if you are going to descend into hell it's important you've been to paradise first'. Michael loves the slowness with which the film begins, the time Spielberg takes immersing his audience in the Devon countryside and introducing them to the characters around whom the story will revolve. And he admires Spielberg's 'spontaneity and genius' in introducing moments of levity and humour even amidst the trenches and the Flanders mud. 'He has mined the best of the book, and the best of the play, and then brought his own ingenuity to it. It's a triumph.' Michael looks dazed, but very happy. 'I wonder,' he says to Léa and Eloïse, 'whether it will still be around for your grandchildren.'

Now nearly seventy, Michael is aware that he is living his 'last few chapters', and he thinks ahead to a time when his story will have come to an end. His ashes, like his father's, will be buried in two places. Half will lie in the churchyard in Iddesleigh, near Seán Rafferty and Wilf Ellis – 'a lot of what I am is there', he says. Half will join Kippe, Tony and Jack beneath the hornbeam. The best of him, he hopes, will live on in his stories. When asked which of these he most hopes will endure, he homes in not on particular books, but on moments within books. All of them are moments of reconcilia-tion: the moment in *Why the Whales Came* when the islanders finally lay aside their suspicions of the Birdman and help him to save Bryher from the curse of Samson; the moment in *Kensuke's Kingdom* when Michael realises that Kensuke, his erstwhile enemy and captor, has become his saviour; the moment in *War Horse* when a German and an English soldier meet in No Man's Land and work together to free Joey from the barbed wire. 'Reconciliation,' Michael says, 'is what I yearn for most.' Kay's recent return to the family has brought home to him 'just how wonderful it is when people who have been divided find common cause again'. He has known, first as a son and then as a father, 'how painful separation can be'.

His relationships with his grandchildren have, by contrast, been a source of simple and straightforward joy. 'The bond is looser, easier, kinder,' he has written. 'There is less baggage, less complexity, altogether less angst.' Age bestows a kind of freedom: 'The older you get, the less you feel you need to pretend.' Léa and Eloïse share the Fulham flat where Michael and Clare stay when they come to London. Léa, a psychology graduate, is training to be a Montessori teacher, Eloïse working towards a degree in International Relations. 'To have known them from babies,' Michael says, 'and now to be able to see the future through them, is a wonderful thing.'

For Léa and Eloïse, meanwhile, Michael and Clare have been a source of unfailing strength. 'I can't think of them separately,' says Eloïse. 'I think of them together, solid as a rock. We cling on to this solidity.' Their memories of staying at Langlands as children are blissful and uncomplicated. Michael liked to show them off to the visiting children at Nethercott, who liked, in turn, to make a fuss of them. He read to them at bedtime. They loved the sense of order and routine in their grandparents' lives. Even on holiday in Scilly, they remember, time was always tidily organised. At breakfast Michael

Clare and Michael with four of their granddaughters.
Left to right: Lucie, Eloïse, Léa and Alice.

would ask, 'OK, what's the programme?', and would draw up a time-table for the day. This clear planning created a sense of security, as well as allowing for spontaneity and fun.

Both girls feel grateful to their grandparents 'for taking us seri-ously since we were very young'. At thirteen, Eloïse went to stay with Michael and Clare during 'a shaky patch'. They encouraged her to talk – 'they have always allowed us a lot of space to be ourselves' – and Michael gave her one of his orange exercise-books in which to write down her thoughts. But at a certain point each day, she remembers, he would insist that they put on their gumboots and coats. 'We'd zip our coats up to our chins, and go and roll down hills together, through cowpats and everything. We'd always be giggling after that.'

In some ways it is now Léa and Eloïse who look after their grandparents. They call Michael and Clare 'the students' because of their hectic lives; they tidy up after them in the flat; they worry when Michael pushes himself too hard, gets too exhausted. 'Sometimes he's so stressed,' says Léa, 'that you think he *must* stop. But the next moment, he's feeding off it, loving it.' One of the things that impresses her most about her grandfather is the generosity with which he has responded to fame: 'It's not the grand moments and the meetings with glamorous people that light him up,' she says. 'It's the feeling he's enhancing ordinary lives.' So it is moving, in a separate conversation, to hear Michael reflect on what piece of wisdom he would most like to hand on to his grandchildren. 'I suppose,' he says, after an unusually long pause for thought, 'it would have to be this. That joy is to be found not in receiving, but in giving – the giving of yourself.'

Michael's greatest dread, as he grows older, is that he should find himself locked into an illness that leaves him unable to communicate. But, while health is on his side, the list of things he hopes still to achieve is almost endless. He would like to help Farms for City Children open a fourth centre, this time in Scotland, 'in Stevenson country – that landscape of castles, rivers, lochs and sea that I first fell in love with reading *Kidnapped*'. His belief in the importance of the charity has, if anything, grown over the years. 'I really do think that one day can change a whole life – whether you are standing by a river looking at a heron, or watching a buzzard soaring over a hillside, or learning about friendship away from home for the first time.'

He is brimming with ideas for new books. Recently he and Clare spent a fortnight in Orkney. On the windswept island of Lamb

Holm, they visited the tiny chapel which Italian prisoners of war, working on the construction of the Churchill Barriers in the early 1940s, built to help ease their homesickness. He would like to write a story about these little-known heroes – about how they made a tabernacle from timber salvaged from a wreck and pooled their cigarette money to buy curtains for the sanctuary. And he would like to write 'a book about the great people who have really moved mankind on, from Jesus to Mandela'. He nurses a quiet ambition that he might one day write 'a small, iconic book like *The Tiger Who Came to Tea*'. No amount of effort or hard work can make this happen. 'Sparks of genius like that come from spontaneity, not design. So I'm trying to banish it from my thoughts.'

He hopes he will always 'keep talking to children, trying to help them to think and ask questions and deal with doubt; to unravel the complexities of the world with understanding rather than prejudice'. But he suspects that in the years ahead he may well spend less time writing for children, and more performing and adapting his stories for the stage.

On his first visit to Ypres, Michael met a trio of 'a cappella' English singers, Coope, Boyes and Simpson. He loved their music – a mixture of folk songs, hymns and carols – and kept in touch with them. After *Private Peaceful* was published he suggested that they work together on a concert version of the story – readings by Michael interwoven with songs. Since then, they have added to their repertoire two more of Michael's stories, *On Angel Wings* and *The Best Christmas Present in the World*, for performances of which Michael shares his readings with an actress – Jenny Agutter, Joanna Lumley, Virginia McKenna or Juliet Stevenson. They have performed them all over the country, at festivals, and in village churches, cathedrals and the National Theatre. With the songwriter John Tams, too, Michael has developed a concert version of *War Horse*, and with the London Symphony Orchestra an adaptation of *The Mozart Question*. The composer Colin Matthews is now working on a score to accompany Michael's retelling of *The Pied Piper*, which Michael will perform with the LSO in the Royal Festival Hall. 'When I'm on that stage, speaking my words,' he says, 'I lose all sense of time. I love that. I feel it's what I should be doing.'

The more he speaks to enormous audiences, however, the more aware Michael becomes of the importance of keeping up what Thomas Hardy called 'the old associations', of remaining in touch with his roots. 'As you get older, you can very easily begin to feel that you are losing your connection to the world, that you are becoming isolated from some of the people who mean most to you. Connection with people and places is what makes a writer feel alive.' In the autumn of 2011, an unusual ceremony in Iddesleigh village hall brought home to him that this was the place, and the community, where he really belonged.

In an Author's Note at the beginning of *War Horse* Michael describes 'a small dusty painting of a horse' that hangs in the village hall.

> To many who glance up at it casually … it is merely a tarnished old oil painting of some unknown horse by a competent but anonymous artist. To them the picture is so familiar that it commands little attention. But those who look more closely will see, written in fading black copperplate writing across the bottom of the bronze frame: 'Joey. Painted by Captain James Nicholls, autumn 1914.'

The painting, like the story that followed, was imaginary. But on 30 November a 'real' painting of 'Joey by Captain James Nicholls' was unveiled by one of the village children. Local ladies laid on tea and scones, and ahead of the ceremony somebody climbed up and set the clock above the village hall to one minute past ten, as it is at the start of the book. A fictional story became part of the real story of the village from which it had sprung. Of all the excitement and celebrations that *War Horse* has inspired in the last few years, Michael says, 'that was the high spot'.

Both Michael and Clare are certain now that they will never move from Iddesleigh. But, as Clare says, 'neither of us is ready to sit by the fire in our slippers yet'. A few years ago Michael read *Travels with Charley*, John Steinbeck's account of a road trip he made around America with his dog in 1960. Setting off from Long Island in a converted camper van, Steinbeck drove to Maine, on to California, through Texas, up through the Deep South and back to New York. Michael would like to make a similar journey with Clare, stopping in small towns along the way and telling stories. 'It would be like living in a road movie,' he says, 'an invitation to engage with the unexpected.' It would also be a chance to spend a good stretch of time alone with Clare – a kind of repeat of their long drive down to the South of France in Michael's MG when they were in their early twenties.

In the summer of 2013 it will be fifty years since Michael and Clare were married at Kensington Register Office, and Michael hopes to celebrate by marrying Clare in church – 'I want, finally, to have a good wedding.' There are hurdles to be overcome. 'Clare won't stand for any kind of ballyhoo', so Michael will need to find a church that is really small and private. St Peter-on-the-Wall near Bradwell is one possibility, the Italian Chapel on Lamb Holm another. He will also need – and this is a greater challenge – to find the right person to take the service, somebody with whose beliefs both he and Clare feel in tune.

Michael's own beliefs remain uncertain. When his aunt Jeanne wrote a biography of her father, she called it *Seeking and Finding*

– an apt title, because Emile Cammaerts was very sure of what he believed and of what he had 'found'. 'But I am still seeking,' says Michael. 'And I think I always will be.' There are moments, joining the Sunday congregation in the little church on Bryher for example, when he recognises 'a truth that I cannot deny'. He sees then that religion can be a force for great good, binding communities together. But all too often this binding together slides into exclusivity – 'shutting people out and judging them, and that's dangerous'. The memory of the misery visited on Kippe by the Bradwell vicar who refused her Holy Communion remains painful for Michael and, as he dwells on it, doubts about the established Church pour out with fierce simplicity and eloquence.

'People like that vicar need to be taken aside and shaken, because if Jesus Christ was about anything at all he was about forgiveness of sins. It worries me so much that, rather than follow what Jesus Christ said and did, the Church just follows the dictates of the institution it has made itself.' Just occasionally, Michael says, 'you meet a monk or priest or holy person who truly follows the example of Jesus Christ, and when that happens you immediately recognise a great truth. But it seems to me that in general the Church takes his name massively in vain.'

He worries not only about shortcomings within the Christian churches, but about divisions between Christianity and other religions. Recently he and Clare watched the DVD of *A Month in the Country*, whose director, Pat O'Connor, has now directed *Private Peaceful*. Based on a novel by J. L. Carr, the film revolves around a First World War soldier, Tom Birkin (played by Colin Firth), who comes home shell-shocked and stuttering from fighting in the trenches to find that his wife has deserted him for another man. In order to recuperate and collect his thoughts, he goes to spend the summer in the small rural community of Oxgodby in Yorkshire, in whose church there is said to be a medieval mural that has been hidden for generations under thick layers of plaster. Very slowly, as the weeks pass, Birkin peels away the layers until the mural is revealed.

Michael was deeply moved by the film, and by the image at its heart. Every religion, he suggests, has played its part in plastering over the truth. But, if we could just peel away the layers, we might find that the thing of beauty we all long to see is the same for every one of us.

In the absence of clear beliefs, for the moment, he holds hard to a piece of advice impressed upon him by his godmother, Mary Niven. 'She sometimes says to me, "Michael, never forget that people *matter*, everyone *matters*." She means, I think, that whatever some-one has done, they are God's creature. They matter in His eyes, and they should matter in ours. It's all about not judging people. I think of it often.'

Outside Michael's family, Mary Niven is the only person still alive who has known him from birth. Now ninety-seven, she lives in sheltered accommodation in Edinburgh. She is neat, courteous and thoughtful. When I visit her one afternoon in late summer, she has taken the trouble to find out that I have two young daughters, and has bought each a packet of pan drops. Her memories are very clear. Looking back to 1945, she talks about the breakdown of Kippe's marriage as if it happened yesterday. Perhaps because of the war, she herself has never been a wife or a mother, so for Kippe to have abandoned Tony and hurt 'those two wonderful boys' remains for her a baffling tragedy. Yet she speaks of it more in sorrow than in anger. 'I think she hardly knew what she was doing, poor Kippe. Poor lass.'

She has set aside for me a pile of newspaper cuttings, in perfect order, charting Michael's public life step by step, from the founding of Farms for City Children, through the publication of his books, to the phenomenon of *War Horse*. She has followed his success every inch of the way, and is justly proud. Yet she is devoted still to the child Michael once was, and perhaps in part remains. 'Dear Michael,' she says as I get up to leave. 'It's been a muddled life, but a marvellous one. Really marvellous.'

Muddle and marvel, woven together. Mary, my dear godmother, says it as she sees it, as usual. The muddle bit is certainly true. Her words remind me of John Tams's lines from 'Rolling Home', my favourite song from the wonderful stage production of *War Horse*:

> The summer of resentment
> The winter of despair
> The journey to contentment
> Is set with trap and snare …

I have so much now to be content about, but it's somehow in my nature to dwell on 'trap and snare'. I think this final story speaks for itself.

A Proper Family

Central Park was bright and fresh that morning too, I remember.
The day before, we'd been out on the boat to see the Statue of
Liberty, and afterwards we'd walked through Greenwich Village.
We sat here for a while that evening, on this very bench, next to the
bronze statue of Hans Christian Andersen, in Central Park, not far
from our hotel. You liked to see the kids sailing their boats on the
lake; I liked the ducks.

The whole of New York City was simply a movie set for us then.
Every cop was a film extra. We knew it had to be Cary Grant we
saw getting into the yellow cab outside that swanky hotel on Fifth
Avenue, and Audrey Hepburn was there too, down the alleyway
looking for her cat in the rain.

It is not a movie set any more. Ten years to the day, I'm back,
sitting here early in the morning on our bench next to Hans
Christian Andersen, and I'm writing you a letter. I want to write it
out of me, once and for all. For ten whole years, I've thought about
precious little else. It's about time I did, don't you think? Or else
they win.

Your arm was around my shoulder that morning, your
breathing warm on my ear, and we were talking. Hans Christian
Andersen was there too, sitting nearby, much larger than life, a
book open on his knee. All three of us were looking out over the
lake at the ducks. A pair of them waddled out of the lake and

stood at our feet demanding to be fed. You told them that all you had were Swiss cough sweets, so there wasn't much point in hanging around, was there? After some complaining they sidled over to Hans Christian Andersen to see if they could do any better with him. And you, in your best Donald Duck voice – which, I have to say, sounded to me more like Groucho Marx – called after them.

'OK, Hans, so you haven't got no bread. So, how 'bout you give us a story instead, but not that old Ugly Duckling story, right? Ugly? Ugly? You should take a look at yourself in the mirror some day, Hans. I mean, who's talking? Y'ain't exactly Robert Redford, y'know.'

On and on you went. You wanted me to go on laughing and I did, helplessly, and that only encouraged you to greater heights of silliness.

Silliness was important to us, wasn't it? The distraction we both needed. It helped us to set aside the bitterness, the regret, and all the recriminations. But on this bench, that morning, it could only do so for a while.

We lapsed into silence, a comfortable enough silence at first, but then I knew the old wound was starting to throb inside you. I could see it in your eyes as you turned away from me. On the trip down through North Carolina and Virginia, both of us had kept to our bargain. We wouldn't mention it, we said. We'd promised ourselves to put the meeting with Josh, and everything to do with it, out of our minds entirely. And we'd done it. Neither of us had said a word about Josh or Margot or the pain of those long and wasted years. I could feel the tension in you rising as the minutes ticked by before you had to go.

'I don't know if I can do this, Ginny,' you said. 'It's been seven years. What am I going to say to him? What if he just walks away when he sees me? He was so angry. But you were there: I was only saying what I thought was right at the time, wasn't I, Ginny? That there might be other ways out of the situation, other ways of dealing with it. What did he expect? They were far too young to get married, you said it yourself. Josh was nineteen! How were they going to manage with a baby? What were they going to do for money? Surely I wasn't being that unreasonable?'

I couldn't have let you go off to the meeting in that frame of mind, still excusing yourself. We'd been given this one chance and I had to speak up or things were never going to work out.

'We've talked about this over and over,' I said. 'We have to understand that to Josh, and to Margot, it was unreasonable. Anyway, it's not what I think that matters, nor what you think. It's how they feel that counts. They wanted our support, our blessing if you like. And you didn't give it. Neither did I. I didn't stand up for them, and I should have done. It was their life they were making together, their baby. You have to remember what we agreed: that you are going to meet him in a spirit of forgiveness. It's the only way. You can't keep raking over all the old arguments and hope Josh will agree with you. He won't. They've come to America and they've made their life. You have to acknowledge that, embrace it, and forget the rest. If we want our son back, if we want to see our granddaughter again, then that's what you're going to have to do. It's that simple. Put your arms around him, and say sorry. Just do it. Please.'

I was shaking when I finished, and in tears. You took my hands in yours, told me how sorry you were for everything, how you were going to put it right. 'I wish you were coming with me,' you said. 'I've never felt so nervous about anything in my life.'

I reached out and touched your cheek. 'It'll be fine,' I said. 'I've talked to Margot. She told me it's what Josh wants. He's ready for it. They want the silence to end just as much as we do, for us all to be together again, like a proper family. She told me.'

You looked at your watch. 'Six forty-five already. I'd better find a cab,' you said. 'The lobby of the Marriott Hotel, wasn't it? Meet you back here in a couple of hours, as planned.'

'Phone me,' I said.

We hugged, tight, not wanting to let go, and then you walked away, patting Hans Christian Andersen on the knee as you went. 'Wish me luck, Hans,' you said, and you were off. You turned and waved back at me, as I hoped you might. Then you were gone.

I strolled around the lake for a while, and sat down outside that café opposite to wait for you. A roller blader swept past me, leaning forward, hands behind his back like an ice skater, wonderfully graceful.

The waiting was long, and my mind, as the minutes passed, filled with doubt. But instead of going back over those seven long years of angry silence, I thought of what Margot had said. She'd always done her best to keep in touch with us. Before they left for America, when Molly was four, Margot was the one who insisted on bringing her over to stay with us in Sussex. Just the two of them; Josh wouldn't come. And you read her *Tintin*. I told you she was far too young for it. You only did it because it had been Josh's favourite book. 'Capt'n Haddock' Josh loved to call you, remember? You went down to the village pond with Molly the morning before they left, and you sailed the Viking boat with the striped sail that you'd made for Josh when he was little.

Margot was our only hope. It was she who wrote to us all those years, sending photos of their home in New York, and of Molly. She phoned so we could speak to Molly on her birthday. And she was the one who'd set up this whole meeting. 'Come to New York,' she'd said on the phone, a couple of weeks before. 'Josh has agreed to see his dad. I really think he's ready to move on.'

It had taken us a while, a fortune in phone calls, to sort out how and when the meeting might best be arranged. But we managed it. You would see him on your own, at the Marriott Hotel just below his office in the World Trade Center and if all went well we'd phone one another and meet up by the statue in Central Park afterwards, and have a picnic together, a proper family reunion.

The last time I'd spoken to Margot she'd said everything would work out fine, she was sure of it. I tried to be as optimistic about it as she had sounded, but I found it hard.

To stop myself worrying – I kept checking my watch every few minutes – I looked up through the trees at the clear blue of the sky beyond. I watched two vapour trails as they met and crossed one another; caught a glimpse of a squirrel running along a branch, tail twitching – that was probably what set me off, remembering our trip down south.

'Let's not just go to New York,' I'd said, poring over the map back home. 'New York's not America. Why don't we make the most of the journey? If we flew out earlier we'd have time to get a proper feel for the place. It would take your mind off the meeting, wouldn't it? We could hire a car and make it up as we go along: our own road movie. We could go to Virginia – it's my name after all. I've always wanted to go there.'

* * *

All the way along the Parkway, the winding road down through the Blue Ridge Mountains, through North Carolina and Virginia, we wondered at the wildness of it all, at the hugeness of this country. There were squirrels everywhere, and deer, and eagles floating up over the treetops. Once, we came round a bend and saw three bears, a mother and two cubs, wandering nonchalantly along the side of the road. They ignored us completely, even when we stopped to take a photo of them.

At Monticello, Thomas Jefferson's grand house near Charlottesville, you sat under a tree in the gardens and read me the Declaration of Independence. I marvelled at the power of Jefferson's words – the way you spoke them brought tears to my eyes. There were squirrels there too, playing in the trees above our heads. And you said: 'Even those squirrels know all about "the pursuit of happiness". Look at them. They're all-American squirrels.'

On the trip back up through the Shenandoah Valley to Washington, and on the train back to New York – you were fed up with driving by then and we'd returned the hire car – we were quieter together, our thoughts drifting ahead of us to the meeting with Josh on the morning of the 11th.

Whether I wanted them to or not, my thoughts took me to the lobby of the Marriott Hotel. I closed my eyes and felt my heart lift with joy as I saw the two of you, walking towards one another in the lobby. You smiled and cried and clung to one another. Perhaps sitting down, over coffee and a plate of breakfast pancakes – how you both loved pancakes – the two of you reminisced about the cricket you used to play in the garden, the Viking boats you'd made, and the runes you had painted together on the work shed. 'Viking graffiti' I'd called it. 'Graphic literature' you and Josh agreed.

'Never paint over it, Mum,' he'd said, do you remember? And we never had.

Just then, my mobile rang. As usual it was hidden away in the deepest recess of my bag and I didn't reach it in time. A text came in. It was from you: 'All's well that ends well.'

I felt like running round the lake and proclaiming it to the entire world. It was over. I had my family back. Life could go on. But instead I did it the English way: I walked all the way round with a silly smile on my face. As I passed Hans Christian Andersen, I had to stop to tell him the good news. Then I did a crazy thing. I climbed up and kissed him on his cold, cold cheek. I heard the sound of hooves behind me. Two cops on horseback were looking up at me quizzically.

'I just felt like it,' I explained, with a shrug. 'Lovely day, and Hans is a lovely man. Great storyteller.' They rode off, one shaking his head, the other laughing.

I settled down again on the bench and waited for you and Josh to arrive. A call came through from Margot. She sounded so happy. She and Molly would be ten minutes. Ten minutes seemed like an hour. Then they were here.

'Grandma Haddock!' Molly called out, running round the lake towards me. 'Look, Grandma, I've brought my boat.' She handed me the Viking ship you'd made for Josh all those years ago – hers now.

The three of us sat there, chatting away together on the bench. I was telling them all about our trip down south. I remember noticing smoke rising from beyond the trees, we heard fire engines, wailing through the streets, but we were so caught up with one another that we didn't give it a second thought. But after a while there were more sirens, and the two cops on horseback came trotting past us in a hurry, one of them shouting something about the Twin Towers.

I went cold. I knew even then. You didn't phone. Josh didn't phone. I did, again and again. Margot did. But your phones were dead.

Ten years have passed, and Margot, Molly and I are here together on our bench again. I've written my letters, one for you and one for Josh. And Molly and Margot have written theirs. It was Molly's idea: in a moment, we'll post them, put them all in the Viking ship and set the sail alight, push it out on to the lake, a proper Viking funeral. Together we'll watch it burn, see the smoke rise, and hope that all our hurt will rise with it too. Only our love for you both will remain.

Bibliography

It Never Rained (1974)

Long Way Home (1975)

Thatcher Jones (1975)

Friend or Foe (1977)

Do All You Dare (1978)

What Shall We Do with It? (1978)

All Around the Year (with poems by Ted Hughes) (1979)

The Day I Took the Bull by the Horn (1979)

The Ghost-Fish (1979)

Love at First Sight (1979)

That's How It is (1979)

The Marble Crusher and Other Stories (1980)

The Nine Lives of Montezuma (1980)

Miss Wirtles Revenge (1981)

War Horse (1982)

*The White Horse of Zennor and Other Stories from Below the Eagle's
     Nest* (1982)

Twist of Gold (1983)

Little Foxes (1984)

Why the Whales Came (1985)

Tom's Sausage Lion (1986)

Conker (1987)

Jo-Jo the Melon Donkey (1987)

King of the Cloud Forests (1987)

Mossop's Last Chance (1988)

My Friend Walter (1988)

Albertine, Goose Queen (1989)

Mr Nobody's Eyes (1989)

Old Sticky (1989)

Jigger's Day Off (1990)

Waiting for Anya (1990)

And Pigs Might Fly! (1991)

Colly's Barn (1991)

The Sandman and the Turtles (1991)

The Marble Crusher (1992)

Martians at Mudpuddle Farm (1992)

The King in the Forest (1993)

The War of Jenkins' Ear (1993)

Arthur, High King of Britain (1994)

The Dancing Bear (1994)

Snakes and Ladders (1994)

Stories from Mudpuddle Farm [1] (1994)

Blodin the Beast (1995)

Mum's the Word (1995)

Stories from Mudpuddle Farm [2] (1995)

The Wreck of the Zanzibar (1995)

The Butterfly Lion (1996)

The Ghost of Grania O'Malley (1996)

Robin of Sherwood (1996)

Sam's Duck (1996)

Farm Boy (1997)

Cockadoodle-doo, Mr Sultana! (1998)

Escape from Shangri-La (1998)

Joan of Arc (1998)

Red Eyes at Night (1998)

Wartman (1998)

Kensuke's Kingdom (1999)

The Rainbow Bear (1999)

Wombat Goes Walkabout (1999)

Billy the Kid (2000)

Black Queen (2000)

Dear Olly (2000)

From Hereabout Hill (2000)

The Silver Swan (2000)

Who's a Big Bully Then? (2000)

Mairi's Mermaid (2001)

Out of the Ashes (2001)

Toro! Toro! (2001)

Cool! (2002)

The Last Wolf (2002)

Mr Skip (2002)

The Sleeping Sword (2002)

Cool as a Cucumber (2003)

Gentle Giant (2003)

Private Peaceful (2003)

The Best Christmas Present in the World (2004)

Dolphin Boy (2004)

Little Albatross (2004)

The Orchard Book of Aesop's Fables (2004)

Sir Gawain and the Green Knight (2004)

The Amazing Story of Adolphus Tips (2005)

Fox Friend (2005)

I Believe in Unicorns (2005)

Alone on a Wide Wide Sea (2006)

Beowulf (2006)

BIBLIOGRAPHY

On Angel Wings (2006)

Singing for Mrs Pettigrew: a Story-maker's Journey (2006)

Born to Run (2007)

The Mozart Question (2007)

Alien Invasion! (2008)

Animal Tales (2008)

Cock-a-doodle-doo! (2008)

Hansel and Gretel (2008)

Kaspar, Prince of Cats (2008)

Pigs Might Fly! (2008)

This Morning I Met a Whale (2008)

The Voices of Children (2008)

The Best of Times (2009)

The Kites are Flying! (2009)

Mudpuddle Farm: Six Animal Adventures (2009)

Running Wild (2009)

An Elephant in the Garden (2010)

It's a Dog's Life (2010)

Not Bad for a Bad Lad (2010)

Shadow (2010)

Little Manfred (2011)

The Pied Piper of Hamelin (2011)

Homecoming (2012)

Acknowledgements

'There's no point in doing this if we don't have *fun*,' said Michael as we signed our contracts. My first thanks go to him and to Clare for their infinite kindness, hospitality and patience, and for making all our meetings, email exchanges and telephone conversations feel much more like pleasure than work.

I would like to thank my editor, Clare Reihill, for her unfailing support and steady nerve, and my agent, Gillon Aitken, for his clear thinking and sage advice.

My employers at the Royal Society of Literature have been extraordinarily generous in enabling me to find time to write. I am particularly grateful to Anne Chisholm and Colin Thubron.

Anne Chisholm also read the book in draft, and so did Anthony Gardner. Their comments and suggestions were invaluable. I am indebted to my kind and sharp-eyed sister-in-law Madeline Fergusson for her painstaking proofreading and fact-checking, and her help in compiling the bibliography. I am grateful to Carol Hughes for permission to quote from letters from Ted Hughes to Christopher Reid, and to Michael and Clare Morpurgo.

I would like to thank Robin Ravilious for permission to use the photograph of Michael Morpurgo on the front cover; Carol Hughes for permission to reproduce the photograph of Ted Hughes and herself; Matt Writtle for permission to reproduce the photograph of Michael Morpurgo in Ypres; Apex News and Pictures for permission

ACKNOWLEDGEMENTS

to reproduce the photograph of Michael Morpurgo reading to children from St John the Baptist School, Hoxton; the National Theatre for permission to reproduce photographs from the set of the theatrical production of *War Horse*; Charles Green for permission to reproduce the photograph of Michael and Clare Morpurgo after the MBE ceremony; and the CBC Still Photograph Collection/Dale Barnes for permission to reproduce the photograph of Tony van Bridge on the set of *Great Expectations*. I am grateful for permission to use photographs of Michael Morpurgo and 'Joey', and Michael and Clare Morpurgo with Steven Spielberg on the set of *War Horse*, © DreamWorksII Distribution Co., LLC All Rights Reserved; and to the University of Bristol Library Special Collections for permission to reproduce the photograph of Allen and Clare Lane (DM1294/1/6/p57). The photograph of Michael and Clare Morpurgo and their grandchildren is © Frank Baron/*Guardian*. Lines from Walter de la Mare's 'The Listeners' are reproduced with kind permission of the Literary Trustees of Walter de la Mare, and the Society of Authors as their representative. All other photographs and quotations are reproduced with the kind permission of Michael and Clare Morpurgo.

Among the many others to whom I owe thanks are Clare Alexander; Karin Altenberg; Christine Baker; Stephen Barlow; Sebastian Barker; Jane Batterham; Veronique Baxter; Louise Beere; Daniel Bennett; Marian Bennett; Emily Berry; Anthony Bilmes; Quentin Blake; Peter Campbell; Helen Chaloner; Paul Chequers; Emma Chichester Clark; Piet Chielens; Susannah Clapp; Mick Csaky; Laura de Lisle; John Dunne; Julia Eccleshare; Robin Edmonds; Tabitha Elwes; Ted Emerson; Gill Evans; Jane Feaver; William Fiennes; Adam Finn; Peter Florence; Michael Foreman; Anne and Ronald Graham-Clarke; Nick Grant; Peter Henderson; David Hicks; Helen Hillman; Sir Michael Holroyd; Lady (Jean)

ACKNOWLEDGEMENTS

Hyde Parker; Sir Nicholas Hytner; Paula Johnson; Denise Johnstone-Burt; Judith Keenlyside; Lady (Elizabeth) Leslie; Jeanne Lindley; Hannah Lowery; Joanna Lumley; Roger McGough; Virginia McKenna; Edna Macleod; Elizabeth Manners; Jane Manners; Eloïse Morpurgo; Kay Morpurgo; Léa Morpurgo; Linda and Mark Morpurgo; Pieter Morpurgo; Rosalind Morpurgo; Tom Morris; John and Virginia Murray; Ann-Janine Murtagh; Henrietta Naish; Mary Niven; Guy Norrish; John and Patricia Owens; Simon Owens; Rachel Page; Joy Palmer; Seonaid Parnell; Philippa Perry; Gina Pollinger; Cally Poplak; Philip Pullman; Robin Ravilious; Simon Reade; Anne and Patrick Robbé; Richard Roberts; Robin Robertson; Olly Rowse; Beaty Rubens; Juliet Stevenson; Daniel Swift; Kris Taylor; Christine and David Teale; David Ward; Graham Ward; Hetty Ward; Neil Warrington; Tim Waterstone; Stephen Webster; Joan Weeks; and Laura West.

Last, and most of all, I thank my husband, James Fergusson, and our daughters, Flora and Isabella. This book is for them.

Spell veterinary - songs!

WAR HORSE

In the Village Hall, *below the clock that* ~~old school they use now for the~~ *has stood* always
at one minute past ten, hangs a small *dusty* painting of a horse.

He stands, a splendid red bay with a remarkable white cross *and with four perfectly matched white socks*
emblazoned on his forehead. He looks mistfully out of the picture,
his ~~eyes~~ *ears* pricked forward, his head turned as if he has just noticed
us standing there.

To many who glance up at it *casually* as they might do
when the Hall is opened up for ~~Parish meetings~~, for Harvest Suppers
or evening socials, it is merely an tarnished old oil painting of
some unknown horse by a *competent* but anonymous artist. To
them the picture is so familiar that it commands little attention.
But those who look more closely will see, written in fading
copperplate writing across the bottom of the bronze frame:
"Joey, *Painted* by Captain James Nicholls, *autumn* 1914."

Some of us in the village, only a very few now and fewer
as each year goes by, remember Joey as he was, *the story it is written*
nor the war they lived and died in
so that neither he nor those who knew him, *will* *be* forgotten. This
is his story, so he must tell as it was and as only he knows it to be

Iddesleigh

Albert Narracott. 1925.